Student Manual

Generalist Practice with Organizations and Communities

FOURTH EDITION

Karen K. Kirst-Ashman
University of Wisconsin, Whitewater

Grafton H. Hull, Jr.
University of Utah

Prepared by

Karen K. Kirst-Ashman
University of Wisconsin, Whitewater

Grafton H. Hull, Jr.
University of Utah

Vicki Vogel
University of Wisconsin, Whitewater

BROOKS/COLE
CENGAGE Learning

Australia • Brazil • Japan • Korea • Mexico • Singapore • Spain • United Kingdom • United States

BROOKS/COLE
CENGAGE Learning

For product information and technology assistance, contact us at
Cengage Learning Customer & Sales Support,
1-800-354-9706

For permission to use material from this text or product, submit all requests online at **www.cengage.com/permissions**
Further permissions questions can be emailed to
permissionrequest@cengage.com

ISBN-13: 978-0-495-80703-2
ISBN-10: 0-495-80703-6

Brooks/Cole
10 Davis Drive
Belmont, CA 94002-3098
USA

Cengage Learning is a leading provider of customized learning solutions with office locations around the globe, including Singapore, the United Kingdom, Australia, Mexico, Brazil, and Japan. Locate your local office at: **www.cengage.com/international**

Cengage Learning products are represented in Canada by Nelson Education, Ltd.

To learn more about Brooks/Cole, visit **www.cengage.com/brookscole**

Purchase any of our products at your local college store or at our preferred online store **www.ichapters.com**

Printed in the United States of America
1 2 3 4 5 6 7 12 11 10 09 08

Table of Contents

Chapter 1
Introduction to Generalist Practice with Organizations and Communities

I. **Why Do You Need the Content in this Book?**

    A.   Community issues have major impacts

    B.   Every community is subject to social, economic, and political forces

    C.   Social services—the tasks that social workers and other helping professionals perform to help people solve problems, increase independence, sustain families, improve personal well-being, and enhance functioning in the social environment

    D.   Generalist practitioners require a sound understanding of the organizational environments in which they practice

II. **The Generalist Intervention Model**

    A.   Foundation for generalist practice: Knowledge, skills, values

    B.   Figure 1.1: Planned Change Steps in the Generalist Intervention Model

        1.   Step 1: Engagement

        2.   Step 2: Assessment

        3.   Step 3: Planning

        4.   Step 4: Implementation

        5.   Step 5: Evaluation

        6.   Step 6: Termination

        7.   Step 7: Follow-up

    C.   Figure 1.2: Steps in the Planned Change Process—Initiating Macro Change

    D.   A micro approach

    E.   A mezzo approach

    F.   A macro approach

III.   What Does Generalist Practice Mean?

A.   The application of an eclectic knowledge base, professional values, and a wide range of skills to target any size system for change within the context of four primary processes

   1.   Emphasizes client empowerment—the process of increasing personal, interpersonal, or political power so that individuals can take action to improve their life situations

   2.   Working effectively within an organizational structure

   3.   Requires the assumption of a wide range of professional roles

   4.   Application of critical thinking skills to the planned change process

B.   Figure 1.3: Definition of Generalist Practice

C.   Highlight 1.1: Dimensions in the Definition of Generalist Practice

   1.   Acquisition of an eclectic knowledge base

      a.   Theoretical foundation: Systems theories

      b.   Human behavior and the social environment

      c.   Social welfare policy and services

      d.   Social work practice

      e.   Research

      f.   Human diversity

      g.   Promotion of social and economic justice

      h.   Populations-at-risk

   2.   Emphasis on client empowerment

   3.   Acquisition of professional values

      a.   National Association of Social Workers Code of Ethics

      b.   Awareness of personal values

      c.   Clarification of conflicting ethical dilemmas

      d.   Understanding of oppression

      e.   Respect for diverse populations

2

4. Use of a wide range of practice skills

    a. Micro

    b. Mezzo

    c. Macro

5. Orientation to target any size system

    a. Micro

    b. Mezzo

    c. Macro

6. Effective work within an organizational structure

7. Assumption of a wide range of professional roles

    a. Enabler

    b. Mediator

    c. Integrator/Coordinator

    d. General manager

    e. Educator

    f. Analyst/Evaluator

    g. Broker

    h. Facilitator

    i. Initiator

    j. Negotiator

    k. Mobilizer

    l. Advocate

8. Employment of critical thinking skills

9.   Use of a planned change process

      a.   Engagement

      b.   Assessment

            1)   Defining issues

            2)   Collecting and assessing data

      c.   Planning

            1)   Identifying alternative interventions

            2)   Selecting appropriate courses of action

            3)   Contracting

      d.   Implementation of appropriate courses of action

      e.   Evaluation

            1)   Using appropriate courses of action

            2)   Applying appropriate research-based knowledge and technological advances

      f.   Termination

      g.   Follow-up

IV.   Defining Generalist Practice

IV.1.   Acquisition of an Eclectic Knowledge Base

A.   Systems theories

1.   System—a set of elements that are orderly and interrelated to make a functional whole

2.   Conceptualizing systems in macro practice

3.   Client system—any individual, family, group, organization, or community that will ultimately benefit from generalist social work intervention

4.   Macro client system—involves larger numbers of clients, families, or groups of clients with similar characteristics or qualifications for receiving resources or services, or an agency or community that will be the beneficiary of the macro intervention process

5.   Target system—the system that social workers must modify or influence in order to reach their goals and have clients benefit from the planned change process

6.   Change agent system—individual who initiates the macro change process (you assume the role of the change agent throughout the book)

7.   Action system—includes those people who agree and are committed to work together in order to attain the proposed macro change

B.   Human behavior and the social environment (HBSE)

1.   Social work has a person-in-environment focus—interactions among individuals, systems, and the environment are critical

2.   Council on Social Work Education standard that social workers should have knowledge about biological, social, psychological, cultural, and spiritual dimensions of human functioning

C.   Social welfare policy and services

1.   Social policies involve the actions of government that have a direct impact on the welfare of people by providing services and income

2.   Agency policies include those standards adopted by individual organizations and programs that provide services

3.   Historical and analytical perspective concerning how well services meet basic human needs and support the development of human capacities

D.   Social work practice

1.   The *doing* of social work

2.   Ability to determine what skills will be most effective in a given situation

E.   Social work research

1.   Guides social workers to become more effective in practice and get better and clearer results

2.   Helps to build an effective knowledge base for the social work profession

3.   Evidence-based practice—the careful, thoughtful, and conscientious use of the best evidence available to implement interventions that have been proven effective in specific practice situations

4.   Four major purposes of social work research:

a.   Exploration

b.   Description

c.   Explanation

d.   Evaluation

F. Human diversity

    1. Discrimination—the act of treating people differently based on the fact that they belong to some group rather than on their own merit

    2. Oppression—putting extreme limitations and constraints on some person, group, or larger system

    3. Economic deprivation—the condition of having inadequate or unjust access to financial resources

    4. Stereotype—a fixed mental picture of members of some specified group based on some attribute or attributes that reflect an overly simplified view of that group, without consideration or appreciation of individual differences

    5. Highlight 1.2: Empowerment of Lesbian and Gay People at the Macro Level

G. Promotion of social and economic justice

    1. Social justice—the idea that, in a perfect world, all citizens would have the same rights, protection, opportunities, obligations, and social benefits

    2. Economic justice—the idea that, in a perfect world, resources would be distributed in a fair and equitable manner

H. Populations-at-risk

    1. Groups of people, based on some identified characteristics, are at greater risk of social and economic deprivation than the general mainstream of society

    2. Social workers need information about the factors that contribute to and constitute being at risk, and insight concerning these populations' special issues and needs

IV.2. Emphasis on Client Empowerment

A. Empowerment—the process of increasing personal, interpersonal, or political power so that individuals can take action to improve their life situations

B. Strengths perspective—focuses on client system resources, capabilities, knowledge, abilities, motivations, experience, intelligence, and other positive qualities that can be put to use to solve problems and pursue positive changes

C. Highlight 1.3: Resiliency: Seeking Strength Amid Adversity

    1. Resiliency—the ability of an individual, family, group, community, or organization to recover from adversity and resume functioning even when suffering serious trouble, confusion, or hardship

2.   Two dimensions of resiliency

      a.   Risk—involves stressful life events or adverse environmental conditions that increase the vulnerability (defenseless or helplessness) of individuals or other systems

      b.   Protection—concerns those factors that buffer, moderate, and protect against those vulnerabilities

3.   Resiliency at the organizational level

4.   Resiliency in a community

IV.3.   Assimilation of Professional Values and Ethics

A.   Values—principles, qualities, and practices that a designated group, individual, or culture deems inherently desirable (what you consider to be right or wrong)

B.   Ethics—principles based on a set of values that serve to guide one's behavior (how you behave based on values)

C.   National Association of Social Workers (NASW) Code of Ethics

      1.   Six core values:

      a.   *Service*: The provision of help, resources, and benefits so that people may achieve their maximum potential

      b.   *Social justice*: An ideal condition in which all members of society have the same basic rights, protection, opportunities, obligations, and social benefits

      c.   *Dignity and worth of the person*: Holding in high esteem and appreciating individual value

      d.   *Importance of human relationships*: Valuing the dynamic interpersonal connections between two or more persons or systems that involve how they think about, feel about, and behave toward each other

      e.   *Integrity*: Maintaining trustworthiness and sound adherence to moral ideals

      f.   *Competence*: Having the necessary skills and abilities to perform work with clients effectively

D.   Awareness of personal values—professionally obligated to prevent personal values that conflict with professional values from interfering with practice

E.   Clarification of conflicting ethical dilemmas

F.   Understanding oppression—recognize the injustice of putting extreme limitations and constraints on some group or institution

G.   Respect for diverse populations

IV.4. & 5. Mastery of a Wide Range of Practice Skills to Target Any Size System

A.   Historically, skills were clustered into three categories:

   1.   Casework

   2.   Group work

   3.   Community organization

B.   Highlight 1.4: Before Macro Practice: Three Models of Community Organization

   1.   Locality development—community change pursued through broad participation of a wide spectrum of people at the local community level

   2.   Social planning—a technical process of problem-solving regarding basic social problems, such as delinquency, housing, and mental health

   3.   Social action—coordinated effort to advocate for change in established laws, customs, or patterns of behavior to benefit a specific population (e.g., homeless people), solve a social problem (e.g., illicit drug use), correct unfairness (e.g., racism), or enhance people's well-being (e.g., improve access to health care)

C.   Generalist perspective assumes a multiple level approach to intervention

   1.   Micro practice—generalist social work practice focusing on planned change with and for individuals

   2.   Mezzo practice—generalist social work practice with small groups

   3.   Macro practice—generalist social work practice intending to affect change in large systems, including organizations and communities

IV.6.   Effective Work Within an Organizational Structure

A.   Organizational structure—the formal and informal manner in which tasks and responsibilities, lines of authority, channels of communication, and dimensions of power are established and coordinated within an organization

B.   Agency structure

   1.   Formal—by the book and according to the rules

   2.   Informal—based on the way the agency really works

IV.7. A Wide Range of Roles

A. Role—a culturally expected behavior pattern for a person having a specified status or being involved in a designated social relationship

B. Four types of systems involved in generalist practice

   1. Client system—those people who will ultimately benefit from the change process

   2. Change agent system—the individual who initiates the macro change process

   3. Action system—those people who agree to and will work together to attain the proposed macro change

   4. Target system—the system that social workers must change or influence in order to accomplish their goals

C. Enabler—provides support, encouragement, and suggestions to members of a macro client system so that system may complete tasks or solve problems more easily and successfully

D. Figure 1.4: The Enabler Role in Macro Practice

E. Mediator—resolves arguments or disagreements among micro, mezzo, or macro systems in disagreement

F. Figure 1.5: The Mediator Role in Macro Practice

G. Integrator/Coordinator—brings people involved in various systems together and organizes their performance

H. Figure 1.6: The Integrator/Coordinator Role in Macro Practice

I. Manager—assumes some level of administrative responsibility for a social services agency or some other organizational system. Administrators utilize three levels of skills:

   1. Technical skills—those used to direct an agency's basic activities such as overseeing counseling techniques, developing programs, or evaluating the agency's effectiveness

   2. People skills—concern interpersonal effectiveness such as oral communication, listening, conflict management, leading, and motivating

   3. Conceptual skills—those oriented toward assessing and understanding the overall operation of the agency and how it fits into its larger macro environment

J. Figure 1.7: The General Manager Role in Macro Practice

K. Educator—conveys information and teaches skills to other systems

L. Figure 1.8: The Educator Role in Macro Practice

M.   Analyst/Evaluator—determines whether a program or agency is effective

N.   Figure 1.9: The Analyst/Evaluator Role in Macro Practice

O.   Broker—links any size system with community resources and services

P.   Figure 1.10: The Broker Role in Macro Practice

Q.   Facilitator—guides a group experience

R.   Figure 1.11: Facilitator Role in Macro Practice

S.   Initiator—calls attention to an issue

T.   Figure 1.12: The Initiator Role in Macro Practice

U.   Negotiator—intermediary who acts to settle disputes and/or resolve disagreements, clearly taking the side of one of the parties involved

V.   Figure 1.13: The Negotiator Role in Macro Practice

W.   Mobilizer—identifies and convenes community people and resources and makes them responsive to unmet community need

X.   Figure 1.14: The Mobilizer Role in Macro Practice

Y.   Advocate—steps forward and speaks out on the behalf of the client system in order to promote fair and equitable treatment or gain needed resources or services

Z.   Figure 1.15: The Advocate Role in Macro Practice

IV.8. Critical Thinking Skills

A.   Critical thinking—the careful scrutiny of what is stated as true or what appears to be true and the resulting expression of an opinion or conclusion based on that scrutiny, and the creative formulation of an opinion or conclusion when presented with a question, problem, or issue

B.   A formula for critical thinking

1.   Triple A approach

a.   Ask questions

b.   Assess the established facts and issues involved

c.   Assert a concluding opinion

C.   Fallacies to avoid

1.   Charisma, charm, and possibly even glamour

2. Newness and experience

3. "Fact" that if something is written down, then it must be true

4. Highlight 1.5: More Fallacies to Avoid When Using Critical Thinking

    a. Irrelevant conclusion

    b. Hasty generalization

    c. Overlooking the role of chance

    d. Personalization

    e. Invalid disjunction (either/or-ing)

    f. Fallacies based on availability

    g. Argument from ignorance

    h. Mental filter

    i. Emotional reasoning

    j. Appeal to authority

    k. Argumentation ad populum

    l. Appeal to tradition

    m. Influence by testimonials

    n. Assume that good intentions result in good services (e.g., protect clients from harm)

5. A final note on critical thinking and generalist practice

IV.9. Use of a Planned Change Process

A. Engagement

1. Four tasks of engagement

    a. Involve yourself in the situation

    b. Establish communication with everyone concerned

    c. Begin to define the parameters within which the worker and the client(s) will work

    d. Create an initial working structure

2. Outcomes of engagement

    a. Practitioner should become an integral facet of the problematic situation

    b. Those involved in the process should establish effective communication among themselves

    c. The practitioner and the client system should establish some agreement concerning the problematic issue and how to go about addressing it

    d. The practitioner should develop an understanding about what to do next

B. Assessment: Identifying issues and collecting information

    1. Assessment—involves identifying the nature and extent of client needs and concerns, as well as critical information about client resources and supports and other environmental factors, thus forming the basis for an intervention plan

    2. Identifying your client system

    3. Assessing the client system's problems and needs from a macro perspective (including diversity)

    4. Identifying client strengths

C. Planning in macro practice

    1. Planning—the process of identifying goals, rationally considering various ways to implement them, and establishing specific steps to achieve them

    2. Macro practice assessment and planning steps often blend to some degree

D. Implementation and evaluation in macro practice

    1. Implementation—the actual undertaking of the plan

    2. Evaluation—the process of determining whether a given change effort was worthwhile

E. Termination in macro practice—the ending of a designated macro practice process

F. Follow-up in macro practice—checking on whether the macro intervention process has succeeded or whether the same old problems have resurfaced in another form

V.   **Specific Steps for Pursuing Planned Change in Macro Practice**

       A.   Figure 1.16: Macro Practice Planned Change

       B.   PREPARE model for assessment and planning in macro practice

             1.   **P**REPARE Step 1—Identify **Problems** to address

             2.   P**R**EPARE Step 2—Review your macro and personal **Reality**

             3.   PR**E**PARE Step 3—**Establish** primary goals

             4.   PRE**P**ARE Step 4—Identify relevant **People** of influence

             5.   PREP**A**RE Step 5—**Assess** potential costs and benefits to clients and agency

             6.   PREPA**R**E Step 6—Review professional and personal **Risk**

             7.   PREPAR**E** Step 7—**Evaluate** the potential success of a macro change process

       C.   IMAGINE model for implementation and evaluation in macro practice

             1.   **I**MAGINE Step 1—Start with an innovative **Idea**

             2.   I**MA**GINE Step 2—**Muster** support and formulate an action system

             3.   IM**A**GINE Step 3—Identify **Assets**

             4.   IMA**G**INE Step 4—Specify **Goals**, objectives, and action steps to attain them

             5.   IMAG**I**NE Step 5—**Implement** the plan

             6.   IMAGI**NE** Step 6—**Neutralize** opposition

             7.   IMAGIN**E** Step 7—**Evaluate** progress

VI.   **Postscript**

       A.   Highlight 1.6: The History of Generalist Practice with Organizations and Communities in the Professional Context

             1.   Three major economic and social changes in United States (between the Civil War and World War I)

                   a.   Industrialization

                   b.   Urbanization

                   c.   Explosive immigration

2.   Two social and ideological movements that became the foundation for social work practice in the 1880s

     a.   The Settlement House Movement

         1)   Settlement houses—places where ministers, students, or humanitarians "settled" to interact with poor slum dwellers with the purpose of alleviating the conditions of capitalism

         2)   Formed a strong partial foundation for generalist social work practice

         3)   Emphasized the empowerment of people

         4)   The concept of community organization and group work developed within the settlement house context

         5)   Jane Addams and Ellen Gates Starr began Hull House in Chicago in 1889

     b.   The Charity Organization Societies (COS)

         1)   COS emphasis was not on lay communal expertise but on scientific practice and expert knowledge

         2)   "Friendly visitors" tried to help people figure out how to solve their problems

         3)   Focused on curing individuals rather than on empowering communities—traditional casework developed from this approach

3.   Three method tracks (casework, group work, and community organization) characterized social work through the 1950s

4.   The Great Depression of the 1930s and the Social Security Act switched many aspects of service provision from the private to the public sector

5.   During the 1950s social workers turned again to psychotherapy and case work

6.   The 1960s produced a new focus on social change versus individual pathology

7.   Accountability became a key word when talking about social service provision

8.   In 1955, seven separate professional organizations came together to form the National Association of Social Workers

9.   The Council on Social Work Education (CSWE), the field's accrediting body, was born in 1952 when several predecessor organizations merged

10.   The prolific development of BSW programs in the late 1960s and early 1970s emphasized the need for a generalist foundation for social work practice

11.   Current thinking is that the BSW is the entry-level degree and the MSW provides advanced, specialized training

Exercise 1.1: What Does Generalist Practice Mean?

A.   Brief Description
Students discuss the nine major concepts inherent in the definition of generalist practice.

B.   Objectives
Students will:
1.   Recognize the basic concepts inherent in the definition of generalist practice.
2.   Examine the significance of each concept for social work practice.

C.   Procedure
1.   Review the material on the definition of generalist practice, an outline of which is provided in the box below under "Instructions for Students."
2.   Divide the class into small groups of four to six.
3.   Ask the groups to discuss the subsequent questions, select a group representative, and be prepared to report to the entire class the small group's findings.
4.   After about 20 minutes, ask the small groups to terminate their discussions and participate in a full class discussion.
5.   Ask the representative from each group to share her or his summary of the discussion. Encourage comments from all class members.

D.   Instructions for Students
Discuss the reasons why each concept inherent in the definition of generalist practice is important in social work. The box below provides an outline of the definition.

AN OUTLINE OF THE DEFINITION OF GENERALIST PRACTICE

1.   **Acquisition of an eclectic knowledge base**
    A.   Theoretical foundation: systems theories
    B.   Human behavior and the social environment
    C.   Social welfare policy and services
    D.   Social work practice
    E.   Social work research
    F.   Human diversity
    G.   Promotion of social and economic justice
    H.   Populations-at-risk
2.   **Emphasis on client empowerment**
3.   **Acquisition of professional values and ethics**
    A.   NASW Code of Ethics
    B.   Awareness of personal values
    C.   Clarification of conflicting ethical dilemmas
    D.   Understanding of oppression
    E.   Respect for diverse populations

---

4. **Use of a wide range of practice skills**
   A. Micro
   B. Mezzo
   C. Macro
5. **Orientation to target any size system**
   A. Micro
   B. Mezzo
   C. Macro
6. **Effective work within an organizational structure**
7. **Assumption of a wide range of professional roles**
   A. Enabler
   B. Mediator
   C. Integrator/coordinator
   D. General manager
   E. Educator
   F. Analyst/evaluator
   G. Broker
   H. Facilitator
   I. Initiator
   J. Negotiator
   K. Mobilizer
   L. Advocate
8. **Employment of critical thinking skills**
9. **Use of a planned change process**
   A. Engagement
   B. Assessment
      1) Defining issues
      2) Collecting and assessing data
   C. Planning
      1) Identifying alternative interventions
      2) Selecting appropriate courses of action
      3) Contracting
   D. Implementation of appropriate courses of action
   E. Evaluation
      1) Using appropriate research to monitor and evaluate outcomes
      2) Applying appropriate research-based knowledge and technological advances
   F. Termination
   G. Follow-up

E. Commentary
This activity may also be conducted by holding a full class discussion without breaking students down into small groups.

16

A. Brief Description
In a large group discussion students apply critical thinking skills to a series of scenarios occurring in macro practice contexts.

B. Objectives
Students will:
1. Use critical thinking to identify fallacies.
2. Articulate the reasons for their choices.

C. Procedure
1. Review the content on critical thinking, "fallacies and pitfalls" (Gibbs & Gambrill, 1996, p.71). Principles are summarized in the box below under "Instructions for Students."
2. Read the scenarios below under "Instructions for Students."
3. Lead a full class discussion focusing on the ensuing questions.

D. Instructions for Students
1. Read the summary of potential fallacies and pitfalls provided in the box below.

"Fallacies and Pitfalls" for Practitioners[1]

1. Trusting case examples instead of scientific research including surveys given to or observations made on representative samples to illustrate effective treatment approaches.
2. Trusting individual testimonials about personal experience as absolute fact. Just because a person says and, perhaps, even thinks that a treatment has been effective, it may not be. Without scientific inquiry something entirely unrelated may have caused the improvement.
3. Nebulous, inexact descriptions of problems, treatments, and evaluation mechanisms that make it impossible to determine what actually happened or if it did any good.
4. Hearing only one side of an argument or approach to treatment and automatically believing it without hearing and evaluating other approaches.
5. Depending on the idea that if the treatment approach is new and innovative, it must be good.
6. On the other hand, believing that if a practice approach has been around a long time and used by a lot of people, it must be good.
7. Believing that if a "fact" is cited or written down in a book, article, magazine, or newspaper, it must be the truth.

---

[1] Gibbs, L., & Gambrill, E. (1996). *Critical Thinking for Social Workers: A Workbook.* Thousand Oaks, CA: Sage, 71.

2.   For each of the following two scenarios, identify which fallacies and pitfalls might characterize the scenario and explain the reasons for your choices.

Scenario A: Re-elect the mayor. Your mayor states that you and other citizens should trust in his good judgment about how to allocate the city's resources, although he does not as yet have a detailed plan or budget in place. He stresses that this is his second term in office and he has a sound track record for making decisions in the past. He mentions that the major newspaper in town consistently supports him and his decisions.

What fallacy(ies) may apply?

Explain:

Scenario B: A famous expert. You are a social worker in a county department of social services. Your colleague Allison has just attended a seminar presented by Dr. B. S. Smock, a renowned expert in radical approaches to crisis intervention. This expert has published two books and several articles on the subject. Allison vehemently states that she thinks all the agency workers should be trained in Dr. Smock's techniques and use his suggestions. She indicates that several clients spoke at the seminar and provided testimony concerning the effectiveness of the approach. Allison is clearly a loyal and enthusiastic disciple of Dr. Smock.

What fallacy(ies) may apply?

Explain:

Scenario C: Supervisor Talking to Supervisees: "We've always scheduled our appointments with clients during the daytime working hours. It's always worked in the past. My motto is, 'If it ain't broke, don't fix it.'"

Which fallacy(ies) does this illustrate?

Explain:

Scenario D: Worker Complaining to a Colleague: "I think agency administration is all wet about their programming recommendations. They don't know what they're talking about."

Which fallacy(ies) does this illustrate?

Explain:

Scenario E: Governor Talking to Reporters: "My new welfare plan is the answer to all our problems with welfare mothers: Make them work to be eligible for their benefits and you'll solve the Temporary Assistance to Needy Families financial crisis in a hurry."

Which fallacy(ies) does this illustrate?

Explain:

> Scenario F: Worker Talking to a Colleague: "I've had the best luck with the Gung-ho Intervention technique on Ollie Hopnoodle. I'm going to use it with all my clients. I think the whole agency should adopt it."

Which fallacy(ies) does this illustrate?

Explain:

> Scenario G: Worker Giving an Informative Speech to Co-workers: "The Harvard Scripture of Social Work states that doing casework with individual clients is the most important aspect of social work practice."

Which fallacy(ies) does this illustrate?

Explain:

> Scenario H: Administrator Talking to His Staff: "Absolute Attainment Management is the wave of the future. It beats everything about the old bureaucratic approach to running social service organizations. Every in-the-know agency is starting to use it. Let's go for it! We don't want to be left behind."

Which fallacy(ies) does this illustrate?

Explain:

> Scenario I: Worker Talking to Agency Director: "I heard Ernie over at Moneyplenty Mental Health Center absolutely rave about their grant-writing seminars. I've got to get myself enrolled—but the fee is about 750 big ones. Do you think the agency might pay for at least half?"

Which fallacy(ies) does this illustrate?

Explain:

E.   Commentary
This exercise may also be conducted using the small group format described in Exercise 1.1.

Exercise 1.3: The Generalist Approach

A.   Brief Description
For a series of vignettes, students identify the potential micro, mezzo, and macro approaches to practice, in addition to the client, action, and target systems for each.

B.   Objectives
Students will:
1.   Assess micro, mezzo, and macro approaches to social work practice.
2.   Define and identify client, action, and target systems within the context of social work practice.

C.   Procedure

    1.   Review the material on micro, mezzo, and macro levels of practice, in addition to the definitions of client, action, and target systems. Definitions are briefly summarized in the box below.

Basic Definitions

Micro practice: Generalist social work practice focusing on planned change with and for individuals. The focus of attention of the individual and how to communicate and work on a one-to-one basis.

Mezzo practice: Generalist social work practice with small groups. In macro settings, this primarily involves task groups, where understanding group dynamics and communication patterns among several people is important.

Macro practice: Generalist social work practice intending to affect change in large systems, including organizations and communities. Skills involved include changing agency and social policies, planning and implementing programs, and initiating and conducting projects within agency and community contexts.

Client system: Any individual, family, group, organization, or community that will ultimately benefit from generalist social work intervention.

Action system: Those people who agree and are committed to working together in order to attain the proposed macro change. This may include you and/or others who are actively involved.

Target system: The system that social workers must modify or influence in order to reach their goals and have clients benefit from the planned change process.

---

    2.   Divide the class into small groups of four to six.

    3.   Ask the groups to discuss the following vignettes, answer the questions, select a group representative, and be prepared to report to the entire class the small groups' findings.

    4.   After about 20 minutes, ask the small groups to terminate their discussions and participate in a full class discussion.

    5.   Ask the representative from each group to share her or his summary of the discussion. Encourage comments from all class members.

D.   Instructions

The following vignettes illustrate case situations you might encounter in generalist practice. Each case could be addressed in a variety of ways, using a micro, mezzo, or macro approach. In each instance, decide how you would approach the case at each level—micro, mezzo, and macro. For each intervention level, identify the potential client, the action system, and the target system.

Vignette 1: You are a rural county social services worker for Lowater County, Iowa. Your job is to complete assessments on families needing services, make appropriate referrals, and provide short-term counseling when necessary. The Mississippi River has flooded, displacing two dozen families from their homes. After intake, a family with two preschool children has been assigned to you for assessment and referral. Other families in distress have been assigned to other workers in your department and other agencies. The family assigned to you has lost virtually everything it owns in the flood and, lacking flood insurance, has only a few hundred dollars left in savings. The mother worked as a waitress and the father as a mechanic in small, locally-owned businesses. The flood has literally wiped out their places of employment, eliminating both of their jobs. Although it was devastating for those involved, the flood was not serious enough to warrant state or national emergency assistance.

1A.   What potential alternative can you pursue at the micro level to help this family?

1B.   For this alternative, identify the following:

*Client system*_____

*Action system*_____

Target system _____

1C.   What potential alternative might you pursue at the mezzo level?

1D.   For this alternative, identify the following:

*Client system*_____

Action system _____

Target system _____

1E.   What can you do to help at the macro level?

1F.   For this alternative, identify the following:

Client system _____

Action system _____

Target system _____

Vignette 2: You are a school social worker in a large urban high school. You provide individual and group counseling to students, consultation to teachers dealing with students' behavioral and emotional issues, family assessments, short-term family counseling, assessments for individual programming, and referrals to appropriate community services. You find that teachers and administrators are referring increasing numbers of students to you because of drug use. There is currently no formal drug education program in the school.

2A.   What can you do to help at the micro level?

2B.   For this alternative, identify the following:

Client system _____

Action system _____

Target system _____

2C.   What can you do to help at the mezzo level?

2D.   For this alternative, identify the following:

Client system _____

Action system _____

Target system _____

2E.   What can you do to help at the macro level?

2F.   For this alternative, identify the following:

Client system _____

Action system _____

Target system _____

Vignette 3: You are a county social services worker in a large urban county in the Southwest. Four Hispanic refugee families from politically turbulent Central American countries have been assigned to your caseload. Each has children ranging in age from two to fifteen. Almost no one in these families speaks English, your county's school system emphasizes an English-language-only approach (rather than bilingualism), and most of the children are not yet enrolled in public school. All four families are living in very overcrowded apartments, receive only meager public assistance, and can barely afford food and clothing. There is no readily available public housing because the waiting lists are extraordinarily long. You are familiar with many facets of Mexican-American culture, but you know little about the specific Hispanic culture from which these clients come.

3A.   What can you do to help at the micro level?

3B.   For this alternative, identify the following:

Client system _____

Action system _____

Target system _____

3C.   What can you do to help at the mezzo level?

3D.   For this alternative, identify the following:

Client system _____

Action system _____

Target system _____

3E.   What can you do to help at the macro level?

3F.   For this alternative, identify the following:

Client system _____

Action system _____

Target system _____

E.   Commentary
        This activity may also be conducted by holding a full class discussion without breaking the class down into small groups.

Exercise 1.4: Roles in Macro Practice

A.   Brief Description
        Students assess a range of social work practice situations and propose the appropriate macro practice roles that can be used in each.

B.   Objectives
        Students will:
        1.   Describe a range of social work roles in macro practice.
        2.   Examine the significance of each role in a social work practice situation.

C.   Procedure
        1.   Review the material below on social work roles in macro practice.
        2.   Divide the class into small groups of four to six.
        3.   Ask the groups to identify the appropriate potential social work roles in macro practice for each vignette.
        4.   After about 20 minutes, ask the small groups to terminate their discussions and participate in a full class discussion.
        5.   Ask the representative from each group to share her or his summary of the discussion. Encourage comments from all class members.

D.   Instructions
        1.   Review the following content on roles social workers can assume in macro practice.

Social Worker Roles in Macro Practice

Generalist social work practitioners may assume a *wide range of professional roles* in macro practice. A *role* is a culturally expected behavior pattern for a person having a specified status or being involved in a designated social relationship. For example, people have certain expectations of how social workers will act and of the activities they will pursue.

Note that professional roles are not necessarily mutually exclusive. A worker may perform the functions of more than one role at a time. The roles include enabler, mediator, integrator/coordinator, manager, educator, analyst/evaluator, broker, facilitator, initiator, negotiator, mobilizer, and advocate.

An *enabler* provides support, encouragement, and suggestions to members of a macro client system, thus allowing the system to operate more easily and more successfully in completing tasks and/or solving problems. In the enabler role, a worker helps a client system become capable of coping with situational or transitional stress. Specific skills used in achieving this objective include conveying hope, reducing resistance and ambivalence, recognizing and managing feelings, identifying and supporting personal strengths and social assets, breaking down problems into parts that can more readily be solved [partialization], and maintaining a focus on goals and the means of achieving them (Barker, 1991, p. 74). For example, an enabler might help a community develop a program for identifying and shutting down crack houses. Community citizens do the work, but the enabler provides enthusiastic encouragement and helps participants identify their strengths and weaknesses and work out their interpersonal conflicts while keeping on task. Enablers, then, are helpers. Practitioners can function in the role of enabler for micro, mezzo, or macro systems.[2]

A *mediator* resolves arguments or disagreements among micro, mezzo, and/or macro systems in conflict (Toseland & Rivas, 2005; Yessian & Broskowski, 1983, pp. 183-84). At the macro level mediators help various factions (subsystems) in a community or community systems themselves work out their differences. For example, a community (or neighborhood) and a social services organization may require mediation over the placement of a substance abuse treatment center. Perhaps the social services organization has selected a prime spot, but the community or neighborhood is balking at the establishment of such a center within its boundaries.

The social worker may have to improve communication among dissident individuals or groups, or help those involved arrive at a compromise. A mediator remains neutral, does not side with either party in the dispute, and understands the positions of both parties. This allows her to clarify positions, recognize miscommunications, and help all parties present their cases clearly.

Integration is the process of assembling different elements to form a cohesive whole. *Coordination* involves bringing components together in some kind of organized manner. An *integrator/coordinator*, therefore, brings the people involved in various systems together and organizes their performance (Hardcastle & Powers, 2004; Yessian & Broskowski, 1983). A generalist social worker can function as an integrator/coordinator "in many ways, ranging from … advocacy and identification of coordination opportunities, to provision of technical assistance, to direct involvement in the development and implementation of service linkages" (Yessian & Broskowski, 1983, p.184). Integrator/coordinators function in macro systems in somewhat the same way that case managers function on behalf of individual clients or families.

A *manager* in social work is one who assumes some level of administrative responsibility for a social services agency or some other organizational system (Brody, 2005; Yessian & Broskowski, 1983, pp. 183-84). Administrators utilize three levels of skills— technical, people, and conceptual (Lewis, Lewis, Packard, & Souflee, 2001, p. 8. *Technical skills* include those used to direct an agency's basic activities such as overseeing counseling techniques, developing programs, or evaluating the agency's effectiveness. *People skills* concern "interpersonal effectiveness such as oral communication, listening, conflict management, leading, and motivating" (p. 8). *Conceptual skills* are those oriented toward assessing and understanding the overall operation of the agency and how it fits into its larger macro environment. These also concern being able to solve complex problems and develop creative solutions. The term *management* refers to all "the tasks and activities involved in directing an organization or one of its units: planning, organizing, leading, and controlling" (Hellriegel, Jackson, & Slocum, 2002, p. 7).

---

[2] Note that this definition of "enabler" is very different from that of the "enabler" as applied to cases of substance abuse. There the term refers to a family member or friend who facilitates the substance abuser in continuing to use and abuse the drug of his or her choice.

An *educator* gives information and teaches skills to other systems (Yessian & Broskowski, 1983, pp. 183-84). To be an effective educator, the worker must be knowledgeable about the topics being taught and a good communicator so that information is conveyed clearly.

An *analyst/evaluator* analyzes or evaluates effectiveness (Yessian & Broskowski, 1983, pp. 183-84). An analyst determines whether a program or agency is effective (Brody, 2005; Yessian & Broskowski, 1983). Generalist social workers with a broad knowledge base can analyze or evaluate how well programs and systems work. Likewise, they can evaluate the effectiveness of their own interventions.

A *broker* links any size system (individuals, groups, organizations, or communities) with community resources and services. Such resources might be financial, legal, educational, psychological, recreational, or health-oriented.

A *facilitator* is one who guides a group experience. Although the facilitator role is very common in mezzo practice, workers also frequently assume it in macro practice. In the macro context a facilitator brings participants together to promote the change process by improving communication, helping direct their efforts and resources, and linking them with needed information and expert help.

An *initiator* is the person who calls attention to an issue (Netting, Kettner, & McMurtry, 2004). The issue in the community may be a problem, a need, or simply a situation that can be improved. It is important to recognize that a problem does not have to exist before a situation can be dealt with. Often preventing future problems or enhancing existing services is a satisfactory reason for creating a change effort. Thus, a social worker may recognize that a policy has the potential to create problems for particular clients and bring this to the attention of her supervisor. Likewise, a client may identify ways that service could be improved. In each case, the worker is playing the role of initiator in terms of beginning the actual change process. Usually, this role must be followed up by other kinds of work, because merely pointing out problems does not guarantee they will be solved.

A *negotiator* is an intermediary who acts to settle disputes and/or resolve disagreements. However, unlike mediators, negotiators clearly take the side of one of the parties involved.

A *mobilizer* identifies and convenes community people and resources and makes them responsive to unmet community needs (Halley, Kopp, & Austin, 1992, p. 256). The mobilizer's purpose is to match resources to needs in the community context. Sometimes, a mobilizer's goal involves making services more accessible to those in the community who need them. Other times, a goal is initiating and developing services to meet needs that heretofore were unmet.

An *advocate* is one who steps forward and speaks out on behalf of the client system in order to promote fair and equitable treatment or gain needed resources. In macro practice, of course, it would be on the behalf of some macro client system. This may be especially appropriate when a macro client system has little power to get what it needs.

2.   Identify the Macro Practice Role(s) assumed in the following case scenarios. As indicated above, the potential roles include **enabler, mediator, integrator/coordinator, manager, educator, analyst/evaluator, broker, facilitator, initiator, negotiator, mobilizer,** and **advocate.** Note that in some scenarios the worker may play more than one role. Explain how each role functions in the scenario.

     A.   A social worker employed by a neighborhood center determines that the various workers and other professionals dealing with adolescent clients are not communicating with each other. For example, school social workers have no established procedure for conveying information to protective services workers who, in turn, do not communicate readily with probation and parole workers— despite the fact that these professionals are working with many of the same clients. The neighborhood center social worker decides to bring together representatives from the various agencies that serve the center and establish more clearly defined communication channels.

Macro Practice Role(s):

Explanation:

B. A worker in a Child Protective Services Unit has developed special skills in family counseling by participating in a two-year training program. Her agency's Assistant Director asks her to provide a series of six in-service training program for other Child Protective Services staff.[3]

Macro Practice Role(s):

Explanation:

C. The main tasks of a Foster Care Unit are to assess potential foster parent applicants, monitor placement, manage cases as children move in and out of foster care, and train foster parents in parenting and behavior-management skills. The unit social workers hold biweekly meetings to discuss how to improve agency service provision. The workers take turns organizing the meetings and running the discussions.

Macro Practice Role(s):

Explanation:

D. A social worker employed by a large private family services agency specializes in international adoptions, especially those involving countries from Northeastern Europe, Central Asia, and China. He discovers that many of the adoptive children suffer from health problems caused by early nutritional deprivation. The worker is convinced that this is not a matter of one or two problem cases, but a disturbing pattern. No automatic referral process is in place to assess these adoptive children and direct their families to needed resources, including designated medical specialists. The worker devises a systematic process for assessment and referral.

Macro Practice Role(s):

Explanation:

E. Agency administration asks one of three social workers in a large residential health care complex for older adults to assess the effectiveness of its social services program.

Macro Practice Role(s):

Explanation:

---

[3] *In-service training programs* are educational sessions provided by an agency for its staff to develop their skills or improve their effectiveness.

F.   A social worker employed at a sheltered workshop for people with developmental disabilities[4] is assigned by her supervisor to oversee a new program that will teach anger management and appropriate assertiveness skills to clients. She will also be responsible for supervising two other social workers and training them to implement the program with their clients.

Macro Practice Role(s):

Explanation:

G.   A group of clients inform their social worker that the community is trying to enforce a housing maintenance ordinance in a punitive and excessively picky manner. Enforcers have been sent to these clients' homes and have cited them for such minuscule matters as having pieces of siding that need repainting and rusted rain gutters. These clients are poor and have almost no access to resources for anything other than basic necessities. They implore their social worker to help them. She learns that the original intent of the ordinance was to ascertain the safety of the clients' living conditions: Were steps and railings broken? Were windows broken? Had lead paint been used? The worker, therefore, judges that both the client group and the community are trying to do the best they can, so she attempts to referee the dispute between the community client group and the community leaders imposing the ordinance.

Macro Practice Role(s):

Explanation:

H.   A social worker employed by a large public social services department increasingly hears client complaints about drug houses popping up in their residential neighborhoods. The worker identifies clients and other concerned citizens, and organizes a community meeting. He then assists community residents in formulating a plan to identify drug house locations and establish a procedure for reporting such houses to the authorities.

Macro Practice Role(s):

Explanation:

I.   A social worker at a public assistance agency is terribly troubled by the conditions in the clients' waiting room and by the tedious process of client intakes. She explores the issue, develops a proposed plan for improvement, and makes an appointment to speak with the agency's executive director about it.

Macro Practice Role(s):

Explanation:

---

[4] *Sheltered employment* such as this workshop for people with developmental disabilities is a program involving work in a safe, closely supervised work environment for people who have trouble functioning more independently.

J.   A local charitable organization cuts off its contribution to a Planned Parenthood agency[5] with a large, centrally located main clinic and three satellite clinics. The result will be a severe cutback in services and the closure of at least two satellite clinics. A huge number of clients will find it difficult if not impossible to receive adequate services. A social work counselor at one of the clinics, with the support of her supervisor, gathers facts to show the importance of the funding and arranges a meeting with the funding organization's leaders. She hopes to discuss the cuts and persuade the charitable agency to reverse its decision.

Macro Practice Role(s):

Explanation:

K.   A juvenile probation officer is distressed by proposed legislation that will shut down a vocational training program for juvenile offenders because of its expense. He talks to other workers and administrators in his state agency, and gathers facts and statistics that demonstrate the program's cost effectiveness. He then calls and writes to influential legislators, and meets with the chairperson of the legislative committee that recommended closing the program. He also contacts other concerned social workers and encourages them to join his effort.

Macro Practice Role(s):

Explanation:

L.   A group of community residents approaches a social worker to ask about starting a Neighborhood Watch program.[6]   The worker provides them with encouragement and information.

Macro Practice Role(s):

Explanation:

E.   Commentary
This activity may also be conducted by holding a full class discussion without breaking the class down into small groups.

---

[5] *Planned Parenthood* agencies assist people in making decisions about pregnancy and promote birth control and contraception.
[6] *Neighborhood Watch* programs bring neighborhood residents together to find ways to prevent crime in their neighborhood. They devise a system for observing any suspicious behavior, especially on the part of strangers, and for alerting the proper authorities. Members also educate new people moving into the neighborhood about the program and publicize the program's existence via window decals and signs.

I. **Introduction**

    A. Assertiveness

    B. Conflict

    C. Working with Supervisors

II. **Beginning Relationships in Macro Practice**

    A. An interview in macro practice includes communicating and problem solving with groups of clients, agency administrators, your colleagues, politicians, community residents, and professionals from various other community agencies

    B. Figure 2.1: The Worker in the Organizational, Community, and Political Macro Environments

III. **A Review of Basic Micro Skills**

IV. **Verbal and Nonverbal Behavior**

    A. Eye contact

        1. Direct eye contact with an occasional glance away is most appropriate

        2. People with different cultural backgrounds may have different expectations in terms of appropriate nonverbal behaviors

            a. Direct eye contact can signify disrespect in Thai culture

            b. Persons from Asian, Latin American, Caribbean, and American Indian backgrounds may offer respect by avoiding eye contact

            c. Traditionally Puerto Ricans have been taught to avoid eye contact with authority figures such as mental health providers, although the provider is expected to look directly at the client

    B. Attentive listening

        1. Hearing is the audio perception of spoken words; listening means that you try both to hear and to understand most of what another person is saying

        2. Three barriers to attentive listening involve three aspects of communication

            a. Intent—some meaning he or she wishes to convey

    b. Impact—what the receiver thinks the sender said

    c. Environmental barriers—potential noise and distractions

   3. Figure 2.2: Barriers to Attentive Listening

 C. Facial expressions

 D. Body positioning

   1. Tense/relaxed continuum

   2. Formal/informal continuum

   3. Personal space

    a. Intimate zone—from skin contact to about eighteen inches

    b. Personal zone—about eighteen inches to approximately four feet

    c. Social zone—four to twelve feet

    d. Public zone—outward from twelve feet

 E. Multicultural sensitivity and nonverbal behavior

   1. Russians say yes by shaking the head from side to side and no by moving the head up and down. Most Europeans do exactly the opposite

   2. People from certain Arabic cultures prefer to be only 18 inches apart when they talk; Arabs experiencing interaction in the 4 to 8 foot zone may interpret European behavior as exceptionally cold and aloof

   3. In Japan, smiling may indicate discomfort

 F. Highlight 2.1: Nonverbal Behavior, Communication, Empowerment, and People Who Have Physical Disabilities

   1. People with visual impairment

   2. People with hearing impairment

   3. People with mobility disabilities

V. **Warmth, Empathy, and Genuineness**

 A. Warmth—conveying a feeling of interest, concern, well-being, and liking to another individual

 B. Empathy—being in tune with how the other person feels, conveying the idea that you understand how he or she feels

1.   Uses of empathy

    a.   Help establish an initial rapport

    b.   Elicit feelings and begin talking about issues

    c.   Make confrontations more palatable

2.   Highlight 2.2: Practicing Empathic Responses in Macro Practice Contexts

C.   Genuineness (Authenticity)—sharing of self by relating in a natural, sincere, spontaneous, open and genuine manner

VI.   Communicating with Other People in Macro Contexts

A.   Simple Encouragement

B.   Be Sensitive to Cultural Differences

C.   Paraphrasing—restating what the other person is saying, but using different words

D.   Reflective Responding—translating into words what you think the other person is feeling

E.   Clarification—making certain that what another person says is understood

F.   Interpretation—seeking meaning beyond that of clarification

G.   Providing Information

H.   Emphasizing People's Strengths

I.   Summarization—briefly covering the main points of a discussion or series of communications

J.   Eliciting Information

1.   Closed-ended questions seek simple yes or no answers, or when there are a number of clearly defined answers to choose from

2.   Open-ended questions seek more extensive thoughts, ideas, and explanations for answers

K.   The Use of "Why?"

1.   It often implies that the person to whom it's directed is at fault

2.   It can put the burden of seeking a solution on the individual to whom it is directed

L.   Overlap of Techniques

VII. **Appropriate Assertiveness in the Macro Environment: Empowering Yourself and Others**

    A.   Assertiveness involves expressing yourself without hurting others or stepping on their rights

    B.   Highlight 2.3: Each of Us has Certain Assertive Rights

        1.   You have the right to express your ideas and opinions openly and honestly

        2.   You have the right to be wrong. Everyone makes mistakes

        3.   You have the right to direct and govern your own life

        4.   You have the right to stand up for yourself without unwarranted anxiety and make choices that are good for you

        5.   You have the right not to be liked by everyone

        6.   You have the right, on the one hand, to make requests and, on the other, to refuse them without feeling guilty

        7.   You have the right to ask for information if you need it

        8.   You have the right to decide not to exercise your assertive rights

VIII. **Nonassertive, Assertive, and Aggressive Communication**

    A.   Assertive communication—verbal and nonverbal behavior that permits a speaker to get points across clearly and straightforwardly, considering own rights and rights of others

    B.   Nonassertive communication—devaluing self completely, feeling that the other person and what that person thinks is much more important than one's own thoughts

    C.   Aggressive communication—bold and dominant verbal and nonverbal behavior, own view taking precedence above all others' points of view

    D.   Passive-aggressiveness—secretly or covertly aggressive

    E.   Figure 2.3: The Assertiveness Continuum

    F.   Highlight 2.4: What Would You Do?

    G.   Advantages of assertiveness

    H.   Assertiveness training

    I.   Final note on assertiveness training

IX. Conflict and Its Resolution

A. Interpersonal Conflict—occurs any time people involved in relationships, such as friends, family members, coworkers, or neighbors, have differing needs, wants, desires, expectations, goals, or means of achieving certain ends

B. The Pros of Conflict

1. Can help us explore a situation more thoroughly

2. Can cause us to make improvements in our behavior and communication

3. Can generate new energy to solve a problem

4. Can make daily routines more exciting

5. Can improve the quality of problem resolution and decision-making

6. Can release emotional "steam"

7. Can enhance self-awareness

8. Can be fun when it is not taken too seriously

9. Can facilitate the development and depth of relationships

C. The Cons of Conflict

1. Takes energy

2. May result in winners and losers instead of compromise

3. Decreased collaboration and team work

D. Personal Styles for Addressing Conflict

1. Turtle—withdraws into his or her shell to avoid conflicts

2. Shark—a power-hungry aggressor; will do almost anything to win

3. Teddy bear—values the relationship with the opponent much more than achieving his or her own goals

4. Fox—a compromiser; tries to reach an agreement that satisfies both parties

E.   Steps in Conflict Resolution

1.   Step 1: The Confrontation

   a.   Confrontation—a face-to-face encounter where people come together with opposing opinions, perspectives, or ideas in order to scrutinize or compare them

   b.   Two major issues when engaging in a confrontation

      1)   Clearly identify and examine your personal goals

      2)   Nurture your interpersonal relationship with the other person

   c.   Case Example—Step 1: Setting the Stage for a Confrontation

2.   Step 2: Establish common ground

   a.   Most important is to keep trying to empathize with your opponent's position

   b.   Case Example—Step 2: Establish Common Ground

3.   Step 3: Emphasize the importance of communication

   a.   Communication guidelines

      1)   Do not begin a confrontation when you are angry

      2)   Do not enter into a conflict unless you have a clearly established reason for doing so

      3)   If you absolutely despise your opponent or have immense difficulty reaching for any positive, empathic feeling about him, do not confront him

      4)   Include positive statements and feedback along with the negative aspects of confrontation

      5)   Be certain to explain your concerns regarding the conflict in a "descriptive and nonjudgmental" manner

      6)   Supply relevant data in support of your stance

      7)   Use "I-messages" frequently

   b.   Case Example—Step 3: Emphasize Communication

c. Suggestions for how to respond when someone confronts you

   1) Pay very close attention to what the confronter is telling you

   2) Explain to the confronter exactly how you will respond to his feedback

   3) Tell your confronter that you appreciate his effort and his feedback

   4) Approach your confronter later, and tell him how you have responded to his feedback

   5) At the time of the confrontation, do not reproach the confronter with a criticism of your own

4. Step 4: Emphasize your willingness to cooperate

   a. Stress the commonalities you have with your opponent

   b. Case Example—Step 4: Emphasize Your Willingness to Cooperate

5. Step 5: Empathize with your opponent's perspective

   a. Work to understand why your opponent feels the way she or he does

   b. Case Example—Step 5: Empathize with Your Opponent's Perspective

6. Step 6: Evaluate both your own and your opponent's motivation to address the conflict

   a. In many situations it is possible to change the degree of motivation on your own or your opponent's part

   b. Case Example—Step 6: Evaluate Both Your Own and Your Opponent's Motivation to Address the Conflict

7. Step 7: Come to some mutually satisfactory agreement

   a. Suggestions

   1) Articulate exactly what your agreement entails

   2) Indicate how you will behave toward the other person in the future as compared with the past

   3) Specify how the other person will behave toward you

        4)   Agree on ways to address any future mistakes

        5)   Establish how and when you and the other will meet in the future to continue your cooperative behavior and minimization of conflict

    b.   Case Example—Step 7: Come to Some Mutually Satisfactory Agreement

X. Working Under Supervisors

    A.   Highlight 2.5: Workers' General Expectations of Supervisors: Keys to Empowerment

        1.   Be readily available for consultation on difficult cases

        2.   Make certain that workers are knowledgeable about agency policy

        3.   Provide input to higher levels of administration regarding line workers' needs

        4.   Facilitate cooperation among staff

        5.   Nurture workers and give them support when needed

        6.   Evaluate workers' job performance

        7.   Facilitate workers' development of new skills

    B.   Administrative Functions of Supervisors

    C.   Educational Functions of Supervisors

    D.   Other Functions of Supervisors

    E.   Using Supervision Effectively

        1.   Use your communication skills with your supervisor

        2.   Keep your records up-to-date

        3.   Plan your supervisory agenda ahead of time

        4.   Put yourself in your supervisor's shoes

        5.   Display an openness to learning and improving yourself

        6.   Demonstrate a liking for your work

        7.   Work cooperatively with other staff

        8.   Give your supervisor feedback

9. Forewarn your supervisor about problematic situations

10. Learn your supervisor's evaluation system

F. Problems in supervision

    1. Highlight 2.6: Games Supervisors and Supervisees Sometimes Play

        a. I'll be nice to you if you'll be nice to me

        b. Therapize me

        c. Good buddies don't evaluate

        d. Of course, I know much more than you do

        e. Poor, helpless, little old me

        f. Information is power

        g. Avoiding the issue

        h. Pose questions to answer questions

    2. Simple misunderstandings between supervisor and supervisee

    3. Supervisors who take credit for your work

        a. Highlight 2.7: What Would You Do?

        b. There is no perfect answer

    4. Supervisory incompetence

    5. Laziness

    6. Problems with delegation

    7. Inability to deal with conflict

    8. Postscript

Exercise 2.1: Practicing Empathic Responses in Macro Practice Contexts

A. Brief Description
Students practice empathic responses for a range of macro practice situations.

B. Objectives
Students will:
1. Define empathy.
2. Propose empathic responses in a range of challenging macro practice situations.

C. Procedure
1. Review the content on empathy. (*Empathy* is not only being in tune with how other people feel, but also conveying to people both verbally and nonverbally that you understand how they feel.)
2. Either in a full-class discussion or in small groups followed by a full-class discussion, ask students to discuss the following vignettes and propose two empathic responses for each.

D. Instructions for Students
Below are several vignettes illustrating macro situations. Formulate and write down two empathic responses for each situation. **Vignette #1 provides an example.**

Vignette #1: You are a school social worker in an urban neighborhood. Residents inform you that a vacant lot in the neighborhood—two houses away from the school—was used as a dump for dangerous chemicals between ten and twenty years ago. In the past fifteen years, a dozen children attending the school have gotten cancer.

Addressing this type of issue is not part of your job description, but you see it as your professional and ethical responsibility to help the neighborhood residents explore their options for coping with this problem. For instance, a class-action lawsuit could be brought against the companies that dumped the chemicals. If it could be proved that the companies are at fault (that is, that they acted knowingly or negligently), they could be held financially liable for their actions.

The mother of one child (Eric, 14) who has leukemia makes an appointment to see you. When she enters your office, she bursts into tears: "I am so angry! How could people do this to little children? They must have known that dumping those wastes so close to children was dangerous."

How do you respond empathically?
- "You sound really angry. I don't blame you. What are your thoughts about what to do?"
- "I'm hearing you say that you are furious about this situation. What can I do to help you?"
- "This whole situation has been a horror story for you. Where do you think we can go from here?"

Vignette #2: You are a social worker in a health care facility for older adults. You want to start a program that will bring middle-school children to visit your senior clients. You believe that such interactions will be mutually beneficial for both your clients and the children. You have approached Kimberly, the other social worker in the facility, with this idea, but her response was hesitant and—in your opinion—negative. You think she is worried that this proposal will create a lot more work for her, work that she is neither ready nor willing to undertake.

In fact, you have pretty much paved the way for implementing the plan: You have contacted school administrators and teachers to obtain their permission and support. You've come up with a transportation plan and a proposed form for parental permissions. Before you have the chance to approach Kimberly again, she initiates a conversation with you: She states, "I know you're trying to do the right thing with this student visitation project [this is an empathic response on Kimberly's part], *but* you're pushing me into it. I don't have enough time to do my own work, let alone get involved in some petty little program you propose."

How do you respond empathically? (Remember that you *do not have to solve the problem* right now. You simply need to let Kimberly know that you understand how she feels.)

Alternative Response #1:

Alternative Response #2:

Vignette #3: You are a social worker at a diagnostic and treatment center for children with multiple physical disabilities. Your primary function is helping parents cope with the pressures they are under and connecting them with needed resources. The Center's staff includes a wide range of disciplines such as occupational therapy,[1] physical therapy,[2] speech therapy, psychology, and nursing. Sometimes the professionals from these other disciplines ask you to talk parents out of asking them questions, especially when a child's condition is getting worse. One day a physical therapist approaches you and asks, "Do you think you could talk to Mrs. Harris? She keeps asking me these uncomfortable questions about Sally [Mrs. Harris's daughter]. Sally's condition is deteriorating. I don't know what to say."

How do you respond empathically?

Alternative Response #1:

Alternative Response #2:

Vignette #4: You are an intake worker at a social services agency in a rural area. Your job is to take telephone calls, assess problems, and refer clients to the most appropriate services. You identify a gap in the services available to people with developmental disabilities. You think that a social activities center would help to fill this gap by meeting some hitherto unmet needs. You talk with administrators in your agency, and they generally support the idea—but they don't know where the funding would come from. They suggest that you talk with some local politicians. You make an appointment with the President of the County Board to explain your idea and ask about possible funding. She responds, "It certainly sounds good, but who's going to pay for it and run it?"

How do you respond empathetically?

Alternative Response #1:

Alternative Response #2:

---

[1] *Occupational therapy* is "therapy that utilizes useful and creative activities to facilitate psychological or physical rehabilitation" (Nichols, *Random House Webster's College Dictionary,* 1999, p. 914).

[2] *Physical therapy* is "the treatment or management of physical disability, malfunction, or pain by physical techniques, such as exercise, massage, hydrotherapy, etc." (Nichols, 1999, p. 887).

Exercise 2.2: Responding to Others in the Macro Environment

A. **Brief Description**
Students practice a range of responses in various macro practice situations.

B. **Objectives**
Students will:
1. Identify nine types of verbal responses.
2. Propose responses in a range of challenging macro practice situations.

C. **Procedure**
1. Review the material below on communicating with people in macro contexts. Nine common verbal responses are briefly defined in the box below.

USING VERBAL RESPONSES IN MACRO CONTEXTS

1. **Simple Encouragement:** *Any verbal or nonverbal behavior intended to assure, comfort, or support the communication.*
2. **Paraphrasing:** *Stating what the other person is saying, but using different words.*
3. **Reflective Responding:** *Translating into words what you think the other person is feeling.*
4. **Clarification:** *Choosing and using words to make certain that what another person has said is clearly understood.*
5. **Interpretation:** *To seek meaning beyond that of clarification by helping bring a matter to a conclusion, to enlighten, or to seek a meaning of greater depth than that which has been stated.*
6. **Providing Information:** *The communication of knowledge.*
7. **Emphasizing People's Strengths:** *Articulating and emphasizing other people's positive characteristics and behaviors.*
8. **Summarization:** *Covering the main points of a discussion or series of communications both briefly and concisely.*
9. **Eliciting Information:** *Requesting knowledge you need.*

---

2. Either in a full-class discussion or in small groups followed by a full-class discussion, ask students to discuss the following vignettes and propose two empathic responses for each.

D. **Instructions for Students**
Below are statements illustrating what might come from colleagues, supervisors, administrators, and others in the macro working environment. For each statement, give examples of the different types of possible responses. (Types of responses are listed under each statement.) **Statement #1 provides an example.**

Statement #1: (**From a worker at another agency**) "I've been meaning to talk to you about your agency's policy regarding the treatment of poor clients."

Possible Responses:

Simple encouragement: "I see. Please go on."

Rephrasing: "You have some concerns about my agency's procedures for working with impoverished clients."

Reflective responding: "You're upset about the way my agency treats poor clients."

Clarification: "You're concerned about the effect of our sliding fee scale on clients who can't afford it."

Interpretation: "You have some ethical concerns about our policy on treatment of poor clients."

Providing information: "Let me give you a copy of our new policy and some data on how it affects clients."

Emphasizing people's strengths: "You always have been an exceptional advocate for the poor."

Summarization: (Since it is almost impossible to summarize one line, assume that there has been an ongoing discussion of this matter.) "Over the past few weeks, we've talked about a number of your concerns about agency policy, including treatment of staff, of people of color, and of the poor."

Eliciting information: "Can you tell me exactly which policy you are referring to?"

Statement #2: **(From a colleague at your agency)** "I'm furious with my supervisor. He never gives me credit for anything!"

Simple encouragement:

Rephrasing:

Reflective responding:

Clarification:

Interpretation:

Providing information:

Emphasizing people's strengths:

Summarization: (Since it is almost impossible to summarize one line, assume that you have had an ongoing discussion on this matter.)

Eliciting information:

Statement #3: **(From another agency's director)** "I think your agency ought to get more involved in our program."[3]

Simple encouragement:

Rephrasing:

---

[3] _Vocational rehabilitation_ involves training people who have physical or mental disabilities "so they can do useful work, become more self-sufficient, and be less reliant on public financial assistance" (Barker, 2003, p. 457).

Reflective responding:

Clarification:

Interpretation:

Providing information:

Emphasizing people's strengths:

Summarization: (Since it is almost impossible to summarize one line, assume that you have had an ongoing discussion on this matter.)

Eliciting information:

Statement #4: **(From a local politician who has significant influence over your agency's funding)** "I'd like to know why your agency's staff hasn't submitted any grants for external funding."

Simple encouragement:

Rephrasing:

Reflective responding:

Clarification:

Interpretation:

Providing information:

Emphasizing people's strengths:

Summarization: (Since it is almost impossible to summarize one line, assume that you have had an ongoing discussion on this matter.)

Eliciting information:

Exercise 2.3: Avoiding the Use of "Why?"

A.   Brief Description
Students consider the effects of using the word "Why?" and propose alternatives.

B.   Objectives
Students will:
1.   Discuss the reasons for the word "Why?" being threatening.
2.   Propose alternative responses instead of asking "Why?".

C.   Procedure
        1.   Review the content on the use of "Why?"
        2.   Either in a full-class discussion or in small groups followed by a full-class discussion, ask students to discuss the following vignettes and propose two empathic responses for each.

D.   Instructions for Students
        Rephrase the following "why" questions.

Question #1: *"We agreed at the last meeting that you'd talk to Fred—why didn't you?"*

Alternative Phrasing:

Question #2: *"Why are you always complaining about that policy?"*

Alternative Phrasing:

Question #3: *"Why did the Director reject our petition?"*

Alternative Phrasing:

Question #4: *"Why are public assistance and social security so complicated?"*

Alternative Phrasing:

Exercise 2.4: Nonassertive, Aggressive, and Assertive Responses

A.   Brief Description
        Students are presented with vignettes portraying uncomfortable situations and asked to suggest aggressive, nonassertive, and assertive responses.

B.   Objectives
        Students will:
        1.   Propose appropriate assertive responses for scenarios occurring in macro settings.
        2.   Evaluate the potential benefits and costs of such responses.

C.   Procedure
        1.   Review the material on appropriate assertiveness in the macro environment. Brief definitions are provided in the box below.

Brief Definitions Regarding Assertiveness *Nonassertive communication:* Meek verbal and nonverbal behavior coming from a speaker who devalues herself completely, feeling the other person and what that person thinks are much more important than her own thoughts. *Aggressive communication:* Bold and dominating verbal and nonverbal behavior whereby a speaker presses her point of view as taking precedence above all other points of view, considering only her own views important, not the views of others.

> *Assertive communication*: Verbal and nonverbal behavior that permits a speaker to get her points across clearly and straightforwardly, taking into consideration both her own value and the values of whomever is receiving her message.

2.   Using a full-class discussion format or a small group format followed by a full-class discussion, ask students to respond assertively to the vignettes below.

D.   Instructions for Students
        Read each of the following and respond to the subsequent questions.

> *Scenario A:* You are a social worker for Heterogeneous County Department of Social Services. Paperwork recording your activities with clients is due promptly the Monday following the last day of each month. For whatever reason, you simply forget to get it in by 5:00 p.m. Monday the day it's due. Your supervisor Enrique calls you at noon the next day. He raises his voice and reprimands, "You know that reports are due promptly so that funding is not jeopardized. How many times do I have to tell you that?"

Nonassertive Response:

Aggressive Response:

Assertive Response:

Costs and benefits of each type of response:

> *Scenario B:* You work with a colleague who consistently comes late to your social work unit's biweekly meetings. He typically saunters leisurely into the meeting room with a cup of decaf in hand, noisily situates himself in a chair at the rectangular meeting table, and casually interrupts whomever is speaking, asking for a brief review of what he missed. You are sick and tired of such rude, time-wasting behavior.

Nonassertive Response:

Aggressive Response:

Assertive Response:

Costs and benefits of each type of response:

> *Scenario C:* You represent your social services agency at a community meeting where twelve community residents and five workers from other agencies are discussing what additional social services the community needs. Some possible grant funding has become available to develop services. The person chairing the meeting asks for input from each person present except you. Apparently, she simply overlooked that you had not gotten an opportunity to speak.

Nonassertive Response:

Aggressive Response:

Assertive Response:

Costs and benefits of each type of response:

Scenario D: Mohammed, a school social worker, applies for a state grant to start a summer activity program for adolescents in an urban neighborhood. Although he has already solicited support from his direct supervisor and from the school board, a principal from another school in the district objects to Mohammed's proposal: "Trying to get money for that project is inappropriate. It will result in significant differences in services between one school district and another, which is completely unfair. I think we should forget the idea."

Nonassertive Response:

Aggressive Response:

Assertive Response:

Costs and benefits of each type of response:

Scenario E: Audrey directs a group home for adults with physical disabilities. The home is run by a conservative religious organization which has publicly declared its anti-abortion stance. Her direct supervisor, the organization's director, is also strongly anti-abortion. Audrey, however, maintains a pro-choice position.

A pro-choice rally is being held this weekend, and Audrey plans to attend and participate. She even expects to carry a pro-choice banner and march in a planned procession through the main area of town. Audrey's supervisor finds out about her plans, calls her aside, and says, "I forbid you to participate in that rally. Our agency has a reputation to maintain, and I won't allow you to jeopardize it."

Nonassertive Response:

Aggressive Response:

Assertive Response:

Costs and benefits of each type of response:

Scenario F: Hiroko is a public assistance worker for a large county bureaucracy. She is very dedicated to her job and often spends extra time with clients to make certain that they receive all possible benefits. Her colleague Bill, who has the same job title, tells Hiroko, "Either you're a fool and a drudge to work overtime like that, or you're trying to be a 'star' to feed your ego."

Nonassertive Response:

Aggressive Response:

Assertive Response:

Costs and benefits of each type of response:

Exercise 2.5: Assertiveness Training for You

A.   Brief Description
Students are asked to review situations in which they might behave more assertively.

B.   Objectives
Students will:
1.   Identify situations where they did not act assertively and contrast these with situations where role models acted assertively.
2.   Propose assertive responses for relevant situations.

C.   Procedure
1. Review the material on assertiveness and assertiveness training.

2. Either in a full-class discussion in small groups followed by a full-class discussion, or as an individual assignment, ask students to discuss the following vignettes and propose two empathic responses for each.

D.   Instructions for Students
1.   Recall a situation in which you could have acted more assertively. Perhaps you were too nonassertive or too aggressive. Describe the situation below.

2.   Analyze the way you reacted in this situation. Critically examine both your verbal and nonverbal behavior. Describe and explain that behavior.

3.   Choose a role model for assertive behavior in a situation similar to the one you have described. Identify the person you've chosen, then describe what happened and how she reacted assertively.

4.   Identify two or three other assertive verbal and nonverbal responses that you could have employed in the situation you described.

5.   Imagine yourself acting assertively in the situation you described. Explain what you would say and do.

6.   After you have completed these five steps, try behaving assertively in real life. Continue practicing until assertiveness becomes part of your personal interactive style. Give yourself a pat on the back when you succeed in becoming more assertive. Be patient with yourself—it's not easy to change long-standing patterns of behavior.

Exercise 2.6: What's Your Style of Conflict?

A.   Brief Description
Students are asked to define their own personal style of conflict.

B.   Objectives
Students will:
1.   Discuss the various ways people address conflict.
2.   Identify their own personal approaches to conflict.

C.   Procedure
1.   Review the material on conflict and its resolution. *Interpersonal conflict* occurs "any time people involved in relationships, such as friends, family members, coworkers, or neighbors, have differing needs, wants, desires, expectations, goals, or means of achieving certain ends " (Nugent, 2001, p. 304). Review material on the five styles of addressing conflict presented in the box below. Review the content on the use of "Why?"s

---

Personal Styles for Addressing Conflict

Johnson (2006) proposed the following five styles of addressing conflict:
1.   *Turtles* "withdraw into their shells to avoid conflicts" (p. 208). For them, this is easier than mustering up the initiative and energy needed to address a conflict. Turtles typically have relatively poor self-concepts and are nonassertive.
2.   *Sharks,* unlike turtles, are aggressors. They move into conflict boldly, pushing aside any opponents. Sharks like power and want to win. They have very little interest in nurturing a relationship with an opponent.
3.   *Teddy bears* are essentially the opposite of sharks. They value their relationships with their opponent more than the achievement of their own goals. Teddy bears are more assertive than turtles because they do value their own ideas, but they will put those ideas aside in deference to an opponent's beliefs if they believe their relationship is threatened.
4.   *Foxes* are compromisers. Slyly, they work toward an agreement acceptable to them and to their opponent. Foxes are willing to relinquish some of their demands in order to come to a reasonable compromise. They are pretty slick at finding ways to satisfy everyone.
5.   *Owls,* like foxes, believe in compromise, but they are much more assertive in conflict. Their style can be called confrontational. Owls walk willingly, even eagerly, into conflict situations because they value *the conflict itself* as a means of brainstorming solutions, attacking problems, and enhancing relationships.

---

2.   Either in a full-class discussion or in small groups followed by a full-class discussion, ask students to discuss the following questions concerning their own individual styles for handling conflict.

D.   Instructions for Students
Answer the following questions:

1.   What style of conflict—or combination of styles—described above comes closest to the way you usually handle a conflict?

2.   To what extent is your approach to handling conflict effective? Explain.

3.   In what ways would you like to change your approach to conflict management? (If you are satisfied with your behavior in conflict situations, say so.)

A.   Brief Description
Students identify a conflict situation in which they were involved and apply the steps of conflict resolution to it.

B.   Objectives
Students will:
1. Explore the dimensions of conflict.
2. Apply the steps of conflict resolution to their own situations.

C.   Procedure
1.   Review the material on confrontation and conflict resolution. A *confrontation* is a face-to-face encounter where people come together with opposing opinions, perspectives, or ideas in order to scrutinize or compare them. See the material summarized in the box below on conflict resolution.

Steps in Conflict Resolution

The following seven steps of conflict resolution are proposed (Ivey & Ivey, 2007, 2008; Johnson, 1986, 2006):

Step 1:   *Confront the opponent.* First, clearly identify and examine your personal goals. Second, keep in mind that it's important to nurture your relationship with your opponent.

Step 2:   *Agree on a definition of the problem.* This definition should make neither you nor your opponent defensive or resistant to compromise. Emphasize how important the issue is to both of you.

Step 3:   Recognize the importance of maintaining communication with your opponent(s) in the conflict. Use the good communication techniques you have learned including the following (Sheafor and Horejsi (2006, pp. 404-405):
  a. Do not begin a confrontation when you're angry.
  b. Do not enter into a conflict unless you have a clearly established reason for doing so.
  c. If you absolutely despise your opponent or have immense difficulty reaching for any positive, empathic feelings about him, do not confront him.
  d. Include positive statements and feedback along with the negative aspects of confrontation.
  e. Be certain to explain your concerns regarding the conflict in a "descriptive and nonjudgmental" manner (Sheafor & Horejsi, 2006, p. 405).
  f. Supply relevant data in support of your stance.
  g. An additional suggestion is to use "I-messages" frequently.

Step 4:   *Indicate your own willingness to work with your opponent to find a mutually satisfactory solution.* To minimize disagreement (or at least to develop a viable plan of action) stress whatever you and your opponent have in common.

Step 5:   *Empathize with your opponent.* Think carefully about why she thinks, feels, or acts as she does.

Step 6:   *Evaluate both your own and your opponent's motivation to address the conflict.* Is it worthwhile to expend the energy necessary to resolve this conflict?

> **Step 7:** Come to some mutual agreement by following these five suggestions (Johnson, 2006).
>
> a. Articulate exactly what your agreement entails.
>
> b. Indicate how you will behave toward the other person in the future as compared to in the past.
>
> c. Indicate how the other person has agreed to behave toward you.
>
> d. Outline ways of addressing any future difficulties (such as might arise if you or the other person violates the agreement).
>
> e. Decide how and when you and the other person will meet to continue your cooperative behavior and to minimize future conflict.

2. Either in a full-class discussion or in small groups followed by a full-class discussion, ask students to answer the following questions.

D. Instructions for Students

Recall a conflict in which you have been involved. For the purposes of this exercise, it may be work-related, school-related, or personal. Answer the following questions:

1. Describe the conflict in detail. Who was involved? What was the issue? Explain the positions taken by the opposing sides. What were the circumstances of the actual confrontation?

2. Did you follow the suggestions in Step 1 for beginning a confrontation—that is, did you identify your goals and nurture your relationship with your opponent? What, if anything, could you have done differently to improve your handling of this conflict?

3. Did you follow Step 2 by finding some common ground with your opponent? What, if anything, could you have done differently to discover some common ground?

4. Did you follow Step 3 by maintaining communication with your opponent? What, if anything, could you have done differently to improve communication?

5. Did you follow Step 4 by indicating your willingness to cooperate with your opponent? What, if anything, could you have done differently to demonstrate this willingness?

6. Did you follow Step 5 by empathizing with your opponent and trying to understand his or her perspective? What, if anything, could you have done differently to achieve this empathy and understanding?

7. Did you follow Step 6 by evaluating both your own and your opponent's motivations in this conflict? What, if anything, could you have done differently to discern and evaluate those motives?

8. Did you follow Step 7 by arriving at some mutually satisfactory agreement? What, if anything, could you have done differently to make such an agreement possible?

A. Brief Description
Students formulate responses to supervisory scenarios by applying various communication techniques.

B. Objectives
Students will:
1. Apply communication techniques to macro practice scenarios.
2. Propose appropriate responses in a supervisory context.

C. Procedure
1. Review the material on communicating with other people in macro contexts and working under supervisors. Communication techniques are summarized in the box below.

USING VERBAL RESPONSES IN MACRO CONTEXTS

1. **Simple Encouragement:** *Any verbal or nonverbal behavior intended to assure, comfort, or support the communication.*
2. **Paraphrasing:** *Stating what the other person is saying, but using different words.*
3. **Reflective Responding:** *Translating into words what you think the other person is feeling.*
4. **Clarification:** *Choosing and using words to make certain that what another person has said is clearly understood.*
5. **Interpretation:** *To seek meaning beyond that of clarification by helping bring a matter to a conclusion, to enlighten, or to seek a meaning of greater depth than that which has been stated.*
6. **Providing Information:** *The communication of knowledge.*
7. **Emphasizing People's Strengths:** *Articulating and emphasizing other people's positive characteristics and behaviors.*
8. **Summarization:** *Covering the main points of a discussion or series of communications both briefly and concisely.*
9. **Eliciting Information:** *Requesting knowledge you need.*

2. Using a full-class discussion format or a small group format followed by a full-class discussion, ask students to respond to the following vignettes involving experiences in supervision.

D. Instructions for Students
Following are a number of statements made by supervisors to their supervisees. For each, give examples of the different types of possible statements you might make or questions you might ask as a supervisee making a response. Label which verbal response or combination of responses indicated in the box above each statement reflects. Formulate as many types of the nine verbal responses as possible. Because the statements are vague, feel free to make up facts in your responses.

Supervisor Statement A: I'm concerned about the quality of your work lately. It seems you've taken a lot of sick days and your record keeping has fallen behind.

As a supervisee, how might you respond?
What type(s) of verbal response or responses does this reflect?
Explain why.
(For example:
"You sound like you're frustrated with me." *Reflective responding*

"What work are you most concerned about?" *Eliciting information*)

Supervisor Statement B: "There's an important staff meeting scheduled after work on Friday. I wouldn't make you attend if I didn't have to."

As a supervisee, how might you respond?

What type(s) of verbal response or responses does this reflect?

Supervisor Statement C: "Could you work up a one-hour in-service training program[1] on some aspect of your practice for the general agency staff meeting next month?"

As a supervisee, how might you respond?

What type(s) of verbal response or responses does this reflect?

Supervisor Statement D: "Funding has been drastically cut. I surely wish someone around here knew more about grant writing."

As a supervisee, how might you respond?

What type(s) of verbal response or responses does this reflect?

Supervisor Statement E: "There's a growing group of community residents complaining about the efficiency of our service provision."

As a supervisee, how might you respond?

What type(s) of verbal response or responses does this reflect?

---

[1] *In-service training programs* are educational sessions provided by an agency for its staff to develop their skills or improve their effectiveness.

A.   Brief Description
Students evaluate a supervisor they've had in the past.

B.   Objectives
Students will:
1.   Examine realistic expectations of supervisory behavior.
2.   Assess a prior supervisory experience.

C.   Procedure
1.   Review the material on supervision. A summary of worker's general expectations of supervisors is presented in the box below.

> **Workers' General Expectations of Supervisors**
>
> Workers generally expect supervisors (Dolgoff, 2005; Halley, Kopp, & Austen, 1998; Kadushin & Harkness, 2002; Sheafor & Horejsi, 2006):
> - To be readily available for consultation—i.e., to provide help based on professional or expert opinion
> - To ascertain that workers are knowledgeable about relevant agency policies and are aware of what they should and should not do
> - To inform higher levels of administration about line workers' needs
> - To facilitate cooperation among staff and resolve disputes
> - To nurture workers, provide support, and give positive feedback whenever possible
> - To evaluate workers' job performance
> - To facilitate workers' development of new and needed skills

2.   Using a full-class discussion format or a small group format followed by a full-class discussion, ask students to discuss a supervisor they've had in the past.

D.   Instructions for Students
Think of a supervisor you have or one you had in the past. You may choose someone you consider very good or downright terrible. In this exercise, you will evaluate that supervisor in terms of the expectations listed above, so choose someone you remember well. If you've never had a supervisor, imagine one of your instructors in that role. In this evaluation, cite pros, cons, and suggestions for improvement. It may help to mention specific interactions you had or issues you confronted with this supervisor.

1.   How readily available was this supervisor to provide help based on professional or expert opinion?

Pros:

Cons:

Suggestions for Improvement:

2. Did this supervisor fulfill your expectations in ascertaining that you were knowledgeable about relevant agency policies so that you could do your jobs as well as possible?

   Pros:

   Cons:

   Suggestions for Improvement:

3. Did this supervisor fulfill your expectations in informing higher levels of administration about line workers' needs?

   Pros:

   Cons:

   Suggestions for Improvement:

4. Did this supervisor fulfill your expectations in facilitating cooperation among staff and helping to resolve disputes?

   Pros:

   Cons:

   Suggestions for Improvement:

5. Did this supervisor fulfill your expectations in nurturing you, providing support, and giving positive feedback?

   Pros:

   Cons:

   Suggestions for Improvement:

6. Did this supervisor fulfill your expectations in accurately and effectively evaluating your job performance?

   Pros:

   Cons:

   Suggestions for Improvement:

7.   Did this supervisor fulfill your expectations in facilitating your development of new and needed skills?

Pros:

Cons:

Suggestions for Improvement:

Exercise 2.10: Addressing Problems in Supervision

A.   Brief Description

Students discuss ways in which to address and cope with problems in supervision.

B.   Objectives
Students will:
1.   Examine potential problems with supervisors.
2.   Propose approaches to deal with problematic situations.

C.   Procedure
1.   Review the material on supervision.
2.   Using a full-class discussion format or a small group format followed by a full-class discussion, ask students to discuss a supervisor they've had in the past.

D.   Instructions for Students
Sometimes, for whatever reason, problems develop with supervisors. They may be your own, your supervisor's, or no one's fault, but when they occur, you must address them, adjust to them, or leave for another job.

The following scenarios are taken from actual supervisory experiences. Each involves real problems that you too could confront. In each case, think about how you might address the problem. Then answer the questions that follow.

Scenario A: Taking Your Credit
        You are a social worker at a large urban diagnostic and treatment center for children with multiple developmental and physical disabilities. Your primary role includes helping parents cope with their child's disability, making referrals to appropriate resources, offering some family counseling, and interpreting the physicians' and other therapists' findings and recommendations to parents in words the parents can understand.
        The city abruptly cuts off funding for transportation to the center. Many of your parents are very poor and don't own vehicles. Most of the children have such extreme physical difficulties that city buses can't accommodate them. After compiling some facts, you call various local political leaders and share with them your serious concerns. Because of your efforts, the local City Council Chairperson convenes a meeting to address and remedy this transportation problem. You are very proud of yourself because you feel you are primarily responsible for this solution.
        You share the news with your supervisor and indicate enthusiastically that you are planning to attend the meeting. She says, "I don't think you need to attend the meeting. I'll go instead." You emphasize how hard you've worked on this project and make clear that you would really like to attend. You suggest that, perhaps, you could both go.

She responds, "No, I don't think so. I'll go." You are devastated.

1. Try to empathize with this supervisor by discerning what her reasons might be for reacting like this.
2. In this situation, how could you use the suggestions for assertiveness and confrontation described earlier in this chapter?
3. Consider the suggestions for using supervision effectively. Which of them could help you in this case?
4. If you were the supervisee portrayed here, how important would it be to you to receive credit for your accomplishment? Would you feel that it was the goal that mattered rather than *who* achieved it?
5. If you are the supervisee portrayed here and you *do* care about receiving credit for your work, what will you do if all the suggestions you have proposed thus far fail? (For example, will you go to an administrator above your supervisor for help and risk your supervisor's wrath? Will you learn a lesson from the experience and keep your successes to yourself in the future? Will you try to put it out of your mind and go on with your daily business? Will you start looking for another job?) There is no "correct" answer. You must identify various options, weigh the pros and cons of each, and decide what to do.

Scenario B: The Communication Gap

You are a newly hired social worker for a unit of boys, ages 11 to 13, at a residential treatment center for youths with serious behavioral and emotional problems. Your responsibilities include counseling, group work, case management, some family counseling, and consultation with child-care staff on matters of behavioral programming. Two of the twelve boys in the unit have been causing you particular trouble. They are late for their weekly counseling sessions and sometimes skip them altogether. When you do talk to them, they don't respond to your questions. Instead, they walk around the room, tell you that you don't know what you're doing, poke holes in the furniture with their pencils, and call you vulgar names.

You are at a loss regarding what to do with these two clients. In your weekly one-hour session with your supervisor, you explain the situation. He makes several vague suggestions about videotaping some of your sessions, making home visits, and talking about the boys' behavior with them. At the end of the session, you feel you've gotten nowhere, and you still don't understand what you should do. You have difficulty following what your supervisor is saying. You can't "read" him. Sometimes you think he's joking, but you can't be sure.

1. Try to empathize with this supervisor by discerning what his reasons might be for reacting like this.
2. In this situation, how could you use the suggestions for assertiveness and confrontation described earlier in this chapter?
3. Consider the suggestions for using supervision effectively. Which of them could help you in this case?
4. Consider the possibility that you tried a range of approaches and none worked. If you decided that your supervisor was incompetent and really unable to help you, what would you do? Might you consider turning to other people in the agency for help? If so, how would you do so?

Scenario C: The Angry Response

You are a social worker at a health care center (nursing home) who has a variety of clients diagnosed as "mentally ill." Every six months, a staffing is held at which social workers, nurses, therapists (speech, occupational, physical), physicians, psychologists, and psychiatrists summarize clients' progress and make recommendations. It is your job to run the staffing and write a summary of what is said.

You are new at your job and unfamiliar with this agency. During the staffing, the psychiatrist is very verbal—in fact, you would describe him as "pushy." You feel intimidated and are uncomfortable asserting your own opinions when they are different from, or even opposed to, his. Because of his advanced education, his professional status, and his self-confident demeanor, you feel that his views are probably more important and valid than yours. After the staffing, your supervisor calls you aside. His face is red and his voice has a deadly, steel-like calm. He reams you out for letting the psychiatrist take over the staffing. This surprises and upsets you so much that you do not hear many of the specific things he says. You just know that he is furious with you and has implied—or even stated—that you are an incompetent wimp. He walks off in a huff.

1. Try to empathize with this supervisor by discerning what his reasons might be for reacting like this.
2. In this situation, how could you use the suggestions for assertiveness and confrontation described earlier in this chapter?
3. Consider the suggestions for using supervision effectively. Which of them could help you in this case?

Scenario D: Problems with Delegation[5]

You are a caseworker for a social services agency in a rural county. Your job includes a wide range of social work practice, from investigating child abuse cases to working with families of truants to providing supplementary services to older adults who want to remain in their own homes. You have a heavy caseload, but feel very useful. In general, you really like your job.

The problem is that your supervisor insists on reading every letter and report you write before it goes out. You think this is a terribly time-consuming waste of effort. In many instances, it also delays your provision of service, and you feel that it's condescending and implies a lack of confidence in your professional abilities.

1. Try to empathize with this supervisor by discerning what her reasons might be for reacting like this.
2. In this situation, how could you use the suggestions for assertiveness and confrontation described earlier in this chapter?
3. Consider the suggestions for using supervision effectively. Which of them could help you in this case?
4. In the event that your efforts to improve this situation fail, what would you do?

---

[5] A primary administrative task for supervisors is mastering the art of delegation. *Delegation* is "assigning responsibility or authority to others" (Mish, *Webster's Ninth New Collegiate Dictionary*, 1991, p. 336).

Scenario E: No Action

You are a social worker in a large urban community center serving multiple community needs. Services include counseling for emotional and behavior problems, provision of contraception, recreational activities for adults and youth, day care for working parents, meals for older adult citizens, some health care, and a variety of other services. Your job focuses primarily on counseling the center's clients referred for this purpose. You enjoy your job and are proud of being a professional social worker.

The problem is another social worker whose office is next to yours. He has a similar job but is assigned a different caseload and a slightly different range of responsibilities. The bottom line is that you seriously question his professional competence. You've observed him using what you'd describe as "comic book therapy" with the children and adolescents on his caseload. In other words, his clients come in and select comic books from his vast collection instead of receiving any real counseling. He has boasted on several occasions that he only went into social work because he was eligible for a scholarship.

One day you approach one of your clients, a fairly bright and articulate boy of 13. You are surprised to see him reading something in the center's waiting room, and you are disturbed when he obtrusively places his hand over a portion of a picture in the book. It strikes you as odd that his hand is placed over the rear half of a horse. He looks surprised to see you and he comments on the horse's long white mane. The mane is indeed remarkable: it reaches to the ground and extends another foot. When you ask your client what the book is about, he sheepishly shows you the picture, which depicts a castrated horse (hence, the mane and tail elongated due to hormonal changes). The book's title is *Washington Death Trips*. Among other items pictured in the book are dead babies in caskets, people who have butchered over 500 chickens by hand for no reason, and various infamous murderers. The boy tells you that your colleague lent him this book.

You are furious. Not only does this colleague offend your professionalism and your professional ethics, he even has the gall to interfere with your clients. You immediately go to your supervisor, who is also his supervisor, and complain about the incident.

Your supervisor—a well-liked, easy-going, but knowledgeable and helpful person—hems and haws. He implies that methods of counseling are each professional's own business, but you believe that your supervisor is afraid to confront your colleague.

1. Try to empathize with this supervisor by discerning what his reasons might be for reacting like this.
2. In this situation, how could you use the suggestions for assertiveness and confrontation described earlier in this chapter?
3. Consider the suggestions for using supervision effectively. Which of them could help you in this case?
4. If your efforts to improve this situation fail, what will you do? Can you ignore this issue?

E. Commentary

In summary, life with supervisors will not always be ideal. When a problem occurs, all you can do is use your communication skills to your best advantage, identify your alternatives, weigh the pros and cons of each, and choose your course of action.

Fortunately, you will probably also have supervisors who will serve as primary mentors. A *mentor* is someone who encourages you to do your best, exposes you to new knowledge and ideas, and provides you with opportunities to develop your skills and competence.

Exercise 2.11: A Role Play in Supervision

A.   Brief Description

Students participate in a role play involving a supervisory scenario.

B.   Objectives
Students will:
1.   Experience a simulated situation as either a supervisor or supervisee.
2.   Explore the interpersonal dynamics involved and enhance empathy for both supervisor and supervisee.

C.   Procedure
1.   Review the material on assertiveness in the macro environment, and conflict resolution, supervision, and worker's general expectations of supervisors. A summary of worker's general expectations of supervisors is presented in the box below.
2.   Divide the class into pairs with one person playing a supervisee and the other a supervisor. Read the following role play. Allow it to continue for 5 to 10 minutes before discussing results.

D.   Instructions for Students
For this exercise students pair off, with one person playing a supervisee and the other a supervisor. You and your partner choose who will play which role. The supervisee should use the suggestions provided in this chapter to confront the supervisor assertively and use supervision effectively. After five to ten minutes, stop and answer the questions.

Supervisee: *You are a generalist practitioner in a foster care placement unit in a large county social services agency. You received your annual performance review report from your supervisor. The format requires a summary statement by the supervisor. Yours reads, "This worker does a pretty good job of completing her work on time." You feel this is a very negative statement, substantially detracting from a positive evaluation. You believe that you work exceptionally hard, often volunteer to accept difficult cases, and take pride in your performance.*

Supervisor: *You have two dozen supervisees. You don't like to give radically different performance reviews to your workers because these can make for hard feelings and jealousy among staff. You don't think the review is really relevant anyway since salaries are based solely on seniority, not on merit. In your view, your significant communication with workers is carried on during your biweekly individual supervisory conferences, and you think this particular supervisee is doing a good job.*

---

1.   What communication, confrontation, assertiveness, and supervisory techniques did the supervisee use during the role play?
2.   How effective were these techniques in resolving the issue?
3.   What other techniques, if any, might the supervisee have used to improve her effectiveness?

Chapter 3
Group Skills for Organizational and Community Change

I. **Introduction**

II. **Leadership and Leadership Skills**

    A.   Identifying targets for change

    B.   Capacity to inspire

    C.   Assertiveness

    D.   Communication skills

    E.   Leading by example

    F.   Bringing new perspectives

    G.   Use of self

        1.   Self-awareness—recognize and examine your own motivations and actions and continually monitor yourself throughout the process

        2.   Self-disclose—appropriately sharing your thoughts, feelings, and observations with others

        3.   Purposefulness—capacity to deliberately engage in goal-seeking behaviors

    H.   Understanding the media

    I.   Task group leadership skills

    J.   Managing conflict

    K.   Leadership and administration

        1.   Administration is often more concerned with issues of consistency and ensuring that rules are followed

        2.   Leadership may sometimes conflict with the interests of administrators

        3.   Administrators often seek to maintain the status quo while social work leaders often seek vastly different goals

        4.   Do not confuse leadership and administration

L.   Leadership and power

    1.   Leaders must have the capacity to exercise power, but power is not the central theme of leadership

    2.   As a servant-leader, a social worker may both lead and follow, depending upon what the situation requires

    3.   Not using power when it is available can be an important contributor to leadership

III.   Networking

A.   Networks—a number of individuals or organizations that are interconnected to accomplish a goal that each feels is worthwhile

B.   Two related but different meanings for the term networking

    1.   Networking occurs when social workers attempt to strengthen or develop linkages among people, groups, or other organizations

    2.   Professionals use networking to describe relationships they develop with colleagues for the purpose of improving services from social agencies and organizations

C.   Highlight 3.1: Networking in Action

D.   Importance of networking

    1.   Clients benefit from informal helping networks

    2.   Networks reach out to clients

        a.   Cross cultural situations

        b.   Networking roles played by churches

        c.   Networking is critical in rural areas

    3.   Networks augment formal resources

    4.   Networks help navigate formal systems

        a.   Networking to fill a service gap

        b.   Highlight 3.2: Networking for Latchkey Kids

        c.   Service fairs

5. Networks help workers cope

6. Networks: Mutual Aid

E. Types of networks

    1. Classified into categories based on:

        a. Type of relationship among members

        b. Degree of intimacy members share

        c. Difficulty level of the help needed

        d. Size of network

F. Problems with networks

    1. When professionals do not value the contributions of informal networks

    2. When a worker takes such an active leadership role with a client's informal network that the client feels incompetent or left out

    3. Within formal networks when negative or dysfunctional relationships reduce the network's effectiveness

    4. Failure to share information with other network members

    5. Lack of support from all agencies involved in network activities

    6. If some professionals question whether the informal network can maintain an adequate level of confidentiality about the client's situation

    7. Methods for overcoming difficulties in networking

        a. Recognize and acknowledge mutual interests of different agencies and resources

        b. Provide various avenues of communication to bridge the gaps

G. Worker roles in networking

    1. Highlight 3.3: Worker Roles with Self-Help Groups

        a. Providing a place to meet

        b. Contributing or arranging for funds

        c. Providing information to members

        d. Training members as leaders

        e. Referring people to the group

f.   Publicizing group activities

g.   Accepting referrals from the group

h.   Providing credibility in the larger community

i.   Providing credibility in the professional community

j.   Serving as a buffer between the group and other agencies/organizations

k.   Providing social and emotional support for group leaders

l.   Consulting with group leaders

IV.   Working In and With Teams

A.   Interdisciplinary teams—used when service to the client requires the expertise of multiple disciplines

B.   Characteristics of effective teams

1.   Clear goals

2.&3.   Structure and membership tied to goals

    a.   Problem-solving teams—composed of people who trust one another and can stay focused on the issues of importance

    b.   Creative team—has the task to come up with a variety of possible products or ideas and need the autonomy to consider alternatives

    c.   Tactical team—is brought in to carry out a plan

4.   Commitment of all members

5.   Collaborative climate

    a.   Groupthink—occurs when too much emphasis rests on collaboration and conformity and not enough attention is given to thinking critically about alternatives

    b.   Critical thinking—challenging assumptions, verifying facts, questioning opinions not supported by data, and being willing to consider ideas that others have rejected

6.   Standards of excellence—measures of the value and worth of actions

7.   Information-based decision making

8.   External support and recognition

9.   Principled leadership

V. Planning and Conducting Meetings

A. Plan ahead

B. Clarify purpose and establish objectives

C. Select participants

D. Select a time and place

    1. Set meeting times weeks in advance if possible

    2. Don't hold meeting and eat simultaneously

    3. Hold meetings in meeting rooms—not in your office

    4. Choose locations that simplify accomplishment of group business

    5. Meeting location needs to be accessible to those with disabilities

    6. Purpose of meeting should determine seating arrangements and overall room layout

E. Prepare an agenda

    1. Agenda—a list of topics to be addressed at a meeting in some sort of prioritized order

    2. Agenda items

        a. Announcements

        b. Decision items

        c. Discussion items

    3. Highlight 3.4: Example of an Agenda

F. Start meetings on time

G. State the ending time at the start

H. Let people know how much of your time they can have

I.   Keep the group on target

       1.   Focus on goals and operating within time constraints

       2.   Promote harmony but not at the expense of thinking critically about options

       3.   Test for agreement whenever apparent compromises appear to be achieved

       4.   Use humor to relax the group or to break the tension

       5.   Avoid personal attacks and don't let others engage in them

       6.   May need to interrupt a participant who talks too much

       7.   Structure the process

             a.   Identify items on which there is already unanimity and approve them together. Sometimes called a consent agenda

             b.   Approval of a lengthy document might best be done *ad seriatim* (item by item)

             c.   Periodically summarize the areas of agreement and sum up when decisions have been made

             d.   Avoid discussing irrelevant topics or rehashing previous decisions

             e.   If new topics are brought up, it is often better to place them on future agendas

             f.   If appropriate, a new business item can be referred to a committee

             g.   Keep necessary reports brief

             h.   When oral reports are needed, ask for succinctness and place a time limit on each report

J.   End the meeting on time

       1.   Highlight 3.5: Ending Meetings

             a.   Meetings should be ended whenever any of the following is evident

                    1)   More facts are required

                    2)   The group needs the input of people not present

                    3)   Members need more time to talk to others

                    4)   Events may change the direction in the immediate future

                    5)   There is not enough time to deal with the topic adequately

        6)   A subgroup can handle this more easily than the entire group can

        7)   A decision has been reached

K.   Plan for follow-up meetings

     1.   Minutes—official record of actions taken by the group

     2.   Highlight 3.6: Minutes of a Meeting

VI.   Parliamentary Procedure

A.   Parliamentary procedure—a highly structured technique used by groups of various sizes to make decisions and conduct business

B.   *Robert's Rules of Order*—first published in 1876, and the most commonly used set of procedures

C.   Advantages and disadvantages of parliamentary procedure

D.   Basic parliamentary concepts

     1.   Motions—proposed actions that the group is asked to support

     2.   Privileged motions—deal with the agenda itself but not with any particular business before the group. They have the highest priority of the four categories

          a.   Motion to recess

          b.   Motion to adjourn

     3.   Incidental motions—relate to the business under discussion

          a.   Point of order—used when a participant is concerned about some aspect of the way business is being transacted

          b.   Point of information—used when a participant is not clear about something occurring in the meeting

     4.   Subsidiary motions—help deal with motions that are currently on the floor

          a.   Table or Postpone—delays action on the proposed motion

          b.   Amend—used to change the proposed motion in some way

5.   Highlight 3.7: Common Parliamentary Definitions

    a.   Ad hoc committee—a special committee assigned one primary responsibility and then terminated

    b.   Adjourn—to end a meeting officially

    c.   Agenda—an official list of business to be discussed or decided at a meeting

    d.   Amend—to add, delete, or substitute words or portions of a motion

    e.   Bylaws—the major rules of an organization, usually more detailed than the constitution

    f.   Call the question—a motion to stop debate and immediately vote on the matter before a group

    g.   Committee—any portion of the total group assigned a specific task

    h.   Constitution—a document that describes the basic laws and governing procedures of an organization

    i.   Debate—discussion of topics a group is addressing

    j.   Executive committee—a subgroup composed of the chief officers of an organization, often including one or more elected members

    k.   Filibuster—speaking for the primary purpose of taking up time and preventing a group from voting on a topic

    l.   Majority vote—greater than one half of the total of persons voting or ballots cast

    m.   Minutes—the official record of decisions reached by a group

    n.   Motion—a proposal, requiring action, submitted to a group

    o.   Nomination—a formal proposal for some office

    p.   Plurality—the receipt of more votes than any other person, but less than a majority

    q.   Point of order—a statement to the presiding officer of a group that a mistake has occurred or a rule should be enforced

    r.   Proxy—a signed statement giving another person the right to vote in one's place

    s.   Quorum—the minimum number or proportion of members needed to legally transact business

t.   Recess—a short break in a meeting

u.   Refer to committee—a motion to delegate work on some specific matter to a smaller group

v.   Second—an indication of approval of a proposed motion

w.   Seriatim—a method of discussing and voting on a document by section

x.   Standing committee—committee that continually exists and handles certain types of business

y.   Table—a motion to indefinitely postpone action on a motion already on the floor

z.   Unanimous—any vote on which there is no dissent

E.   Main motions

   1.   Introduce the primary issue before the group

   2.   Most motions need a second

   3.   Highlight 3.8: Classes of Motions

      a.   Privileged motions

      b.   Incidental motions

      c.   Subsidiary motions

      d.   Main motions

   4.   Motions that require a two-thirds majority to pass

      a.   Object to consideration of a motion

      b.   Call to suspend the rules

      c.   Call for an immediate vote

      d.   Limit or extend debate

      e.   Rescind a motion under consideration

   5.   Voting on motions

F.   Other parliamentary rules

1.   Quorum—minimum number of members who must be present to conduct business and make decisions

2.   Officers

3.   Committees

a.   Standing—permanent

b.   Ad hoc—temporary committees established to address some specific issue

c.   Steering—sometimes created to help run an organization that does not want to become too formal

4.   Filibustering—endlessly speaking on a matter, thereby preventing a group from conducting its business

VII.   Managing Conflict

A.   Conflict is normal; can be positive or negative; fear and discomfort with conflict is common

B.   Highlight 3.9: Conflict in the Hospital

C.   Forms of Conflict

1.   Interpersonal—occurs when disagreement over a concrete issue escalates to include personal attacks

2.   Scarce resources—occurs over the use of (or access to) money, time, attention, or power

3.   Representational—occurs when one person represents a group whose interests differ from those of other groups

4.   Intercessional—when you must intercede between two or more individuals or groups in conflict

D.   Types of Conflict

1.   Interest/commitment conflict—characterized by basic genuine clashes of opposing interests, values, or commitments

2.   Induced conflict—created to reach goals that could otherwise not be attained directly

3.   Misattributed conflict—based on an honest mistake

4.   Data conflict—occurs when two sides have either inconsistent or inadequate data upon which to make decisions

5.   Structural conflict—dispute arising from differences in such factors as power, time, or physical or other environmental barriers

6.   Illusionary conflict—similar to misattributed conflict, but based on something that was blamed on the wrong person or group

7.   Displaced conflict—directed at people or concerns other than the real source of conflict

8.   Expressive conflict—rests primarily on a wish to express hostility, aggression, or other strong feelings

E.   Highlight 3.10: Steps in Managing Conflict

F.   Advanced Conflict Management: Guidelines and Strategies

    1.   Focusing on power

        a.   Always assess both your power and that of your adversary

        b.   Avoid full disclosure of your power

        c.   Always use power sparingly

    2.   Forestalling or sidestepping conflict

    3.   Generating conflict

    4.   Conflict management by covert means

        a.   Passive resistance—simply drag your feet in ways that create problems for the opponent

        b.   Concealment—do not let the other party know what you are doing

        c.   Manipulation—influence others without their being aware of it

        d.   More specific tactics

            1)   Negativism and noncompliance with rules

            2)   Stonewalling—refusing to act on a matter

            3)   Deceit or deception

            4)   Seduction—offering of inducements to convince neutral parties to join you or to convert opponents to your side

5) Emotional extortion—withholding something valued by the other

6) Divide and conquer—reduces the influence of the adversary and neutralizes opposing players

5. Conflict management by emergent agreement—one side convinces the other to change

6. Conflict management by coactive disputation—both parties are willing to consider joint problem solving, using facts to settle disputes, and remain open to persuasion

7. Conflict management by negotiated agreement

8. Conflict management by indirect means or procedural measures

   a. When both sides cannot or will not negotiate

   b. When other management approaches are unpalatable

9. Conflict management by exercise of authority/power

Experiential Exercises and Classroom Simulations

Exercise 3.1: Identifying Your Own Networks

A. Brief Description
Students will identify and categorize their own networks.

B. Objectives
Students will:
1. Recognize their own personal and professional networks.
2. Understand the ways in which networks can help fill basic human needs.

C. Procedure
1. Ask each student, working alone, to identify the networks of which they are a part. Then ask them to categorize each of them into those which are professional networks and those which are personal.
2. Ask students to identify which of their networks (if any) might be helpful in situations listed in the box below.
3. After about 10-15 minutes ask students to identify their networks and to indicate which, if any, of the boxed situations could be helped by their network.

D. Instructions for Students
1. Identify the networks of which you are a part. Categorize each of them into those which are professional networks and those which are personal. Which networks (if any) would be helpful in the following situations.

Which of Your Networks Might be Helpful in These Situations?

1. You need advice about a personal problem.
2. You want to know how to register to vote in your community.
3. You need to refer a client to a substance abuse program.
4. You need to help a client getting a temporary restraining order.
5. Your car breaks down on the way to your first day at your field placement. You need a ride to work for the next two days.
6. Payday is still a week away and you need another $50 to get a wart removed from your nose.
7. Your computer and printer just quit, you have a paper due tomorrow morning at 8:00 a.m., and the campus computer labs are closed.
8. You have decided to come out of the closet and acknowledge that you are gay (or lesbian). Who is the first person you could depend on for support?

E. Commentary
This exercise can be done in groups of 4-6 students with a recorder reporting back to the larger group. The recorder will report the networks identified by group members and which (if any) of the situations in the box above that could not be resolved by using one's networks.

Exercise 3.2: Leadership

A. Brief Description
Students identify and discuss leadership characteristics that they admire most in other people.

B. Objectives
Students will:
1. Recognize various leadership skills exhibited by other individuals.
2. Describe why they admire the individual's particular leadership skills.

C. Procedure
1. Ask students to look at the list of leadership skills in the box below.
2. Have students discuss which of the leaderships skills they have identified in others.

D. Instructions for Students
1. Review the list of leadership skills in the box below.
2. Identify individuals you know who exhibit one or more of these leadership skills.
3. Share with other students why you admire these particular leadership skills.

Leadership Skills List

Clarity about one's own goals and directions in life
Capacity to persuade other people
Ability to identify problems and challenges involved in a situation
Capacity to inspire others with their vision
Assertiveness
Communication skills

| Leads by example |
| Brings new perspectives to a situation |
| Self-awareness |
| Self-disclosure |

E.   Commentary
This exercise can be done either in small groups or with the full class.

Exercise 3.3: Teamwork

A.   Brief Description
Students discuss groups and teams of which they are a part and compare these to characteristics of effective teams.

B.   Objectives
Students will:
1.   Recognize the many groups and teams of which they are a part.
2.   Learn to evaluate groups and teams using a measure of effectiveness.

C.   Procedure
1.   Review the characteristics of effective teams as described in the chapter.
2.   Ask students to list three groups or teams of which they are a member.
3.   Ask them to compare each of these groups/teams on the basis of the characteristics shown in the box below.
4.   Allow about 15 minutes for this exercise.
5.   Ask class members to report on groups/teams which they believe were especially effective or especially ineffective. Encourage class members to discuss why a particular group was effective or ineffective.

D.   Instructions for Students
List three groups or teams of which you are a member. These can be from your work, class, or personal life. Using the characteristics of effective teams noted in the box below, identify which (if any) of these groups/teams were particularly effective.

| Characteristics of Effective Teams |
| 1.   Clear goals |
| 2.   Structure and membership tied to goals |
| 3.   Commitment of members (team spirit) |
| 4.   A climate of collaboration |
| 5.   Commitment to excellence |
| 6.   External recognition and support |
| 7.   Principled leadership |

E.   Commentary
This exercise can also be done with students working in small groups.

Exercise 3.4: Conflict

A.   Brief Description
Students learn to identify and appropriately categorize types of conflicts.

B.   Objectives
Students will:
1.   Appropriately identify types of conflicts in their own lives.
2.   Develop skill in articulating their opinions.

C.   Procedure
1.   Discuss in class the various forms of conflict encountered in social work practice.
2.   Ask students, working alone, to identify two conflicts in their own lives and to categorize these using the categories interpersonal, resource, representational and intercessional.
3.   Allow about 10-15 minutes for this process.
4.   Ask students to identify a conflict and to give their reasons why they believe the conflict fits into one of the categories shown below.
5.   Invite other students to ask questions or offer their opinion as to an appropriate category.

D.   Instructions for Students
Identify two conflicts in which you have been involved in your school, work, or personal life and indicate whether each conflict was an interpersonal, resource, representational, or intercessional conflict. Be prepared to explain why you chose a particular type of conflict.

E.   Commentary
This exercise can be done in small groups with students presenting their categorization to other group members.

Exercise 3.5: Practicing Team Work

A.   Brief Description
Students learn to appreciate the contributions of other team members.

B.   Objectives
Students will:
1.   Learn to identify what different professionals bring to a team.
2.   Differentiate the contributions of various professions to a team.

C.   Procedure
1.   Read each of the case scenarios below.
2.   Respond to each situation as appropriate.

Case Scenario A

A.   It is your first week of work at a residential treatment center for adolescents with emotional problems.   At 10:00 AM you have your first meeting with the "M" team, which consists of you (the social worker), a Ph.D. psychologist, a psychiatrist, a nurse, and the cottage parents from cottage B (your cottage). Just prior to the meeting your supervisor asks you to list the professional knowledge and skills each of these people will bring to the meeting. This isn't "busy work." She wants you to appreciate the value of all the professionals on this team. List the professional contributions each might bring to this meeting based upon their professions and positions.

Psychiatrist

Psychologist

Nurse

Cottage Parents

Case Scenario B

B.   You have been assigned to work with a team of community citizens seeking to "improve the quality of life in Tanktown." The team has been floundering for several months. Read the information provided about the team and review the characteristics of effective teams. Then identify what you see as the possible problems that may be causing this group's inability to get things done.

The Quality of Life Team (or Q-Team as they like to call themselves) has been meeting for the past four months. They were appointed by the mayor to "improve the quality of life in Tanktown." Members include residents of the community, business owners, students, and several ministers. The mayor chose people who worked in his last election campaign. Meetings have been spent arguing about what the team should focus on. Discussions center around members' very different opinions about what Tanktown's most important problems are. Several members have missed at least five meetings, and the others tend to push ideas that are supported by a majority of the team. The mayor told the group he'd check back in a year to see how they were doing. List the characteristics of effective teams that this group appears to lack. Explain each item.

Exercise 3.6: Planning and Conducting Meetings

A.   Brief Description
Students will begin thinking about steps in planning and conducting meetings.

B.   Objectives
Student will:
1.   Identify steps needed to plan a meeting.
2.   Make decisions about steps in the planning process.

C.   Procedure
1.   Break the class into 3-5 small groups.
2.   Read the case situation aloud for the class.
3.   Ask each group to respond to questions A through C and record their decisions.
4.   After each group has completed its assignment, ask them to report.

D.   Instructions for Students
Respond to each of the questions listed below.

Case Situation

The agency director has asked you to handle the details for a forthcoming meeting. The participants are community representatives interested in services for people with disabilities. Your director wants to impress upon her guests the agency's commitment to serving this population, and she tells you to set the meeting for either August 1st or September 1st at your option. All of the other details are also up to you.

A.   Identify below the decisions you will have to make (for example, setting the meeting date and time).

B.   Now identify specifically what you decided about each item above (for example, set meeting for September 1st).

C.   What further information, if any, do you need from the Director?

Exercise 3.7: Doing a Better Job

A.   Brief Description
Students review and discuss a problematic meeting, identifying needed areas of improvement.

B.   Objectives
Students will:
1.   Identify potential problem areas in a community meeting.
2.   Identify actions that might be taken to improve the effectiveness of the community meeting.

C.   Procedure
1.   Ask students to review the description of the community meeting described below.
2.   Have students identify potential problems or challenges noted in the meeting description.
3.   Ask students to describe how the problem could be solved or the challenge overcome.

D.   Instructions for Students
1.   Carefully read the case situation described below.
2.   Identify problems or challenges noted in the meeting.
3.   List the ways by which the problems might be lessened or the challenges overcome.

Community Coalition Meeting

You are invited to observe a meeting of a community coalition created to reduce street violence. Below is a summary of the minutes of the meeting. Read it, and identify any improvements you think are warranted in the conducting of this group's meetings.

The meeting began at 1:20 p.m. after a short delay to locate the light switches for the meeting room and to accommodate late-comers who were confused about the meeting location. Since agendas were not mailed ahead of time, Chairperson Reno opened the meeting by reading the agenda aloud. The agenda included (1) action on the curfew ordinance, (2) planning for next week's community forum, and (3) discussion of adding to the coalition a representative from the Parents-Teachers Association at the high school. There being no objections, the agenda was adopted as read.

The secretary reminded the group that we had decided at the last meeting to talk about proposing changes to the curfew ordinance. The group discussed this matter and voted to talk to the City Council about changing the curfew. It was agreed that the coalition would meet again later this month to review progress on this matter. The meeting adjourned at 3:00 p.m.

List the actual or potential problems you noted in this brief record. Discuss briefly what should have been done.

Actual or Potential Problems   What Should Have Been Done

Exercise 3.8: Parliamentary Quick Quiz

Without peeking back at the chapter, quickly match the terms on the left with the definitions on the right.

_____	1.	Robert's Rules of Order	A. Official recorder of group decisions
_____	2.	Secretary	B. Accomplish primary business of group
_____	3.	Point of Order	C. Guidelines used in parliamentary procedure
_____	4.	Minutes	D. Minimum number of members needed to transact business
_____	5.	Second	E. Motion indicating proper procedure is not being followed
_____	6.	Amendment	F. Committee that exists continuously
_____	7.	Debate	G. Proposed modification to a motion
_____	8.	Executive Committee	H. Discussion about a motion
_____	9.	Standing Committee	I. Governing rules of an organization
_____	10.	Constitution and by-laws	J. Composed of officers of an organization and charged with acting for the body between meetings
_____	11.	Main Motions	K. An indication of support for a motion which has just been proposed
_____	12.	Quorum	L. Official record of actions taken by a group

Exercise 3.9: Recognizing Types of Conflict

A. Brief Description
Students review snippets from group meetings in which conflict is evident and decide which types of conflict exist.

B. Objectives
Students will:
1. Identify sources of conflict in various groups.
2. Explain the reasoning behind their choices.

C. Procedure
1. Ask students to review the snippets from each group below with a goal of identifying which types of conflict are evident.
2. Have students list their reasons for selecting the specific types of conflict that are evident.

D. Instructions for Students
Read each of the snippets below and identify the type of conflict you believe is being displayed. Then, provide a brief explanation for your choice.

Conflict Snippets

A. "As chair of the homeless coalition, I can't sit here and let this city council tear down the old courthouse without a fight. We have 50 homeless families in this city and the city owns a building that would make a wonderful shelter. Mayor Jones, why can't you see the benefits that using this structure for a shelter would bring to the community?"

"The city council has to be concerned about more than just homeless people, Ed. We need the space occupied by the old courthouse for downtown parking. We're losing business to the mall outside of town because we have no place for people to park downtown. The city council asked me to work with you to find some other solution for this homeless problem."

Type of Conflict:

Explain:

B. "If we add money to the budget so we can hire another building inspector, we won't be able to put another police officer on the force. What with the increase in gang activity here, I believe we need more cops, not more building inspectors."

Figuring out what makes the most sense within the budget is important, Mary. We have only $75,000 left in the personnel budget. I think the money will produce better benefits for the community if we add the inspector. There are too many substandard homes and apartments in the community, some of which are being used as drug houses. An inspector could help us cope with this at least as well as another police officer."

Type of Conflict:

Explain:

C.	"Constanza, I am tired of hearing of the so-called benefits of the DARE program. Show me an ounce of research that proves this program actually keeps school kids from using drugs. The whole thing is just a big public relations program. I think we should concentrate our efforts on something we know works—like the Police Dog Sniffer program. We know the dogs can sniff out drugs in school lockers." "José, police dogs are fine after the fact, but they do nothing to prevent drug use. We should spend our money on prevention, not intervention." Type of Conflict: Explain:

D.	"You're on their side! Why don't you ever see our perspective? All you ever do is agree with the Razers." "Oh, right. Man, if he's on our side we're in big trouble. He can't understand anything 'cause he's not a home boy." "Washington, Alonzo, I'm not on anyone's side. I'm supposed to find a way to keep you from stomping each other and keep you out of jail besides. My point is that I think the Guns' proposal to keep the downtown area off limits to gang activity makes sense. It lets both your groups use the downtown as individuals, and it keeps the police off your butts. The minute you start something downtown, you've got the mayor, the council, and business owners turning up the heat. Both of your gangs get fried whenever that happens. Just because Alonzo suggested it, doesn't make it automatically a bad idea. Now get out of my face unless you have a better idea." Type of Conflict: Explain:

Exercise 3.10: Managing Conflict

A. Brief Description
Students identify potential means of reducing or managing group conflict.

B. Objectives
Students will:
1. Identify conflict situations in a group.
2. Identify strategies for reducing or managing the conflict.

C. Procedure
1. Break students into groups of 5-7 members.
2. Ask each group to read the conflict scenario.
3. Ask each group to discuss possible ways of better managing the conflict and decide the one approach with the greatest likelihood of success.
4. Have the group report back to the full class.

D.   Instructions for Students
In the following case, conflict is occurring within a hospital social work department. Identify what you might say to the group members to build cooperation, encourage compromise, hear their various viewpoints, find a common ground among members, and produce an environment of respect for everyone's ideas. In short, how would you keep the conflict from escalating?

In the following case example, a conflict is brewing within the staff of a hospital social work department. Assume you are a new worker in this unit and that you are concerned about the apparent split developing over the best way to handle a hospital-proposed reduction in patient services.

Miguel, the most senior social worker in the unit, is speaking angrily about the situation: "We have always been a department that offered help to anyone we felt was at high risk. That risk could be financial, emotional, social, or medical. We've never set some group aside and said, 'We won't help you.' That's not what social work is all about."

"Micky, I know you're upset. But we don't own the hospital—we just work here. If the hospital director says we have to focus our services rather than take all comers, I don't see what we can do," says Betty, the acting department director.

"You can't fight city hall," says Mel, another worker.

"Baloney," Todd chimes in. "This hospital has built a fine reputation and we're not going to let it get destroyed without a fight."

I. **Introduction**

II. **Defining Organizations, Social Services, and Social Agencies**

    A.   Organizations (definition)

        1.   Social entities

        2.   Goal-directed

        3.   Deliberately structured and coordinated activity systems

        4.   Linked to the external environment

    B.   Social services

        1.   Institutional—those provided by major public service systems that administer such benefits as financial assistance, housing programs, health care, or education

        2.   Personal social services—address more individualized needs involving interpersonal relationships and people's ability to function within their immediate environments

        3.   Human services, social services, and sometimes social welfare, are often used interchangeably

        4.   Human services—programs and activities designed to enhance people's development and well-being

        5.   Social welfare—the nation's system of programs, benefits, and services that help people meet those social, economic, educational, and health needs that are fundamental to the maintenance of society

    C.   Social agencies—organizations providing social services that are usually staffed by human services personnel (including professional social workers, members of other professions, paraprofessionals, clerical personnel, and sometimes volunteers)

        1.   Public—run by a designated unit of government and are usually regulated by laws that directly affect policy

        2.   Private—privately owned and run by people not employed by a government

            a.   Nonprofit—run to accomplish some service provision goal, not to make financial profit for private owners

            b.   Proprietary or for-profit—provide designated social services, often quite similar to those provided by private social agencies; a major purpose is to make money

III. Organizational Theories

A. Organizational theories—ways to conceptualize and understand how organizations function by stressing specific concepts and explaining how these concepts relate to each other

B. Organizational behavior—the study of human behavior in the workplace, of the interaction between people and the organization, and of the organization itself. The major goals of organizational behavior are to explain, predict, and control behavior

C. Management—the attainment of organizational goals in an effective and efficient manner through planning, organizing, leading, and controlling organizational resources

D. Classical organizational theories—emphasize that specifically designed formal structure and a consistent, rigid organizational network of employees are most important in having an organization run well and achieve its goals

    1. Scientific management

        a. Concept introduced by Frederick W. Taylor and was developed in the early 20th century, when there was often great hostility between management and employees

        b. Four principles

            1) Jobs and tasks should be studied scientifically to develop and standardize work procedures and expectations

            2) Workers should be chosen on a scientific basis to maximize their potential for being trained and turned into productive employees

            3) Management and employees should cooperate with each other and work together following standardized procedures

            4) Management should make plans and task assignments which workers should then carry out as instructed

    2. Administrative theory of management

        a. Proposed by Henri Fayol in the early 20th century, and focused on the administrative side of management rather than the workers' performance

        b. Five basic functions that management should fulfill: planning, organizing, command, coordination, and control

        c. Six basic principles that managers should abide by, but use discretion concerning the intensity

            1) Division of labor

            2) Authority and responsibility

           3)   Centralization

           4)   Delegation of authority

           5)   Unity of command

           6)   Unity of direction

3.   Bureaucracy

    a.   Initiated by Max Weber in the early 20th century, they attain goals with precision, reliability, and efficiency

    b.   Emphases of traditional bureaucracies

           1)   Highly specialized units performing clearly specified job tasks

           2)   Minimal discretion on the part of employees

           3)   Numerous specific rules to maintain control

E.   Neoclassical organizational theories

1.   As reactions to classical management thought, these theories originated in the mid-20th century

2.   In order to achieve coordination and cooperation, organizations offer inducements in exchange for contributions

3.   Chester Barnard proposed that organizations functioned on the basis of two types of motivation

    a.   Motivation to participate—the motivation of an individual to join and stay with the organization and perform at a minimally acceptable level

    b.   Motivation to perform—involves inducements to produce contributions that are greater than minimal performance expectations

F.   Human Relations Theories

1.   Emphasize the role of the informal, psychosocial components of organizational functioning

2.   Important concepts include employee morale and productivity, and the dynamics of small-group behavior

3. Theory X and Theory Y

    a. Theory X

        1) Managers view employees as incapable of much growth, and believe they must control, direct, force, or threaten employees to make them work

        2) Employees are perceived as inherently disliking work and having relatively little ambition

        3) Inconsistent with what behavioral scientists assert are effective principles for directing, influencing, and motivating people

    b. Theory Y

        1) Managers view employees as wanting to grow and develop by exerting physical and mental effort to accomplish work objectives

        2) Believe that the promise of internal rewards are stronger motivations than external rewards and punishments

        3) Most employees are assumed to have considerable ingenuity, creativity, and imagination

        4) Mistakes and errors are viewed as necessary to the learning process

G. Figure 4.1: Classical Organizational, Neoclassical, and Human Relations Theories

H. Feminist theories and organizations

    1. Feminist theories—involve the liberation of women and girls from discrimination based on gender; the goal of women's self-determination

        a. Liberal feminism—grew out of the U.S. liberal political thought, a theory about individual rights, freedom, choice, and privacy

        b. Socialist feminism—grew out of Marxist theories of economy and is particularly concerned with the economic-class aspect of women's lives

        c. Radical feminism—emphasizes how male domination manifests itself in women's sexuality, gender roles, and family relationships, and is carried over into the male-dominated world of work, government, religion, and law

        d. Postmodern feminism—stresses the particularity of women's experiences in specific cultural and historical contexts

    2. Using a gender filter—assumes that sexism is relevant to the experiences of many women and is the basis for many of women's difficulties

3. The end of patriarchy—refers to ending the control by men of a disproportionately large share of the power

4. Empowerment—emphasizes that power should be distributed and equalized to whatever extent possible within an organization

5. Consciousness raising—the development of critical awareness of the cultural and political factors that shape identity, personal and social realities, and relationships, as well as one's position and opinions with respect to these issues

6. The personal is political—women's conditions go beyond one's personal situation; personal problems and conditions have historical, material, and cultural bases and dimensions

7. The importance of process—emphasizes that the process of how things get done is just as important as what gets done; the process of decision making should be based on equality and the participation of all

8. Unity in diversity: Diversity is strength—efforts are made to bridge differences between women based on such factors as race, class, physical ability, and sexual orientation

9. Validation of the nonrational—a feminist perspective does not exclude the importance of rationality, analytical skills, order, and efficiency; however, it also includes aspects of life and human interaction that go beyond structured scientific reasoning

   a. Feelings, emotions, intuition, and spirituality are taken into account

   b. Validation—the process of accepting a person and a person's actions as justifiable and relevant

I. Cultural perspective

   1. Organizational culture—the set of key values, beliefs, understandings, and norms that members of an organization share

   2. Advantage—performance becomes predictable, thus requiring less effort to develop new approaches

   3. Disadvantage—may squelch innovative ideas with pressure to retain the old way of thought

J. Economics theory—emphasizes how organizations should proceed in whatever way necessary to maximize profits or outputs

   1. Poses difficulties for social workers who maintain professional values and ethics

   2. Places primary emphasis on profit and productivity

K.   Chaos theory

1.   Organizational management can no longer maintain an illusion of order and predictability in today's unstable and unpredictable macro global environment

2.   The theory suggests that relationships in the complex, adaptive systems are nonlinear and made up of numerous interconnections and divergent choices that create unintended effects and render the universe unpredictable

3.   It stresses the importance of recognizing the positive aspects of change and flexibility

L.   Contingency Perspective—maintains that each element involved in an organization depends on other elements; therefore, there is no one generally best way to accomplish tasks or goals

1.   Strength—flexibility

2.   Potential weakness—lack of direction

M.   Culture-quality theories

1.   These theories characterized the final two decades of the 20th century

2.   They focused on how to build a strong set of shared positive values and norms, while emphasizing quality, service, high performance, and flexibility

N.   Figure 4.2: A Wide Range of Organizational Theories

O.   Systems theories

1.   Emphasize how all parts of the organization are interrelated

2.   Emphasize the environment and the effects of other systems upon the organization

3.   Emphasize constant assessment and adjustment

P.   Which organizational theory is best?

IV.   **Social Agencies as Systems**

A.   Systems theories involve concepts that emphasize interactions among various systems including individuals, families, groups, organizations, and communities

B.   Systems theories definition of terms:

1.   System—a set of orderly and interrelated elements that form a functional whole

2.   Boundaries—borders or margins that separate one entity from another, and establish how various units in a system relate to each other

3.   Subsystem—a secondary or subordinate system, a smaller system within a larger system

4.   Homeostasis—the tendency for a system to maintain a relatively stable, constant state of balance

5.   Role—the culturally established social behavior and conduct expected of a person having a designated status in a particular group or society

6.   Relationship—the dynamic interpersonal connection between two or more persons or systems that involves how they think about, feel about, and behave toward each other

7.   Input—the energy, information, or communication flow received from other systems

8.   Output—what happens to input after it has been processed by some system

9.   Feedback—a special form of input where a system receives information about that system's own performance

10.   Interface—the contact point between various systems, including individuals and organizations, where interaction and communication may take place

11.   Differentiation—a system's tendency to move from a more simplified to a more complex existence

12.   Entropy—the natural tendency of a system to progress toward disorganization, depletion, disintegration, and, in essence, chaos

13.   Negative entropy—the progress of a system toward organization, growth, and development

14.   Equifinality—there are many different means to the same end

V.   Viewing Organizations from a Systems Perspective

A.   Figure 4.3: Fastbuck and WINK—Similar Processes

B.   Resource input

C.   Process through organizational technology

D.   Output

E.   Outcomes

VI. The Nature of Organizations

A. Agency settings

    1. Predominantly social work settings

    2. Host settings—the main service provided by the agency is not social services

B. Organizational mission statements

    1. Mission statement—a brief declaration of the organization's purpose that establishes broad and relatively permanent parameters within which goals are developed and specific programs designed

    2. A mission statement also includes what client populations are to be served and provides general guidance for what needs should be met

C. Organizational goals

    1. Organizational goals—statements of expected outcomes dealing with the problem that the program is attempting to prevent, eradicate, or ameliorate

    2. Organizational goals serve at least three major purposes:

        a. Provide guidelines for the kinds of functions and activities organizational workers are supposed to pursue

        b. Constitute a source of legitimacy which justifies the activities of an organization and, indeed, its very existence

        c. Serve as standards by which members of an organization and outsiders can assess the success of the organization—that is, its effectiveness and efficiency

    3. Official goals—represent a translation of social welfare legislation and policy direction into programmatic action or activities

    4. Highlight 4.1: Faith-Based Social Services

        a. Spirituality—concerns people's search for meaning, purpose, and value in life

        b. Religion—a set of beliefs and practices of an organized religious institution

        c. Charitable choice section of the Personal Responsibility and Work Opportunity Reconciliation Act permits faith-based service providers to retain their religious autonomy

        d. The social worker does not evaluate a person or group based upon religion, but does evaluate the individual or group's unique expression of that religion

5.   Multiple goals—social service organizations are often complex entities that aim to accomplish multiple goals

6.   Highlight 4.2: Organizational Objectives Indicate How to Achieve Goals

   a.   Goals—provide social service agencies with general direction concerning what should happen, but not with specific guidance regarding how it should be done

   b.   Objectives—smaller, behaviorally specific sub-goals that serve as stepping stones on the way to accomplishing the main goal

   c.   Four basic types of objectives used in social service agencies

      1)   Impact objectives—specify outcomes to be achieved as a result of program activities

      2)   Service objectives—the organization's tally of activities provided or services rendered

      3)   Operational objectives—convey the intent to improve the general operation of the organization

      4)   Product objectives—designed to provide a tangible outcome to benefit a target population or a community

7.   Goal displacement

   a.   Official goals—the general purposes of the organization as put forth in the mission statement, annual reports, public statements by key officials and other authoritative pronouncements (what it is supposed to do)

   b.   Operative goals—designate the ends sought through the actual operating policies of the organization (what it really does day-to-day)

   c.   Goal displacement—often occurs when the means to a goal becomes the goal itself; when an organization continues to function but no longer achieves the goals it's supposed to

   d.   Highlight 4.3: Goal Displacement—Process Superseding Progress

8.   Systems theories, organizations, and goal displacement

   a.   Goal attainment—refers to what is supposed to happen through the intervention process

   b.   Figure 4.4: The Process of Goal Displacement

D.   Organizational culture

     1.   Organizational culture—the set of key values, beliefs, understandings, and norms that members of an organization share

          a.   What kind of attire is considered appropriate within the organization's cultural environment

          b.   Each agency has its own personality

E.   Organizational structure

     1.   Organizational structure—the manner in which an organization divides its labor into specific tasks and achieves coordination among these tasks

     2.   All large agencies and some smaller ones have a formal structure

     3.   Agencies develop informal structures and lines of communication

     4.   Lines of authority—the specific administrative and supervisory responsibilities of supervisors to their supervisees

          a.   Figure 4.5: Multihelp—An Example of a Formal Organizational Chart

          b.   Agencies also develop informal channels of communication

     5.   Channels of communication

     6.   Dimensions of power in the formal structure

     7.   Informal structure: Multihelp—An example

          a.   Figure 4.6: Contrasting Formal and Informal Structures in Agencies

          b.   Being aware of both formal and informal agency structures can provide you with information about where you can turn for help and support

F.   Power and politics in organizations

     1.   Types of power in organizations

          a.   Legitimate power—that attained because of one's position and vested authority

          b.   Reward power—that held because of the ability to provide positive reinforcement and rewards to others

          c.   Coercive power—the capacity of dispensing punishments in order to influence others' behavior

d. Referent power—that held as a result of other group members' respect and high esteem

e. Expert power—that based on established authority or expertise in a particular domain

2. Politics in social service organizations

   a. Organizational politics—activities that people perform to acquire, enhance, and use power and other resources to obtain their preferred outcomes in a situation where there is uncertainty or disagreement

   b. Highlight 4.4: Dynamics Contributing to Political Behavior in Agencies

      1) Organizations are, by nature, political

      2) Some people are more power-oriented than others

         a) Power-oriented managers sometimes cope with the limited amount of power available by expanding their sphere of influence sideways

         b) Machiavellianism—a tendency to manipulate others for personal gain

      3) Decentralized organizations distribute power widely to lower levels in the organizational hierarchy

3. Using agency politics for positive change

   a. Conduct a political diagnosis—an assessment of the location of power in an organization and the type of political behavior that is likely to happen

      1) Coalition—an alliance of individuals who share a common goal

      2) Political network—the system of affiliations and alliances of individuals and coalitions within the social service organization's environment

   b. Develop contacts and relationships with people in power

   c. Form coalitions yourself

   d. Get information about what's going on

   e. Provide positive feedback where warranted

   f. Use assertive communication

4.   Tactics not to use in agency politics: Problematic, unethical behavior

       a.   Don't engage in backstabbing

       b.   Don't set up a person for failure

       c.   Don't divide and conquer

       d.   Don't exclude the opposition

       e.   Don't go over your supervisor's head without first exhausting all other options

G.   Centralized versus decentralized organizations

    1.   Extremely centralized organizations have clearly established lines of authority, units are clearly defined and separated, and workers have little discretion in making decisions

    2.   Extremely decentralized organizations offer and encourage great worker discretion and likely have a wide variety of clients with vastly different problems, issues, and backgrounds

VII.   The Macro Context of Organizations

A.   The shifting macro environment and shrinking resources

    1.   Temporary Assistance to Needy Families (TANF)

    2.   Highlight 4.5: Managed Care and Service Provision: Problems and Ethical Issues

       a.   Managed care is a generic label for a broad and constantly changing mix of health insurance, assistance, and payment programs that seek to retain quality and access while controlling the cost of physical and mental health services

       b.   Managed care fundamentally transformed traditional relationships between clients and workers in mental health settings

       c.   Ethical issues in managed care

           1)   Potential conflict between the gatekeeping role of some managed care organizations and client self-determination

           2)   May conflict with the ethical principle of informed consent

           3)   Potential to violate client confidentiality

d. Managed care and advocacy in social work practice

    1) Guarantee patients the right to choose a doctor outside their health plans' networks if they agree to share the cost of services

    2) Ensure patients' access to detailed information about coverage, treatment options

    3) Require companies to cover emergency care without prior authorization

    4) Make health plans comply with state and federal laws that protect the confidentiality of health information

    5) Require companies to set up procedures under which providers could appeal denials of coverage

B. Necessary resource inputs

C. Legitimation—appropriate status or authorization to perform agency functions and pursue agency goals that are granted by external entities

D. Client sources

1. Highlight 4.6: Organizations in a Global Context: Helping People of Other National Origins

    a. National origin—involves individuals', their parents', or their ancestors' country of birth

    b. Refugees—people who have crossed national boundaries in search of refuge

    c. Immigrants—those individuals who have been granted legal permanent residence in a country not their own

    d. Global network—includes international, national, and local agencies, both public and private, and professionals and paraprofessionals from a variety of disciplines

    e. International organizations

        1) Intergovernmental organizations

        2) Premigration services—include helping migrants get their documents in order, understand and follow required procedures, obtain necessary medical evaluations, and cope with cultural changes and conditions

    f. National organizations

g.   Local organizations

h.   Social services for immigrants and refugees

VIII.   Social Work Organizations in National and International Contexts

A.   ACOSA (Association for Community Organization & Social Administration)—provides a forum for enhancing macro practice theory, research, and skills

B.   IASSW (International Association of Schools of Social Work)—committed to promoting peace, human rights, and social justice through social work education

C.   IFSW (International Federation of Social Workers)—an international organization of national professional social work organizations in 78 countries

D.   ICSW (International Council on Social Welfare)—a global governmental organization which represents a wide range of national and international member organizations that seek to advance social welfare, social development and social justice

IX.   Methods of Management

A.   Management—the attainment of organizational goals in an effective and efficient manner through planning, organizing, leading, and controlling organizational resources

B.   Management style provides important clues for understanding people's behavior in the organizational environment

X.   Working in a Traditional Bureaucracy

A.   Value discrepancies between workers and "the system"

      1.   Highlight 4.7: Orientation Conflicts Between Helping Professionals and Bureaucracies

            a.   Orientation of helping professionals

            b.   Orientation of bureaucratic systems

B.   How to survive in a bureaucracy

      1.   Whenever your needs or the needs of your clients are not met by the bureaucracy, use the following problem-solving approach:

            a.   Precisely identify the need

            b.   Generate a list of possible solutions

            c.   Evaluate merits and shortcomings of the possible solutions

            d.   Select a solution

e.   Implement the solution

f.   Evaluate the solution

2.   Learn how your bureaucracy is structured and how it functions

3.   Remember that bureaucrats are people with feelings

4.   If you are at war with the bureaucracy, declare a truce or the system will find a way to eliminate you

5.   Know your work contract and job expectations

6.   Continue to develop your knowledge and awareness of specific helping skills

7.   Identify your professional strengths and limitations

8.   Be aware that you can't change everything, so stop trying

9.   Learn how to control your emotions in your interactions with the bureaucracy

10.   Develop and use a sense of humor

11.   Learn to accept your mistakes and perhaps even to laugh at some of them

12.   Take time to enjoy and develop a support system with your colleagues

13.   Give in sometimes on minor matters

14.   Keep yourself physically fit and mentally alert

15.   Leave your work at the office

16.   Occasionally, take your supervisor and other administrators to lunch

17.   Do not seek self-actualization or ego satisfaction from the bureaucracy

18.   Make speeches to community groups that accentuate the positives about your agency

19.   No matter how high you rise in a hierarchy, maintain some direct service contact

20.   Do not try to change everything in the system at once

21.   Identify your career goals and determine whether they can be met in this system

XI.   Newer Approaches to Management and Worker Empowerment

    A.   Constructing a culture of caring

        1.   Job ownership

        2.   Seeking a higher purpose

        3.   Emotional bonding

        4.   Trust

        5.   Pride in one's work

    B.   The learning organization—one in which everyone is engaged in identifying and solving problems, enabling the organization to continuously experiment, change, and improve, thus increasing its capacity to grow, learn, and achieve its purpose

        1.   Five primary concepts

            a.   Power is redistributed from higher levels to lower levels in the organizational structure

            b.   Nurture the development of new ideas

            c.   Emphasize the effectiveness of service provision to clients instead of the process of service provision

            d.   Use of multidisciplinary teams is encouraged

            e.   Open information is promoted

            f.   Encourages individuals to lead because they want to serve one another as well as a higher purpose

        2.   Highlight 4.8: "Learning Disabilities" Working Against Learning Organizations

            a.   I am my position

            b.   The enemy is out there

            c.   The illusion of taking charge

            d.   The parable of the boiled frog

            e.   The delusion of learning from experience

            f.   The myth of the management team

C.   Teamwork and team empowerment

  1.   Team—a group of two or more people gathered together to work collaboratively and interdependently with each other to pursue a designated purpose

  2.   Teams are most effective and empowered when used under the following four circumstances

      a.   A clear, engaging reason or purpose should exist for using them

      b.   Should be used when the job can't be done unless people work together

      c.   When rewards can be provided for teamwork and team performance

      d.   When they have clear authority to make recommendations or implement their decisions as a result of their efforts

D.   Managing diversity

  1.   Diversity refers to the degree of differences among members of a group or an organization

  2.   Valuing diversity emphasizes training employees of different races and ethnicities, religions, genders, ages, and abilities to function together effectively

XII.   Specific Management Approaches

A.   Total quality management (TQM)

  1.   Emphasizes organizational process, attainment of excellent quality service, and empowerment of employees

  2.   Clients as customers

      a.   The central theme of TQM is the importance of the customer or client

      b.   Highlight 4.9: The Seven Sins of Service

          1)   Apathy (DILLIGAD—Do I Look Like I Give a Damn?) syndrome

          2)   Brush-off—getting rid of the customer as soon as possible and doing the least work necessary

          3)   Coldness—chilly hostility, curtness, or impatience intended to convey to the customer they are a nuisance and please go away

          4)   Condescension—treating customers with a disdainful patronizing attitude that implies you as the worker are more knowledgeable and better than the customer

5) Robotism—treat each customer identically, without changes in facial or verbal expression

6) Rule book—if you want to think as little as possible, use the rule book to give the organization's rules and regulations absolute precedence

7) Runaround—stalling customers by using as little of your own time as possible, while wasting vast amounts of the customer's time

3. Customer feedback

4. Quality as the primary goal

    a. Lutheran Social Services of Wisconsin and Upper Michigan's six components of quality

        1) Accuracy measures the extent to which actual service provision matches customers' expectations

        2) Consistency is "service accuracy over time"

        3) Responsiveness refers to timeliness of service provision

        4) Availability is the ease with which customers can obtain services

        5) Perceived value is the extent to which customers feel the service is worth it

        6) Service experience sums up the total treatment experience

5. Employee empowerment

    a. Participative management—refers to placing the major responsibility for effective service provision on direct service workers

    b. Highlight 4.10: Empowerment on a Macro Level

        1) Factors working against client empowerment

            a) Expectations of funding sources

            b) Social environment

            c) Intrapersonal issues

            d) Interpersonal issues

	2)	Organizational conditions enhancing client empowerment
		a)	Administrative leadership and support
		b)	Staff development
		c)	Enhanced collaborative approach

     6.   Use of teams and teamwork

     7.   A total quality approach to leadership

     8.   Establishing a culture of quality

          a.   Leaders are responsible for changing the organizational culture from one that dwells on status quo to one that gets excited about change

          b.   A long-term perspective

B.   Servant leadership

     1.   Servant leadership emphasizes that leaders should be attentive to the concerns of their followers and empathize with them; they should take care of them and nurture them

     2.   Qualities of a servant leader

          a.   Calling

          b.   Listening

          c.   Empathy

          d.   Healing

          e.   Awareness

          f.   Persuasion

          g.   Conceptualization

          h.   Foresight

          i.   Stewardship

          j.   Growth

          k.   Building community

XIII. **Common Problems Encountered in Organizations**

    A.   Impersonal behavior

    B.   Rewards and recognition

    C.   Agency policy and worker discretion

    D.   Traditions and unwritten rules

Experiential Exercises and Classroom Simulations

Exercise 4.1: Comparing and Contrasting Organizational Theories

A.   Brief Description
Students compare and contrast various theoretical perspectives on organizations.

B.   Objectives
Students will:
1. Recognize the basic concepts inherent in the theoretical perspectives on organizations.
2. Examine the similarities and differences among the approaches.

C.   Procedure
1. Review the material on theoretical perspectives of organizations.
2. Divide the class into small groups of four to six.
3. Ask the groups to discuss the subsequent discussion questions, select a group representative, and be prepared to report to the entire class the small group's findings.
4. After about 20 minutes, ask the small groups to terminate their discussions and participate in a full class discussion.
5. Ask the representative from each group to share her or his summary of the discussion. Encourage comments from all class members.

D.   Instructions for Students
1. What are the primary concepts involved in each of the following theoretical perspectives on organizations?

> Classical organizational theories
>   Scientific management theories
>   Administrative theory of management
>   Bureaucracy
> Neoclassical organizational theories
> Human relations theories
> Feminist theories
> The cultural perspective
> Economics theory
> Chaos theory
> Contingency theory
> Culture-quality theories
> Systems theories

2. What are the similarities and differences among the six perspectives?
3. Which theoretical perspective(s) is (are) best? Explain why.

E.   Commentary
        This activity may also be conducted by holding a full class discussion without breaking students
        down into small groups.

Exercise 4.2: Identifying and Evaluating Management Concepts

A.   Brief Description
        In a large group discussion students respond to brief descriptions of management approaches.
        They are asked to identify whether each description reflects a traditional bureaucratic or Total
        Quality Management style and to explain the reasons for their answers.

B.   Objectives
        Students will:
        1.   Identify basic concepts in two opposing management styles.
        2.   Assess the pros and cons of principles involved.

C.   Procedure
        1.   Review the content on working in a bureaucracy and a total quality approach to
                management.
        2.   Read the brief descriptions of management approaches below under "Instructions for
                Students."
        3.   Lead a full class discussion focusing on the ensuing questions. Note that each description
                of a management approach may reflect concepts inherent in both traditional
                bureaucracies and total quality management.

D.   Instructions for Students
        For each of the following brief descriptions of a management approach, answer the subsequent
        questions.

Description A: Agency management emphasizes that workers should be consistent in their
service provision, responsive to clients, and readily available when needed.

---

        1.   To what extent does this management approach reflect that of a traditional bureaucracy or
                total quality management?
        2.   What more specific concepts inherent in traditional bureaucracy or total quality
                management are reflected and why?
        3.   What are the pros and cons of this management approach?

Description B: Agency leaders should serve as watchdogs to make certain that the agency
functions smoothly.

---

        1.   To what extent does this management approach reflect that of a traditional bureaucracy or
                total quality management?
        2.   What more specific concepts inherent in traditional bureaucracy or total quality
                management are reflected and why?
        3.   What are the pros and cons of this management approach?

Description C: The agency frequently solicits feedback from clients and other community residents regarding the effectiveness and efficiency of its service provision.

1. To what extent does this management approach reflect that of a traditional bureaucracy or total quality management?
2. What more specific concepts inherent in traditional bureaucracy or total quality management are reflected and why?
3. What are the pros and cons of this management approach?

Description D: The agency is made up of numerous highly specialized units assigned to perform specific job tasks. The intent is to have the service provision process run smoothly and get things done. The rules are there to help practitioners accomplish their tasks in designated and consistent ways. Allowing practitioners much of their own decision-making initiative only paves the way for mistakes.

1. To what extent does this management approach reflect that of a traditional bureaucracy or total quality management?
2. What more specific concepts inherent in traditional bureaucracy or total quality management are reflected and why?
3. What are the pros and cons of this management approach?

E. Commentary
This exercise may also be conducted using the small group format described in exercise 1.1.

Exercise 4.3: Defining Types of Agencies

A. Brief Description
Students are asked to match terms involving types of agencies with their corresponding definitions.

B. Objectives
Students will:
1. Define terms associated with social service agencies.
2. Distinguish among types of agencies.

C. Procedure
1. Either in a full-class discussion, a small group format, or individually, ask students to match the terms below with their respective definitions.
2. Discuss how the terms differ from each other and how they may overlap.
3. **For instructors only:** Answers are: (1) h; (2) d; (3) e; (4) g; (5) a; (6) b; (7) f; and (8) c.

D. Instructions for Students
Match the following terms with their respective definitions:

a. Social services
b. Institutional services
c. Personal social services
d. Social agency

e. Public social agency
f. Private social agency
g. Nonprofit social agency
h. Proprietary agency

1. _____: A social agency that provides designated social services, often quite similar to those provided by private social agencies, but with the additional aim of making a profit for its owners.

2. _____: An organization providing social services that "is usually staffed by human services personnel (including professional social workers, members of other professions, paraprofessionals, clerical personnel" and sometimes volunteers (Barker, 2003, p. 401).

3. _____: An agency run by designated units of government and usually regulated by laws that directly affect its policies.

4. _____: A social agency run to accomplish some service provision goal (not to make financial profit for private owners) that receives funding from a range of sources (from tax money to private donations to grants to service fees) and is governed by a board of directors.

5. _____: Tasks that social work practitioners and other helping professionals perform for improving people's health, enhancing their quality of life, increasing self-sufficiency, "preventing dependency, strengthening family relationships," and helping people and larger systems improve their functioning in the social environment (Barker, 2003, p. 407).

6. _____: Services provided by major public service systems that administer such benefits as financial assistance, housing programs, health care, or education (Barker, 2003).

7. _____: An agency that that is privately owned, is run by people not employed by government, and includes the provision of personal social services.

8. _____: Services that address more individualized needs involving interpersonal relationships and people's ability to function within their immediate environments. Such services usually target specific groups (such as children or older adults) or particular problems (such as family planning or counseling) (Barker, 2003).

Exercise 4.4: Relating Concepts to Theory

A. Brief Description
Students match an organizational theory with one of its theoretical concepts and discuss the concept's significance.

B. Objectives
Students will:
1. Identify the organizational theory characterized by a theoretical concept.
2. Assess the significance of the concept for understanding organizational behavior.

C. Procedure
   1. Review the content on organizational theories and concepts characterizing them.
   2. Either in a full-class discussion or in small groups followed by a full-class discussion, ask students to identify which organizational theory characterizes the identified concept. Ask them to discuss the significance of the concept to the theory and how the concept helps them understand human behavior in organizations.
   3. **For instructors only:** Answers are: (1) Economics theory; (2) Chaos theory; (3) Feminist theories; (4) Neoclassical theories; (5) Classical organizational theories; (6) Contingency theory; (7) Systems theories; (8) Human relations theories; (9) Cultural perspective; (10) Culture-quality theories.

D. Instructions for Students
Each concept listed below characterizes one of the following organizational theories:
- Classical organizational theories
- Neoclassical theories
- Human relations theories
- Feminist theories
- Cultural perspective
- Economic theory
- Chaos theory
- Contingency theory
- Culture-quality theories
- Systems theories

Identify the organizational theory each concept characterizes. Explain the concept's significance to that theory and how it helps you understand organizational behavior.

1. *Concept: Maximization of profits and efficiency*

Organizational theory it characterizes:

Explain the concept's significance for understanding the theory and organizational behavior:

2. *Concept: Complex variables and interactions in and among organizations often with unpredictable effects, and emphasis on the positive aspects of change and flexibility*

Organizational theory it characterizes:

Explain the concept's significance for understanding the theory and organizational behavior:

3. *Concept: Using a gender filter*

Organizational theory it characterizes:

Explain the concept's significance for understanding the theory and organizational behavior:

4. *Concept: Provision of inducements (incentives) to enhance contributions and motivation to perform*

Organizational theory it characterizes:

Explain the concept's significance for understanding the theory and organizational behavior:

5. *Concept: Formal structure and close supervision of employees*

Organizational theory it characterizes:

Explain the concept's significance for understanding the theory and organizational behavior:

6.   *Concept: Use of different means to solve different problems with no one best way to accomplish goals*

Organizational theory it characterizes:

Explain the concept's significance for understanding the theory and organizational behavior:

7.   *Concept: All parts of the organization being related to all other parts, as the organization interacts with its environment*

Organizational theory it characterizes:

Explain the concept's significance for understanding the theory and organizational behavior:

8.   *Concept: Employee morale, employee productivity, motivation, and leadership*

Organizational theory it characterizes:

Explain the concept's significance for understanding the theory and organizational behavior:

9.   *Concept: An organization's unique mixture of values, standards, and presumptions about how things should be done as a context for work*

Organizational theory it characterizes:

Explain the concept's significance for understanding the theory and organizational behavior:

10.   *Concept: Development of a strong set of shared positive values and norms within an organization with emphasis on high quality production and high employee commitment*

Organizational theory it characterizes:

Explain the concept's significance for understanding the theory and organizational behavior:

Exercise 4.5: Assessing Organizations from a Systems Perspective

A.   Brief Description
Students are asked to interview a social worker or administrator in a social services agency. After asking specified questions, they are instructed to write a paper summarizing information received, using systems theories' concepts and terms.

B.   Objectives
Students will:
1.   Define major systems theories' concepts.
2.   Apply systems theories' concepts to the functioning of a social services agency.

C.   Procedure
1.   Review the systems theories' concepts posed below.
2.   Ask students to interview a social services social worker or administrator and ask the questions cited below.
3.   Instruct them to write a paper describing the agency's functioning by using systems theories' terminology and concepts.

D.   Instructions for Students
1.   Review the concepts in the box below which are especially significant in understanding systems in the macro environment.

SYSTEMS THEORIES' CONCEPTS

System: A set of orderly and interrelated elements that form a functional whole.

Boundaries: Borders or margins that separate one entity (for example, a system) from another. They enclose the repeatedly occurring patterns that characterize the relationships within a system and give that system a particular identity.

Subsystem: A secondary or subordinate system within a larger system.

Homeostasis: The tendency for a system to maintain a relatively stable, constant state of balance.

Role: The culturally established social behavior and conduct expected of a person having a designated status in a particular group or society.

Relationship: The dynamic interpersonal connection between two or more persons or systems that involves how they think about, feel about, and behave toward each other.

Output: What happens to input after it has been processed by some system.

Feedback: A special form of input where a system receives information about its own performance.

Negative feedback: Input to a system about negative aspects of functioning that enables that system to correct any deviations or mistakes and return to a more homeostatic state.

Positive feedback: Input to a system about what that system is doing correctly in order to maintain itself and thrive.

Interface: The contact point between various systems including individuals and organizations, where interaction and communication may take place.

Differentiation: A system's tendency to move from a more simplified to a more complex existence.

Entropy: The natural tendency of a system to progress toward disorganization, depletion, disintegration, and, in essence, death.

Negative entropy: The process of a system toward growth and development—the opposite of entropy.

Equifinality: The idea that there are many different means to the same end.

---

2.   Select a social services agency in your area and make an appointment to speak with a social worker or administrator. You may conduct the interview over the phone if necessary. Your goal is to better understand organizational functioning by applying a systems perspective. Ask the interviewee the following questions and record her responses. Note that the questions are rephrased in systems terms in parentheses.

3.   Write a 3 to 5 page paper summarizing the information you received using systems theories' concepts and terminology to describe the agency's functioning.

A.   How is the agency structured—that is, what professional departments or units does it comprise *(what are its various subsystems)*? How many departments or units are there?

B.   How are professional departments or units defined *(what are their boundaries)*? Are they divided according to the problems they address—for example, all staff serving abused children under one umbrella? Or according to function—e.g., intake, assessment, referral, counseling? Or according to some combination of the two?

C.   Do you consider the agency relatively stable *(maintaining homeostasis)*? Are funding sources *(input)* stable? What are the primary funding sources for service provision?

D.   How is the effectiveness of service provision *(output)* measured?

E.   What types of *feedback* are solicited from consumers, such as clients or other agencies purchasing services?

F.   Has the agency recently received any *positive or negative feedback* about its effectiveness? If so, what was this feedback?

G.   Over time, has the agency become more complex—for example, added new services, served new client groups, or added new staff *(differentiation)*? If so, in what ways?

H.   Is the agency generally improving its ability to function and provide effective services *(negative entropy)*? Is it encountering increasing problems—for example, funding, regulations, or changing client needs *(entropy)*? In either case, in what ways?

Exercise 4.6: Comparing Social Service Agencies

A.   Brief Description
Students are asked to contact a social worker or administrator from two different social services agencies. After asking specified questions, they are instructed to write a paper that summarizes, compares, and contrasts the two agencies' input and output.

B.   Objectives
Students will:
1.   Assess the input and output of two different social services agencies.
2.   Compare and contrast the two agencies' inputs and outputs.

C.   Procedure
      1.   Review the material on systems theories, especially the concepts of input and output.
      2.   Ask students to interview a social worker or administrator from two different social services agencies and ask them the questions posed in the box below. (Telephone or email interviews are appropriate.)
      3.   Instruct students to write a 2 to 4 page paper summarizing the information they received and answering the additional questions posed below that compare and contrast the agencies' input and output.

D.   Instructions for Students
      1.   Select two social service organizations and contact workers or administrators. You may use phone or email contact, or an interview. Try to choose two dissimilar agencies—for example, one public and one private, one that serves children and one that serves older adults, one that addresses problems of poverty and one that addresses problems of mental illness. This will allow you to make broader, more striking comparisons. For each agency, find the following information: (1) forms of input, both client and financial support; (2) treatment or service provision process; and (3) output, or how service effectiveness is determined and measured.
      2.   Ask the social worker or administrator for each agency (Agency A and Agency B) the questions posed in the box below:

QUESTIONS TO ASK THE SOCIAL WORKER OR ADMINISTRATOR OF EACH AGENCY

Agency A

1a.   What sources comprise Agency A's financial input?

1b.   What are the characteristics of Agency A's clientele input (for example, problem type, age range, needs, strengths)?

2.   Describe the treatment or service provision process that Agency A employs.

3.   How does Agency A determine or measure its service effectiveness or output?

Agency B

1a.   What sources comprise Agency B's financial input?

1b.   What are the characteristics of Agency B's clientele input (for example, problem type, age range, needs, strengths)?

2.   Describe the treatment or service provision process that Agency B employs.

3.   How does Agency B determine or measure its service effectiveness or output?

---

      3.   Use the information you received to write a 2 to 4 page paper that **(1) summarizes** the information and **(2) discusses the following questions**:

            A.   How are Agencies A and B similar or different in terms of their financial input?

            B.   How are Agencies A and B similar or different concerning their clientele input?

C.   How are Agencies A and B similar or different concerning their process of service provision?

D.   How are Agencies A and B similar or different concerning their determination and measurement of service effectiveness?

Exercise 4.7: Analyzing Formal and Informal Organizational Structure

---

A.   Brief Description
Students are asked to speak with an employee of a social services agency and explore the extent to which formal lines of authority, channels of communication, and the dimensions of power compare and differ. They then write a short paper summarizing their findings.

B.   Objectives
Students will:
1.   Investigate the formal lines of authority, channels of communication, and the dimensions of power in a social services agency.
2.   Compare and contrast how these coincide with each other.

C.   Procedure
1.   Review the material on formal lines of authority, channels of communication, and dimensions of power as they function in a social services agency.
2.   Ask students to interview a staff member of a social services agency and summarize their findings after asking the questions posed below.

D.   Instructions for Students
Choose an organization, preferably some type of social services agency. For the purposes of this assignment, however, any agency—including your university or some segment of the university—will do. Contact an employee, a supervisor, or an administrator in the agency you selected, and ask for a copy of the organizational chart. Explain to your contact person that you want to study the formal *lines of authority,* the *channels of communication,* and the *dimensions of power* illustrated in the chart. Define the terms for your contact, then ask the following questions and summarize the information you gather in a 2 to 4 page paper.

1.   A.   To what extent do the channels of communication in the agency follow the formal lines of authority depicted in the organizational chart?

B.   If there are specific differences between the chart and the reality, describe them.

C.   What are the positive and negative effects of these differences?

2.   A.   How closely do the dimensions of power in the agency match the formal lines of authority depicted in the organizational chart?

B.   If there are specific differences between the chart and the reality, describe them.

C.   What are the positive and negative effects of these differences?

A.   Brief Description
Students are asked to have an employee of a social services organization fill out the questionnaires provided below and then answer several questions about their organizational culture. Students then score the questionnaires and write a short paper summarizing their findings.

B.   Objectives
Students will:
1.   Explore the organizational culture of a social services organization.
2.   Compare and contrast the bureaucratic orientation with the customer/employee orientation of that organization.

C.   Procedure
1.   Review the material on organizational culture, bureaucracy, and styles of management (including Total Quality Management [TQM]).
2.   Instruct students to identify an employee of a social services organization who will fill out the questionnaires posed below and answer several questions.
3.   Ask students to write a brief paper summarizing their findings.

D.   Instructions for Students
1.   The two questionnaires below contain questions you can ask to evaluate organizational culture. They compare two organizational cultures—a traditional bureaucracy and a client/employee centered agency employing Total Quality Management (TQM) principles. This exercise will sensitize you to differences in organizational culture and to how those differences may affect you professionally.
2.   Select a social services agency—large or small, public or private—in your area. You may interview a worker, a supervisor or agency administrator, or both a worker *and* an administrator. (If you choose this last option, you can compare their impressions of the organizational culture. Frequently, workers—who are in direct contact with clients and their views—perceives an organization very differently than do administrators—who are exposed to political, funding, and regulatory pressures from the external macro environment.) This questionnaire will not yield a specific score to precisely define organizational culture, but it will provide you with some thought-provoking information about agency life.

Instruct the interviewee(s) to answer both questionnaires to the best of her ability, using this scale: (1) never; (2) infrequently; (3) sometimes; (4) frequently; and (5) always. Record her responses below.

3.   Add up the scores for each questionnaire separately and divide each by ten. The two average scores will range from 1—low organizational commitment to that management style—to 5—very high commitment to that management style. You may find an inverse relationship between scores on the Bureaucratic and Customer/Employee Orientation questionnaires, reflecting the extreme differences between the two.

***Bureaucratic Orientation Questionnaire*[1]**

1. Most professional employees in this organization hold a clearly defined job with clearly designated responsibilities.

Never	Infrequently	Sometimes	Frequently	Always
1	2	3	4	5

2. Most professional employees in this organization are told straightforwardly and specifically how their jobs should be accomplished.

Never	Infrequently	Sometimes	Frequently	Always
1	2	3	4	5

3. Supervisors closely scrutinize employees' work.

Never	Infrequently	Sometimes	Frequently	Always
1	2	3	4	5

4. The administration considers efficiency to be of the utmost importance.

Never	Infrequently	Sometimes	Frequently	Always
1	2	3	4	5

5. Decisions about agency policy and practice tend to be made by higher administration and flow from the top down.

Never	Infrequently	Sometimes	Frequently	Always
1	2	3	4	5

6. Power in the agency is held primarily by top executives.

Never	Infrequently	Sometimes	Frequently	Always
1	2	3	4	5

7. Communication in the organization flows from the top down.

Never	Infrequently	Sometimes	Frequently	Always
1	2	3	4	5

---

[1]Many of the questions listed below are derived from the conflicts posed by Knopf (1979) that occur between the orientations of helping professionals and bureaucratic systems.

8. There is little communication among horizontal units—that is, units of approximately equal status that perform different functions.

Never	Infrequently	Sometimes	Frequently	Always
1	2	3	4	5

9. The organization emphasizes a rigid structure of power and authority that works to maintain stability and the status quo.

Never	Infrequently	Sometimes	Frequently	Always
1	2	3	4	5

10. The organization and its administration place great importance on specified rules and policies and expect employees to adhere to them.

Never	Infrequently	Sometimes	Frequently	Always
1	2	3	4	5

TOTAL: = _____ ÷ **10** = _____ **(AVERAGE SCORE)**

Customer/Employee Orientation Questionnaire

1. The organization places primary importance on the client (customer) and on effective service to clients.

Never	Infrequently	Sometimes	Frequently	Always
1	2	3	4	5

2. The organization holds in high regard practitioners who provide services directly to clients.

Never	Infrequently	Sometimes	Frequently	Always
1	2	3	4	5

3. The organization's administrative structure is viewed primarily as a support system for clients and direct service workers.

Never	Infrequently	Sometimes	Frequently	Always
1	2	3	4	5

4. The organization's administration considers quality of service—consistency of service provision, responsiveness to clients' needs, and service availability—its major goal.

Never	Infrequently	Sometimes	Frequently	Always
1	2	3	4	5

5. Organizational leadership seeks to empower agency practitioners so that they can do their jobs as effectively as possible.

Never	Infrequently	Sometimes	Frequently	Always
1	2	3	4	5

6. Professional employees are encouraged to provide input into how the organization is run.

Never	Infrequently	Sometimes	Frequently	Always
1	2	3	4	5

7. The organization values client feedback and incorporates it into improving service provision.

Never	Infrequently	Sometimes	Frequently	Always
1	2	3	4	5

8. Professional employees are encouraged to work together to improve service provision.

Never	Infrequently	Sometimes	Frequently	Always
1	2	3	4	5

9. Communication flow is open and frequent among most agency units.

Never	Infrequently	Sometimes	Frequently	Always
1	2	3	4	5

10. Professional employees feel that their input to upper levels of administration is valued and put to use.

Never	Infrequently	Sometimes	Frequently	Always
1	2	3	4	5

TOTAL = _____ ÷ **10** = _____ **(AVERAGE SCORE)**

4.   After calculating scores, explain to the interviewee(s) which organizational culture his agency reflects. Give brief examples of traditional bureaucracy and of TQM. Then ask the following questions about the organization's culture and effectiveness and write a two- to four-page paper summarizing your findings.

A.   How would you describe the organization's culture?
B.   To what extent do you feel the organization's culture enhances or detracts from practitioners' ability to do their work effectively?
C.   What are the strengths of the organization's culture?
D.   What are the weaknesses of the organization's culture?
E.   Ideally, what changes, if any, would you make in the organizational culture?

I. Introduction

II. Change in Organizations

    A.   Highlight 5.1 A word about innovations

    B.   Undertaking specific projects

        1.   Service projects—address needs or issues requiring some new, innovative, or untried approach

        2.   Support projects—involve short-term endeavors aimed at specific ends that support some other agency activity

    C.   Initiating and developing programs

        1.   Program—(also referred to as a social program) an ongoing configuration of services and service provision procedures intended to meet a designated group of clients' needs

        2.   You may see gaps in service delivery system that need to be addressed

    D.   Changing agency policies

        1.   Formal policies—policies that are written down and clearly specified, often in a policy manual (the policy manual may be the most important document in your agency)

        2.   Informal policies—policies that are not overtly stated, yet still guide and influence agency staff's behavior

        3.   Informal agency policies

            a.   Highlight 5.2: Case Example: "Hidden" Informal Policies

            b.   Informal policies on practice procedures

                1)   Practice procedures—refer to the techniques and approaches practitioners use to accomplish their goals with clients

                2)   The way tasks are actually carried out in agencies, as opposed to how they are theoretically supposed to be carried out

            c.   Informal agency goals—often replace formally stated goals and thus become the real goals the agency strives to reach (goal displacement)

            d.   Informal personnel practices

III.   Beginning the Change Process

    A.   Change agent—the person who feels some change within the agency is needed

    B.   Action system—the people and resources you will organize and employ to work toward the needed change

    C.   Innovation proposal—the idea you want to implement

    D.   Action plan—a detailed blueprint for how to go about achieving the desired change

    E.   Two major tasks

          1.   Identify the action system's potential goal

          2.   Think about the opposition you anticipate

IV.   The Process of Organizational Change

    A.   The planned change process

          1.   Engagement—the initial period where you as a practitioner orient yourself to the problem at hand and begin to establish communication and a relationship with others also addressing the problem

          2.   Assessment—the investigation and determination of variables affecting an identified problem or issue and concentration on strengths, both as viewed from micro, mezzo, and macro perspectives, in preparation for formulating a plan of action to help a client system

          3.   Planning—the use of empirically based practice to review potential alternatives, evaluate their pros and cons, and determine what course of action to pursue to promote the well-being of the client system, and pursue social and economic justice

          4.   Implementation—the actual *doing* of the plan and monitoring of its progress

          5.   Evaluation—determination of the effectiveness of the plan's implementation, including the attainment of goals at the micro, mezzo, and macro levels

          6.   Termination—the ending of the professional social worker-client system relationship

          7.   Follow-up—the reexamination of a client system's situation at some point after the intervention's completion in order to monitor the intervention's ongoing effects and to determine potential reassessment for further intervention

    B.   Figure 5.1: PREPARE: An Assessment of Organizational or Community Change Potential

    C.   Case Example—Deciding to Go Macro

V.   **Step 1: _P_REPARE—Identify <u>Problems</u> to Address**

     A.   Substep 1: Decide to seriously evaluate the potential for macro level intervention

          1.   Critical thinking skills required

          2.   Case Example—Substep 1

     B.   Substep 2: Define and prioritize problems

          1.   Case Example—Substep 2

          2.   Figure 5.2: Define and Prioritize Problems

     C.   Substep 3: Translate problems into needs

          1.   Problems—any sources of perplexity or distress

          2.   Needs—physical, psychological, economic, cultural, and social requirements for survival, well-being, and fulfillment

          3.   Figure 5.3: Translate Problems into Needs—Substep 3

          4.   Five phases for clarifying and substantiating an unmet need in order to prepare for program development within your agency

               a)   Get background data and information to clarify exactly what the need is

               b)   Recognize and specify other agencies or programs in the community that already address the need

               c)   Talk to other professionals serving similar clients

               d)   Get clients involved

               e)   Consider the value of a more formal needs assessment (needs assessment—formal evaluations of client needs within the organizational context and of resident needs within the community context)

          5.   Case Example—Substep 3

     D.   Substep 4: Determine which need or needs you will address

          1.   Focus on one at a time

          2.   Case Example—Substep 4

VI. **Step 2: P*R*EPARE—Review Your Macro and Personal <u>Reality</u>**

    A.   Macro reality—the macro environment in which you work

    B.   Personal reality—the personal strengths and weaknesses that might affect your ability to effect a macro intervention in the macro environment

    C.   Substep 1: Evaluate macro variables working for or against you in the macro change process

        1.   Force field analysis—evaluation method that organizes information so that major variables acting for or against macro change can be identified

        2.   Figure 5.4: Evaluate Macro Variables—Substep 1

        3.   Five arenas of variables

            a.   Resources and funding

            b.   Constraining regulations or laws

            c.   Internal political climate

                1)   Factors against change

                      a)   An organization that has undergone a number of major external alterations and upheavals in recent months will probably be more resistant to change

                      b)   An agency that is wedded to a specific philosophy or treatment modality

                      c)   Age of the agency and longevity of its staff

                2)   Highlight 5.3 Bureaucratic Succession: Opportunity for Positive Change

            d.   External political climate

            e.   Other factors

            f.   Case Example—Substep 1

    D.   Substep 2: Review your personal reality—strengths and weaknesses that may act for or against successful change efforts

        1.   Figure 5.5: Evaluating Personal Characteristics for Macro Practice: Macro Practice Builds on Macro Practice Skills

        2.   Case Example—Substep 2

VII.   Step 3: PR_E_PARE—<u>Establish</u> Primary Goals

    A.   Characteristics of goals

        1.   Goals are derived from some identified problem

        2.   The problem can be translated into some specific need

            a.   Three concepts relevant to goal selection

                1)   Potential for permanence

                2)   Greater influence

                3)   Simplicity

            b.   Case Example—**Establish** Primary Goals

VIII.   Step 4: PRE_P_ARE—Identify Relevant <u>People</u> of Influence

    A.   Figure 5.6: PREPARE—Identify Relevant **People** of Influence

    B.   Highlight 5.4: Leadership Styles of Decision-Makers

        1.   Climber—(also referred to as "the narcissist") tends to closely control subordinates to ensure nobody else is seen as a rising star

        2.   Conserver—toils to preserve the homeostatic status quo

        3.   Zealot—a go-getter who exudes energy and loves creative innovation

        4.   Advocate—a person who has exceptionally high commitment to the goals of the organization or unit of which she or he is a member, or to a client population serviced by the agency

        5.   Statesperson—is more concerned with the welfare of society as a whole than with the agency or a particular client population

    C.   Case Example—Identify Relevant **People** of Influence

    D.   Rationales for internal advocacy

IX.   Step 5: PREP_A_RE—<u>Assess</u> Potential Costs and Benefits to Clients and Agency

    A.   Opportunity cost—how you might miss out on other good opportunities where your time would be better spent

    B.   Three questions to ask before pursuing a new project

        1.   Will the results be worth the effort?

2.   Might alternative solutions produce more benefits at less cost?

3.   Who gets the benefits and who pays the costs?

C.   Case Example—**Assess** Potential Costs and Benefits to Clients and Agency

X.   Step 6: PREPA*R*E—Review Professional and Personal <u>Risk</u>

A.   Figure 5.7: PREPARE—Review Professional and Personal **Risk**

B.   Three questions to ask yourself before seriously undertaking macro change in an organization

1.   Could I lose my job?

2.   Will my career path be affected?

3.   Will I strain interpersonal relationship at work?

C.   Highlight 5.5 Consider "Covert Operations"

D.   A strengths perspective on risk

E.   Case Example—Review Your Professional and Personal **Risk**

XI.   Step 7: PREPAR*E*—<u>Evaluate</u> the Potential Success of a Macro Change Process

A.   Substep 1: Review the PREPARE process and weigh pros and cons of proceeding

1.   Three possible conclusions

    a.   You might make a definite commitment to continue the change process

    b.   You might determine that the time is not right

    c.   You might decide that the potential for effective organizational change is too poor to continue your efforts

2.   Figure 5.8: PREPARE—**Evaluate** the Potential Success of a Macro Change Process

3.   Case Example—Substep 1

B.   Substep 2: Identify possible macro approaches to use, estimate their effectiveness, and select the most appropriate one

1.   The transitional stage between deciding to pursue a macro change effort and actually doing it

2.   Case Example—Substep 2

3.   Highlight 5.6: Summary Outline of the PREPARE Process

   a.   **P**: Identify **<u>Problems</u>** to address

      1)   Substep 1: Decide to seriously evaluate the potential for macro level intervention

      2)   Substep 2: Define and prioritize problems

      3)   Substep 3: Translate problems into needs

      4)   Substep 4: Determine which need or needs you will address

   b.   **R**: Review your macro and personal **<u>Reality</u>**

      1)   Substep 1: Evaluate macro variables working for or against you in the macro change process. These variables include:

         a)   Resources

         b)   Constraining regulations

         c)   Internal political climate

         d)   External political climate

         (e)   Other factors

      2)   Substep 2: Review your personal reality—strengths and weaknesses that may act for or against successful change efforts

   c.   **E**: **<u>Establish</u>** primary goals

   d.   **P**: Identify relevant **<u>People</u>** of influence

   e.   **A**: **<u>Assess</u>** potential benefits to clients and agency

   f.   **R**: Review professional and personal **<u>Risk</u>**. Questions you might ask include:

      1)   Could I lose my job?

      2)   Will my career path be affected?

      3)   Will I strain interpersonal relationships at work?

g.   **E**: **Evaluate** the potential success of a macro change process

      1)   Substep 1: Review the PREPARE process and weigh the pros and cons of proceeding

      2)   Substep 2: Identify possible macro approaches to use, estimate their effectiveness, and select the most appropriate one

---

Experiential Exercises and Classroom Simulations

Exercise 5.1: Understanding Change in Organizations

A.   Brief Description
Using a small group format, students investigate the meanings of project implementation, program development, and agency policy change by exploring the major concepts involved, their similarities and differences, and examples of each.

B.   Objectives
Students will:
1.   Recognize the basic concepts inherent in the three types of organizational change.
2.   Examine how the types of organizational change compare and differ.
3.   Identify examples of each.

C.   Procedure
1.   Review the material on change in organizations provided in the text including a word about innovations, undertaking specific projects, initiating and developing programs, and changing agency policies.
2.   Divide the class into small groups of four to six.
3.   Ask the groups to discuss the subsequent questions, select a group representative, and be prepared to report to the entire class the small group's findings.
4.   After about 20 minutes, ask the small groups to terminate their discussions and participate in a full class discussion.
5.   Ask the representative from each group to share her or his summary of the discussion. Encourage comments from all class members.

D.   Instructions for Students
Address the following issues:
1.   Describe the major concepts involved in project implementation, program development, and agency policy change.
2.   In what ways are the three types of organizational change similar?
3.   In what ways are the three types of change different?
4.   Provide some examples of each type of change.

E.   Commentary
This activity may also be conducted by holding a full class discussion without breaking students down into small groups.

Exercise 5.2: Identifying Leadership Styles of Decision-Makers

A.   Brief Description

Using a small group format, students identify the leadership style reflected in each of several leader descriptions.

B.   Objectives

Students will:
1.   Identify which leadership style characterizes examples of leaders.
2.   Compare and contrast the dimensions of leadership styles.
3.   Describe an ideal leadership style and explain why.

C.   Procedure
1.   Review the material on leadership styles of decision-makers provided in the text.
2.   Provide students with copies of the matching exercise under "Instructions for Students."
3.   After allowing students a few minutes to complete the exercise, initiate a full class discussion regarding the following questions and issues:
    a.   What leadership style characterizes each leader description and why?
    b.   In what ways are these five leadership styles different?
    c.   In what ways are these five leadership styles similar?
    d.   What is the ideal leadership style? How does it differ from any or all of these?

D.   Instructions for Students

Match the following leadership styles with the descriptions cited below. Note that some descriptions may apply to more than one leadership style.

A. Climber
B. Conserver
C. Zealot
D. Advocate
E. Statesperson

1.   A leader who is more concerned with the welfare of society as a whole than with the agency or a particular client population.

    a.   What leadership style(s) characterize(s) this leader?
    b.   Explain why.

2.   A leader who is very concerned with and interested in him/herself and his/her own work.

    a.   What leadership style(s) characterize(s) this leader?
    b.   Explain why.

3.   A leader who likes to closely control subordinates to ensure nobody else is seen as a rising star.

    a.   What leadership style(s) characterize(s) this leader?
    b.   Explain why.

4.	A leader who has exceptionally high commitment to the goals of the organization or unit of which she or he is a member.

   a.	What leadership style(s) characterize(s) this leader?
   b.	Explain why.

5.	A leader who is a superduper go-getter, exudes energy, and loves creative innovation.

   a.	What leadership style(s) characterize(s) this leader?
   b.	Explain why.

6.	A leader who is a skilled administrator and is exceptionally committed to the agency and its clients.

   a.	What leadership style(s) characterize(s) this leader?
   b.	Explain why.

7.	A leader who will probably not support subordinates' ideas for change, but might just confiscate them and take them as her/his own.

   a.	What leadership style(s) characterize(s) this leader?
   b.	Explain why.

8.	A leader who is not so much concerned about quality of service provision as following the rules to the letter.

   a.	What leadership style(s) characterize(s) this leader?
   b.	Explain why.

9.	A leader who has excellent public relations skills but is not very good at attending to detail or carrying through with long-term proposals.

   a.	What leadership style(s) characterize(s) this leader?
   b.	Explain why.

10.	A leader who will probably not spend much time listening to your ideas.

   a.	What leadership style(s) characterize(s) this leader?
   b.	Explain why.

E.	Commentary
This activity may also be conducted by holding a full class discussion without breaking students down into small groups.

Exercise 5.3: Evaluating Personal Characteristics for Macro Practice

A. Brief Description
Students are asked to evaluate their personal characteristics for as they might apply while undertaking macro practice activities.

B. Objectives
Students will:
1. Explore and identify their personal characteristics that are relevant to macro practice.
2. Evaluate how these personal characteristics might help them function in assessing whether or not to undertake project implementation, policy change, or program development in macro practice.

C. Procedure
1. Review the material on PREPARE including the various substeps involved.
2. Ask students to respond to the questions posed below.
3. Discuss students' answers using either a small group format or full class discussion.

D. Instructions for Students
Evaluating your own characteristics, strengths, and weaknesses is as important in macro practice as in micro or mezzo practice. Indeed, macro practice skills are built upon micro and mezzo practice skills, and you will use the same interpersonal skills in macro practice as you do at the other levels. Picture yourself working with staff, administrators, and clients in an agency. Answer the questions and follow the instructions below:

1. Complete the following four "Who are you?" statements, using adjectives, nouns, or phrases. If you had to summarize who you are, what would you say?

I am

I am

I am

I am

2. What adjectives would you use to describe yourself? Circle all that apply.

Happy	Sad	Honest	Dishonest	Sensitive
Insensitive	Trustworthy	Untrustworthy	Caring	Uncaring
Outgoing	Shy	Withdrawn	Friendly	Unfriendly
Religious	Not-very-religious	Nervous	Calm	Formal
Informal	Aggressive	Assertive	Timid	Confident
Not-very-confident	Careful	Careless	Capable	Incapable
Independent	Dependent	Affectionate	Cool	Wary
Bold	Cheerful	Witty	Unassuming	Thorough
Easy-going	Determined	Clever	Responsive	Strong-minded
Leisurely	Industrious	Weak-willed (at least sometimes)	Controlled	Spontaneous
Serious	Funny	Tough	Pleasant	Daring
Eager	Efficient	Not-so-efficient	Artistic	Tactful

Intolerant	Vulnerable	Likable	Smart	Understanding
Impatient	Patient	Imaginative	Wordy	Concise
Open-minded	Funny	Organized	Somewhat-disorganized	Conscientious
Late	Emotional	Unemotional	Controlled	Open
Creative	Curious	Sincere	Precise	A-little-haphazard
Cooperative	Ethical	Brave	Mature	Spunky

3.   Cite your four greatest strengths—personal qualities, talents, or accomplishments.

Strength A

Strength B

Strength C

Strength D

4.   Several weaknesses are listed below. To what extent do you suffer from each? Rate yourself on each one by placing the appropriate number beside it.

1. Very serious 2. Moderately serious 3. Mildly serious 4. Not at all serious

Lack of understanding of community service system   _____
Personal stress   _____
Exhaustion and fatigue   _____
Over-involvement with job   _____
Insufficient time   _____
Lack of self-confidence   _____

5.   Cite your four greatest weaknesses.

Weakness A

Weakness B

Weakness C

Weakness D

6.   How do you think your personal strengths will help you work with other staff, administrators, and clients in macro practice situations?

7.   What weaknesses, if any, do you think you need to address to improve your ability to work with staff, administrators, and clients in macro practice situations?

A.   Brief Description
Students apply the PREPARE process to a case example.

B.   Objectives
Students will:
1.   Apply the PREPARE process to a case example.
2.   Assess the potential for macro change.

C.   Procedure
1.   Review the PREPARE process in detail.
2.   Ask students for answer the questions posed below concerning a case example in macro practice.
3.   This exercise may be undertaken by requiring students to write a paper answering the questions, or discuss the case in a small group format.

D.   Instructions for Students
1.   Read the following case vignette and answer the subsequent questions using each step of the PREPARE process. Feel free to add creative ideas and solutions to each phase of the decision-making process.

> **CASE EXAMPLE:** You are a social worker for Shatterproof County Department of Social Services in the Public Assistance Division.[1] Shatterproof is a huge urban county populated primarily by people of color. Following the demise of Aid to Families with Dependent Children (AFDC),[2] your agency is struggling to adapt to new policies, regulations, and requirements concerning the distribution of clients' needed resources. You and your colleagues are working to adjust and conform to new expectations. However, that is not the immediate focus of your concern.
>
> In working for the county these past three years, you have become increasingly disturbed about the way many workers treat clients, most of whom are women of color. You feel that workers are pressured to process clients through the problem-solving process as quickly as possible and that too little emphasis is placed on client empowerment. *Empowerment* is the "process of increasing personal, interpersonal, or political power so that individuals can take action to improve their life situations" (Gutierrez, 1995, p. 205).[3] You feel strongly that if workers assumed an empowerment-oriented approach, more clients would be able to gain control of the solutions to their own problems. Such an approach might involve teaching workers how to focus on empowerment approaches and techniques, including "accepting the client's definition of the problem," "identifying and building upon existing strengths," engaging in a realistic assessment of the client's power in her personal situation, "teaching specific skills" (such as "skills for community or organizational change; life skills," such as parenting, job seeking, and self-defense; and interpersonal skills, such as assertiveness, social competency, and self-advocacy"), and "mobilizing resources and advocating for clients" (Gutierrez, 1995, pp. 208-10).

---

[1] *Public assistance* is financial benefits and in-kind (services of goods versus cash) benefits provided to people who can't support themselves.

[2] *AFDC* is "a former public assistance program, originating in the Social Security Act as Aid to Dependent Children. It was funded by the federal and state governments to provide financial aid for needy children who are deprived of parental support because of death, incapacitation, or absence" (Barker, 2003, p. 14).

[3] Many of the concepts presented here are taken from L. M. Gutierrez (1995). "Working with women of color: An empowerment perspective." In J. Rothman, J. L. Erlich, & J.E. Tropman (eds.), *Strategies of Community Intervention* (pp. 204-220). Itasca, IL: F. E. Peacock.

So you begin to wonder what you might be able to do about this situation. Clients ought to be allowed more input into the definition and solution of their problems, but workers are not as receptive to clients as they should be. Adopting an empowerment approach could greatly help in successfully implementing the new public assistance programs. Of course, this is not the agency's only problem. Workers are overly burdened with paperwork, and computers and programs are already outdated. Nevertheless, in your mind empowerment remains the dominant issue. You think social workers, supervisors, and administrators should be educated about empowerment issues and trained to implement empowerment approaches in practice. Emphasis should be placed on both empowerment values and skills. How can you increase awareness and implementation of a philosophy of empowerment in your huge agency? Upper-level administrators seem to inhabit some unreachable plane. There are only so many hours in your workday. What are your options? Can you start small by trying to reach workers in your own unit? (There are seven of you who report to one supervisor.) Can you initiate training for yourself and the other six workers in your unit?

Will the unit and the agency accept an empowerment approach? What factors will help you and what will hinder you? What will training the unit staff cost? The agency may have some funding available to provide in-service training for workers,[4] because it does require every worker to complete continuing education units (CEUs)[5] on a regular basis. As a matter of fact, you have a flier announcing an empowerment training seminar led by an expert in the field. You also know of a social work professor in the local university who might be able to do some training or to refer you to someone who can. What would that cost? Is there any possibility of getting volunteers to do the training on a limited basis?

Are there other potential barriers to training besides cost? Certainly the agency's CEU requirements are in your favor. Although the agency is in some turmoil due to new programs and requirements, it seems there has always been some degree of hubbub. That's really nothing new. Training a single unit is a relatively small task. Ideally, you'd like to include the entire agency, but that's something to think about in the future. You can think of no one outside the agency who would actively oppose your plan.

Do you think you can "pull off" such a project, even though training programs aren't in your job description? What personal characteristics will work to your advantage in the process? For example, are you capable, responsible, and/or assertive? Do you have exceptionally strong communication or negotiation skills? On the other hand, what weaknesses do you have that might act against a successful change process? For example, is it difficult for you to ask for things? Do you consider yourself shy or lacking in confidence?

The bottom line is that you really want other workers to work with clients more effectively by adopting an empowerment approach. Your goal, then, is to figure out how to provide training to help them do just that. You've discussed the idea with colleagues who seemed mildly positive about it. You don't think they'd be willing to take on primary responsibilities for the project, but it would be worthwhile speaking with some of them further.

Your colleague and friend Ortrude has some difficulties organizing and following through on details, but she usually speaks up for anything she believes in. Maybe you can win her support. There is also Virgilia, a hard, responsible worker who usually keeps her opinions to herself. You don't feel you know her very well, but she might be in favor of your idea. On the downside, there's your colleague and non-friend Bentley who typically "pooh-poohs" any innovative idea.

---

[4] *In-service training programs* are educational sessions provided by an agency for its staff to develop their skills or improve their effectiveness.

[5] Acquiring CEUs often involves successful completion of "qualified academic or professional courses" (Barker, 1995, p. 79). One intent is to keep professionals in a range of professions updated with current knowledge relevant to their fields.

The agency's voluntary In-service Training Committee suggests and plans training for various agency units, so you will have to approach its members, and they might be supportive—even though their funding is limited and fluctuating. Since you don't personally know any committee members, you have no natural "in."

As to people in the community, you've already established that at least one expert is available (though you don't know what her fee would be) and that the professor at the university is another possibility.

What about your own position and how initiating such a project might affect you both professionally and personally. Your supervisor Astral is a "laid-back" type who generally gets her work done in a leisurely fashion. (Actually, you think she's kind of "spacey.") She is not someone to depend upon for high-powered consultations or for strong support for this initiative. On the other hand, if you're willing to do the work yourself, she will probably approve the project and send it up for higher level authorization. All agency in-service training must be approved by the agency's Assistant Director, Harvey. You think Harvey, a scrooge-like accountant at heart, is more likely to approve such a plan if it isn't extremely costly.

2. Answer the following questions with respect to this case example.

Exercise 5.4 (1):

Step 1: Identify Problems to Address
Substep 1.1: Evaluate the potential for macro level intervention. Discuss the seriousness of the identified problem situation in the case example above. In your own words, describe what you see as the core issue(s).

Substep 1.2: Define and prioritize the problems you've identified in the case example.

Substep 1.3: Translate problems into needs.

Substep 1.4: Determine which need or needs you will address if you are in this worker's situation.

Exercise 5.4 (2):

Step 2: Review Your Macro and Personal Reality
Substep 2.1: Evaluate the organizational and other macro variables potentially working for or against you in the macro change process as portrayed in the above case example. Fill out figure 5.3, then explain the reasons for your responses below.

Figure 5.3: PREPARE--Evaluate Your Professional and Personal Risk

To what extent are you in danger of:	No danger	Some danger	Moderate danger	Serious danger
1. losing your job?				
2. decreasing your potential for upward mobility?				
3. seriously straining work relationships?				

Explain the reasons for your responses.

Substep 2.2: Assess your personal reality—that is, the strengths and weaknesses that may act for or against a successful change effort. Exercise 5.1 may help you with this question.

Exercise 5.4 (3):

Step 3: Establish Primary Goals
List the goals you would pursue if you were in the position described above.

Exercise 5.4 (4):

Step 4: Identify Relevant People of Influence

In the following figure, list individuals and groups both inside and outside of the agency.

Figure 5.4: PREPARE--Identify Relevant **People** of Influence

Potential _Action Systems_	_Name_	_Potential Support_			
		Very good	Mildly good	Mildly bad	Very bad
Individuals in the Organization					
Groups in the Organization					
Individuals in the Community					
Groups in the the Community					
Others					

Give a brief explanation of your choices.

Exercise 5.4 (5):

Step 5: Assess Potential Financial Costs and Potential Benefits to Clients and Agency
Use the case example in your response.

131

Exercise 5.4 (6):

Step 6: Review Professional and Personal Risk
Could you lose your job, decrease your potential for upward mobility, and/or seriously strain your work relationships?

Exercise 5.4 (7):

Step 7: Evaluate the Potential Success of a Macro Change Process
Substep 7.1: Review (and summarize) **the prior PREPARE process, and weigh the pros and cons of proceeding with the macro change process.**

PROS
Client need (see Step 1):
Positive organizational and other macro variables (see Step 2):
Your own strengths (see Step 2):
Potential support (see Step 4):
Financial benefits (see Step 5):

CONS
Negative organizational and other macro variables (see Step 2):
Your own weaknesses (see Step 2):
Potential resistance (see Step 4):
Financial costs (see Step 5):
Your risks (see Step 6):

Substep 7.2: Identify possible macro approaches to use in the case example and determine how you would proceed (that is, continue the macro change process, postpone it, or drop the whole idea).

Exercise 5.5: Creative Macro Change

A.   Brief Description
Students are asked to discuss case examples and propose the appropriate avenue of macro change.

B.   Objectives
Students will:
1.   Assess potential macro practice scenarios.
2.   Propose methods of macro change.
3.   Evaluate the pros and cons of such change.

C.   Procedure
1.   Using a small group format or large class discussion, ask students to discuss the case scenarios proposed below and answer the subsequent questions. (Students may also be asked to write a paper concerning their answers.)

D.   Instructions for Students
Below are three case scenarios that might involve project implementation, program development, or policy change. For each, determine what type of change should be pursued, provide a rationale for your answer, and discuss potential benefits and problems of this change.

Case Scenario A: You are the social worker at an elementary school. You notice that an increasing number of children come from turbulent homes. With each passing year these children present more problems with truancy. Their grades deteriorate and their illicit drug use soars. They need help. But what kind? Your job is to intervene individually with children suffering the most severe crises. You do some individual counseling, make some family visits, run a few support and treatment groups, and attend numerous assessment and planning meetings.

In a social work journal, you read about a new type of alternative approach for children at risk for the very problems you're seeing. One idea in particular catches your eye: A school in Illinois developed a "Friendship System" for children-at-risk. Volunteers solicited from among social work students at a nearby university attended a dozen training sessions, learning how to deal with these children. Each volunteer was then paired with a child and became the child's "special friend." The required commitment period was one year. Volunteers' responsibilities included spending time with the child at least once a week, being available when the child needed to talk, and generally being a positive role model for the child.

The program seems similar to Big Brothers/Big Sisters in which volunteers "work under professional supervision, usually by social workers, providing individual guidance and companionship to boys and girls deprived of a parent" (Barker, 1995, p. 35). But children in the Friendship System might or might not be from single-parent homes. The Friendship System's only prerequisite for the children is that school staff designate them as at-risk of problems including truancy, deteriorating school performance, and drug use, and school staff have substantial latitude in determining a child's eligibility for the program. Typical criteria include a recent divorce in the family, extreme shyness and withdrawal, academic problems, or other social problems. You think, "Wouldn't it be great if my school system had something like that in operation?"

What type of change would you consider pursuing—implementing a project, developing a program, or changing a school policy? Provide a rationale for the proposed change and discuss its potential benefits and problems.

A. What type of change should be pursued?
B. Explain your reasons for choosing this change.
C. What are the potential benefits and problems of this change?

Case Scenario B: Your agency requires clients to fill out a 27-page admissions form before they can receive services. A large percentage of the agency's clients are Hispanic, and they speak very little English so the admissions form effectively prohibits Hispanic clients from receiving service. Because of the language difference, the agency blocks clients from receiving service.

What type of change would you consider pursuing—implementing a project, developing a program, or changing an agency policy? Provide a rationale for the proposed change and discuss its potential benefits and problems.

A. What type of change should be pursued?
B. Explain your reasons for choosing this change.
C. What are the potential benefits and problems of this change?

Case Scenario C: You are a social worker in a rural county social services agency. The towns within the county range in size from 1500 to 10,000 people, and the area have become increasingly impoverished as a number of small cheese and leather factories have left the area. Many people are struggling to survive in old shacks with little clothing and food. You know you can't overhaul the entire public assistance system, but you would like to initiate a food drive or collection to temporarily relieve people's suffering.

What type of change would you consider pursuing—implementing a project, developing a program, or changing an agency policy? Provide a rationale for the proposed change and discuss its potential benefits and problems.

A. What type of change should be pursued?
B. Explain your reasons for choosing this change.
C. What are the potential benefits and problems of this change?

I.   **Introduction**

II.   **The Planned Change Process and Organizational Change**

    A.   Figure 6.1: The Relationship Between PREPARE and IMAGINE

    B.   Highlight 6.1: A Word About Engagement

III.   **IMAGINE: A Process for Organizational Change**

    A.   Figure 6.2: IMAGINE—A Process for Initiating and Implementing Macro Change

    B.   **I**MAGINE: Develop an innovative **Idea**

        1.   Case Example: Develop an Innovative Idea

    C.   I**M**AGINE: **Muster** support and formulate an action system

        1.   Conceptualizing the macro practice environment

            a.   The macro client system—includes those people who will ultimately benefit from the change process

            b.   Figure 6.3: The Macro Client System in Macro Practice

            c.   The change agent system—the individual who initiates the macro change process

            d.   A note about the agency as a change agent system—we will generally refer to the agency as the agency system instead of the change agent system

            e.   The target system—the system that social workers must change or influence in order to accomplish their goals

            f.   Figure 6.4: The Target System

            g.   The action system—includes those people who agree and are committed to work together to attain the proposed macro change

            h.   Figure 6.5: The Change Agent, Action, Target, and Macro Client Systems

            i.   Case Example: Conceptualizing the Macro Practice Environment

        2.   Formulate an action system: The application of mezzo concepts to macro practice

3. Composition of the action system

    a. Understanding of and commitment to purpose

    b. Group leadership and participation skills

    c. Case Example: **Muster** Support and Formulate an Action System

D. IM**A**GINE: Identify <u>**Assets**</u>

1. Assets are resources and advantages that will help you to undertake and complete your proposed change process

2. Case Example: Identify **Assets**

E. IMA**G**INE: Specify <u>**Goals**</u>, objectives, and action steps to attain them

1. Primary goals do not usually specify how they will be achieved

2. Objectives—smaller, behaviorally specific subgoals that serve as stepping stones on the way to accomplishing the primary goal

3. Writing clear action steps—the tasks one must complete (in the correct order and within the designated time frame) to achieve the desired objective [who, what, when]

4. Case Example—Specify **Goals**, Objectives, and Action Steps to Attain Them

F. IMA**G**INE: <u>**Implement**</u> the plan

1. The plan will need to be monitored carefully to keep the change process on course

2. Case Example: **Implement** the Plan

G. IMAG**I**NE: <u>**Neutralize**</u> opposition

1. Communicating with decision-makers

2. Logical administrative reactions

3. Phases of resistance

    a. Monumental negativism

    b. Mulled over issues and thought about possibilities

    c. Conflict

    d. Covert resistance possible after proposal is implemented

4. Collaborative and adversarial strategies

    a. Continuum from collaborative to adversarial strategies

    b. Collaboration and persuasion

    c. Four basic steps in persuading

        1) Initiate persuasion by:

            a) Establishing something in common

            b) Sharing honest feelings

            c) Blunt assault—takes sharing honest feelings much farther

        2) Allow time to discuss and answer questions

        3) State proposal clearly and straightforwardly

        4) Summarize progress with the decision makers and any agreement regarding how to proceed

    d. Additional strategies for using persuasion

        1) Educate the decision makers

        2) Discuss options

        3) Ask if a trial or partial policy, project, or program change is possible

        4) Suggest that a committee be formed to discuss and consider the proposed plan

        5) Creatively identify how target and action system members could spend more time together to develop communication channels and become familiar with the issues from both sides

        6) Appeal to the decision makers' sense of fairness, ethics, and right and wrong

        7) Develop a rational argument to support your proposed plan

        8) Specify to decision makers what the negative consequences of ignoring the identified problem might be

5.   Highlight 6.2: Being an Adversary and Pressuring

         a.   Strategies when pressuring for change

                 1)   Circulate a petition to gain collective support and submit it to administration for consideration

                 2)   Stage open confrontations regarding issues with decision makers during regular staff meetings

                 3)   Inform sanctioning agencies from the external environment about the issue

                 4)   Go to the newspapers, television, and radio with information that will bring agency problems to public attention

                 5)   Encourage staff or clients to interfere deliberately with service provision

                 6)   Initiate a strike

                 7)   Organize concerned personnel and others, including clients, to picket the agency

                 8)   Take the issue to the courts

                 9)   Undertake formal bargaining

6.   Case Example—**Neutralize** opposition

H.   IMAGIN**E**: **Evaluate** progress

     1.   Evaluation serves two major purposes

         a.   Monitor the ongoing operation and activities involved in achieving a macro-level change

         b.   Target the end results of your macro intervention

     2.   Case Example—**Evaluate** Progress

IV.   **Application of IMAGINE to Macro Intervention**

A.   Changing Agency Policy

B.   Formal and informal agency policies

C.   Types of Changes in Agency Policy

    1.   Highlight 6.3: Using PREPARE and IMAGINE to Establish a Culturally Competent, Empowering Organization

        a.   Cultural competence in the organizational context—a set of congruent behaviors, attitudes, policies, and structures which come together in a system, an agency, or among professionals and enables that system, agency, or those professionals to work effectively in the context of cultural differences

        b.   Cultural Incompetence: A Case Example

        c.   Assessing cultural competence

            1)   How responsible is the organization in responding effectively and efficiently to the needs of the culturally diverse people it serves?

            2)   In what ways is the agency empowering its staff so that staff may, in turn, empower clients from diverse backgrounds?

            3)   In what ways could services be administered differently in response to the needs of the agency's culturally diverse client population?

            4)   What is the organizational vision with respect to the culturally diverse community?

            5)   How might you determine that the goal of cultural competence has been achieved?

        d.   Recommendations for attaining cultural competence

        e.   Responding to the juvenile justice system critique

    2.   Changing organizational goals

    3.   Changing policies on personnel practices

    4.   Changing policies on practice procedures

    5.   Using IMAGINE to change agency practice procedures

        a.   **I**MAGINE: Start with an innovative **idea**

        b.   I**M**AGINE: **Muster** support and formulate an action system

        c.   IM**A**GINE: Identify **assets**

        d.   IMA**G**INE: Specify **goals**, objectives, and action steps to attain them

e.   IMAG**I**NE: **Implement** the plan

f.   IMAGI**NE**: **Neutralize** opposition

g.   IMAGIN**E**: **Evaluate** progress

Experiential Exercises and Classroom Simulations

Exercise 6.1: Targeting Policies for Change

A.   Brief Description
Using a small group format, students apply the first four steps of IMAGINE model to a university, college, or department policy they feel merits change.

B.   Objectives
Students will:
1.   Review the IMAGINE process for pursuing policy change.
2.   Discuss how the first four steps of the process might be applied to pursue a policy change.

C.   Procedure
1.   Review the IMAGINE process and the material on changing agency policy.
2.   Ask students to identify a university, college, or department policy they would like to see changed. This might involve anything from parking fees to grading procedures to the department's course prerequisites.
3.   Divide the class into small groups of four to six.
4.   Ask the groups to follow the first four steps in the IMAGINE process for pursuing the designated policy change. The model is outlined below in a box under "Instructions for Students." Ask the groups to designate at least one spokesperson to take notes and subsequently share the group's plan with the entire class.
5.   After about 30 minutes, ask the small groups to terminate their discussions and participate in a full class discussion.
6.   Ask group representatives to share their summaries of the discussion. Encourage participation from all class members.

D.   Instructions for Students
An outline of the IMAGINE process for policy change is provided in the box below.

An Outline of the First Four Steps in the Imagine Process: Pursuing Policy Change

IMAGINE Step 1: Develop an Innovative **Idea.**
I**M**AGINE Step 2: **Muster** support and formulate an action system.
       Identify the macro client system.
       Identify the change agent system.
       Identify the target system.
       Identify the action system.
IM**A**GINE Step 3: Identify **assets.**
IMA**G**INE Step 4: Specify **goals** and action steps to attain them.

---

1. Select a university, college, or department policy you feel is in need of change.
2. Discuss how you might apply the first four steps of the imagine process (as summarized in the box above) to initiate change in this policy.
3. Address the following questions:
   a. What difficulties were you faced with in trying to follow the steps?
   b. What additional information would be helpful?
   c. What have you learned about changing policy from this experience?

E. Commentary
This activity may also be conducted by holding a full class discussion without breaking students down into small groups

---

Exercise 6.2: Using Persuasion

A. Brief Description
The class is broken down into pairs for the purpose of a role play. One member of the dyad plays a worker attempting to persuade the other member, playing an agency director, to pursue a policy change. Ensuing discussion focuses on the process, positive aspects, and difficulties of persuasion.

B. Objectives
Students will:
1. Dramatize a simulated macro situation involving persuasion.
2. Appraise the persuasion process.

C. Procedure
1. Review the content in the text on neutralizing opposition, including that on communicating with decision-makers, logical administrative reactions, phases of resistance, and collaborative and adversarial strategies.
2. Read the material included below under "Instructions for Students" including worker role, suggestions for persuasion, and agency director role.
3. Divide the class up into pairs. Instruct one member of the dyad to play a worker and the other an agency director. Students can arbitrarily decide who plays whom. Read the role player descriptions cited below under "Instructions for Students." The worker in the role play should try to use the suggestions for persuasion presented in the text to persuade the agency director to the former's point of view. Inform students that the role play will take about ten minutes.
4. After about ten minutes, arbitrarily halt the role play for a full class discussion. Address the questions identified in "Instructions for Students" below.

D. Instructions for Students
Divide up into pairs where one will arbitrarily play the worker and the other the agency director described below.

> **WORKER ROLE:** You are a case manager at an agency that provides diagnosis, treatment, and residential care for clients who have cognitive disabilities. The agency's policy for interdisciplinary treatment staffings is to include the designated client's MSW social worker (who provides therapy), psychologist, psychiatrist, physician, and nursing staff. Interdisciplinary treatment staffings are meetings held biannually for each client where staff involved with the client report the client's progress, discuss new treatment plans as necessary, and make specific recommendations for service provision.

141

The problem is that you, as the client's case manager, are not invited to the staffings. You feel this is ridiculous because you are the one who works directly with clients on a daily or weekly basis and are charged with overseeing all service provision. The rationale for your exclusion is that you don't have a graduate degree. This makes no sense to you because nursing staff are included and they don't necessarily have graduate degrees either. You approach the agency director who is responsible for establishing much of agency policy and seeing that staff adhere to it.

You have made an appointment to meet with the agency director. Use the suggestions for persuasion proposed in the box below and any others you can think of to persuade the director to amend policy to include you and other case managers in multidisciplinary treatment staffings.

Suggestions For Persuasion

1. Establish something you have in common with the agency director.
   (Suggestion: Concern for the clients' wellbeing and best interests.)

2. Share honest feelings.
   (Suggestions: Share your sincere desire to improve service provision. Empathize with the agency director's position as agency policy is not all that easy to change.)

3. Educate the decision-makers.
   (Suggestions: Elaborate on your role as case manager—without being condescending. Inform the director of the extra time it takes for you and other staff to communicate about treatment plans because you can't attend treatment staffings.)

4. Discuss options.
   (Suggestion: Discuss the potential advantages and disadvantages of your proposed plan.)

5. As if a trial or partial policy change is possible.
   (Suggestion: Is it possible to include the case manager in staffings for a temporary period of time on a trial basis?)

6. Suggest that a committee be formed to discuss and consider the proposed plan.

7. Creatively identify how spending more time with other team members during staffings could develop communication channels and become familiar with the issues from both sides.

8. Appeal to the agency director's sense of fairness, ethics, and right and wrong.
   (Suggestion: What is the most ethical approach to service provision for clients?)

9. Develop a rational argument to support your proposed plan.

10. Specify to the agency director what the negative consequences of the identified problem might be.
    (Suggestion: How will ignoring the problem result in costs to the director, the client, and the agency.)

> **AGENCY DIRECTOR:** You are very busy overseeing numerous aspects of agency functioning. You are plagued by budget cuts, pressure from regulatory agencies to comply with codes, and various staffing problems. (For example, a former employee is suing the agency for sexual harassment by a psychologist who supervised her.)
>
> You are very busy and have little time to waste on complaints or whining. You have agreed to see the case manager because you feel it is your responsibility to be in touch with your staff's issues. You understand this issue is something about a policy change, but you don't know much more than that. In general, you hate policy changes. The process is time-consuming and there are usually unanticipated results, many of which are negative.

After the role play, address the following questions in a full class discussion.

   a. What happened during the role play?
   b. Which suggestions for persuasion worked and which didn't? Explain.
   c. What other suggestions do you have for successful persuasion?
   d. From this experience, what have you learned about the persuasion process?

E. Commentary
This exercise may also be performed by asking two volunteers to conduct the role play before the rest of the class with the other students observing.

Exercise 6.3: Identifying Macro Client, Action, and Target Systems

A. Brief Description
Students are provided a case vignette and asked to identify the macro client, actions, and target systems involved.

B. Objectives
Students will:
1. Recognize macro client, action, and target systems in macro practice scenarios.

C. Procedure
   1. Review the material on macro client, action, and target systems.
   2. Using a small group format or large class discussion, ask students to identify these systems for the case scenario posed below.

D. Instructions for Students
Read the following vignette and identify the systems involved.

> **Case Scenario:** You are a hospital social worker who works with patients in the geriatric unit. Their problems typically include broken bones, onset of diseases such as diabetes, increasing mental confusion, and many accompanying physical difficulties. Patients usually remain hospitalized two days to two weeks. Most patients come to the hospital from their homes, and your job often involves placing patients in more structured settings because injuries or diseases have restricted their ability to function independently. Many are placed in health care centers (nursing homes).

You have been assigned Olga, 82, who fell and broke her hip. She also has diabetes and is increasingly incontinent. Prior to her fall, she barely subsisted in a second story one-room apartment, dependent on her monthly Social Security check for survival, and she has consumed all of her meager savings. She is an extremely pleasant woman who continues to emphasize that she doesn't want to be a burden on anyone. All of her family are dead. You worry that placement in an inferior setting will be tortuous for her if she doesn't receive the relatively intensive care she needs.

You notice that nursing homes vary dramatically in their levels of care, their appearance, the attention they give to patients, their ratios of staff to patients, the activities they offer, and their overall cleanliness. Patients with private insurance can easily enter one of the better facilities, while impoverished patients on Medicaid must go to inferior settings. You consider this both unfair and unethical.

You see yourself as a possible change agent. At least three of your colleagues in the hospital's social work unit have similar concerns about their own clients and the hospital's older adult clients in general. Your immediate supervisor is not really an "eager beaver" when it comes to initiating change, but you think you might be able to solicit some support from her. You are not certain whether upper levels of hospital administration believe that nursing home conditions are any of their business. In your state all nursing homes must be licensed, but licensing regulations require the maintenance of only the most minimal standards.

a.   Identify the macro client system in this case.

b.   Who might make up the action system?

c.   Who might be your target system?

Exercise 6.4: Identifying Assets

A.   Brief Description
Students are asked to identify assets in a macro practice case scenario.

B.   Objectives
Students will:
1.   Examine macro practice scenarios.
2.   Assess the assets involved in each.

C.   Procedure
1.   Review the content on assets.
2.   Read the case scenario presented below to the class.
3.   Ask students to identify the various assets involved in the case scenario posed below.

D.   Instructions for Students
Step 3 in the IMAGINE process involves the identification of assets. Whatever the type of macro level change, a change agent must determine what *assets* are available to implement the change. *Assets* are any resources and any advantages you have that will help in your proposed change process. Assets can include readily available funding, personnel who are able and willing to devote their time to implementing the change, and office space from which the change activities can be managed.
1.   Read the following case scenario and identify the assets it reveals.

Case Scenario: Louise, a financial counselor at a private mental health agency, knows that the agency has access to special funding through personal donations made on behalf of persons "with special needs." She is not certain how the administration defines "special needs." But since the agency is privately owned, it is not subject to the same requirements and regulations that would limit a public agency. Louise learned about this special fund via the informal agency grapevine. It has never been publicly announced.

Louise is working with several families whom she feels are in exceptional need. Their problems—including unemployment, depression, mental illness, poverty, unwanted pregnancy, and truancy—make them truly multiproblem families. Neither her agency nor any local public agency has been able to provide adequate resources for these families. Louise has established clear documentation of their extreme circumstances.

Having worked at the agency for eight years, she feels she has gained substantial respect for her work and her ideas. She knows one member of the agency's board of directors fairly well, because she's worked with him on several projects in the past. (A board of directors is "a group of people empowered to establish an organization's objectives and policies and to oversee the activities of the personnel responsible for day-to-day implementation of those policies," and board members are often highly respected and influential volunteers from the community (Barker, 1995, p. 39). Louise might be able to contact this man to get information about the special-needs funding.

She is aware, however, that her agency administration discourages workers from seeking access to this "secret" fund. Amounts available are limited, so the administration must dispense these funds extremely cautiously. In any case, Louise decides to approach the agency's Executive Director and request funding for the families in need.

2.   Identify the assets available to Louise.

Exercise 6.5: Establishing Goals, Objectives, and Action Steps

A.   Brief Description
Students identify goals, objectives, and action steps for case scenarios in macro practice.

B.   Objectives
Students will:
1.   Recognize the process for achieving goals in macro practice.
2.   Formulate initial goals, objectives, and action steps for three case scenarios in macro practice.

C.   Procedure
1.   Review the content on formulating initial goals and objectives to achieve those goals.
2.   Using a small group format or full class discussion, instruct students to read the case scenarios presented below, and identify goals, objectives, and action steps for the case scenarios presented below.

D.   Instructions for Students

After formulating an innovative idea, mustering support from others, and identifying assets, it is time to specify your goals, objectives, and action steps in the IMAGINE macro change process. A *goal* is "the end toward which effort is directed" (Mish, 1995, p. 499). Goals give you direction, but primary goals are usually so broadly stated that it is virtually impossible to specify how they will be achieved. For example, you might want to improve conditions in the Family Planning Center where you work. In order to accomplish this, you must break down that primary goal into a series of objectives. *Objectives* are smaller, behaviorally specific subgoals that serve as stepping stones on the way to accomplishing the primary goal. *Action steps* are tasks one must complete (in correct order and within the designated time frame) to achieve the desired objective—which, in turn, is designed to achieve your primary goal. The formula for creating an action step is to specify who will do what by when: *"Who"* is the individual that will accomplish the task; *"what"* is the task(s) assigned to that individual; and *"when"* sets a time limit so the task is not delayed or forgotten.

Read the following case scenarios, and identify the initial goals that would lead to the desired ends. Use the **who** will do **what** by **when** formula. Then list some objectives or subgoals that would help in achieving the larger goal. (Note that an arbitrary number of four goals are cited for each case vignette. You are free to establish more or fewer goals as you see fit. You also may establish any number of objectives and action steps to achieve each goal.)

Vignette #1: Horace, a state parole agent, is a member of a Task Force to Curb Substance Abuse in his community.[1] He attends the first of a series of meetings aimed at facilitating a range of educational, prevention, and treatment programs to obliterate substance abuse among youth, especially delinquents. Other members include Bainbridge, a local judge; Uzzia, a lawyer working for the county to represent juveniles accused of felonies; and Wahkuna, a retired social worker who was an alcohol and other drug abuse counselor. They decide they need more information to determine the extent of the problem: How prevalent *is* drug abuse in this area? What prevention tactics are currently in use? What treatment facilities (type and quantity) are now in place? What diagnosis and assessment mechanisms would be appropriate? What treatment approaches are likely to be most effective?

Goal:

       Objectives:

           Action Steps:

Goal:

       Objectives:

           Action Steps:

Goal:

       Objectives:

           Action Steps:

---

[1] A task force is "a temporary group, usually within an organization, brought together to achieve some previously specified function or goal" (Barker, 2003, p. 430).

Goal:

    Objectives:

        Action Steps:

Vignette #2: Marelda is a social worker at a homeless shelter in a large northeastern city. Facilities are simply inadequate to provide the necessary resources—including food, clothing, and shelter—for hundreds of homeless families. Suddenly Marelda has a brilliant idea. Why not make arrangements with the dozens—perhaps hundreds—of fast-food restaurants in the area to collect their unused food and distribute it to people in need? At the end of a day, remaining food is simply thrown out and goes to waste. Marelda begins to consider what support from friends and colleagues she might elicit, and how she might go about contacting fast-food restaurants and persuading them to support her cause.

Goal:

    Objectives:

        Action Steps:

Goal:

    Objectives:

        Action Steps:

Goal:

    Objectives:

        Action Steps:

Goal:

    Objectives:

        Action Steps:

Vignette #3:[2] Brian is a hospice social worker. The hospice movement rests on a philosophy of caring and an array of programs, services, and settings for people with terminal illness. Hospice services are usually offered in nonhospital facilities with homelike atmospheres where families, friends, and the significant other can be with the dying person (Barker, 1995, p. 171).

---

[2] This vignette is based on an account in J. Dworkin & D. Kaufer, "Social Services and Bereavement in the Lesbian and Gay Community," Vol. 2, No. 3/4, 1995, pp. 41-60.

> Brian sees increasing numbers of gay patients entering the facility. He is aware of the special "issues of stigma, homophobia, and the cumulative effects of stress" experienced by gay people along with the devastating effects of their terminal illness (Dworkin & Kaufer, 1995, p. 41). He considers two possibilities. First, can he initiate support groups for patients, their families, and their partners? Second, to what extent are other hospice staff aware of the special issues facing gay people? Could the agency initiate in-service training to address this potential need? Brian thinks the hospice director would probably be very supportive of these his ideas—*if* Brian can figure out just how to implement them.

Goal:

   Objectives:

      Action Steps:

Goal:

   Objectives:

      Action Steps:

Goal:

   Objectives:

      Action Steps:

Goal:

   Objectives:

      Action Steps:

E.   Commentary
Note that, depending on the amount of time available, only one or two of the case scenarios might be addressed.

Exercise 6.6: Applying IMAGINE to Agency Policy Change

A.   Brief Description
Students review a macro practice case example and apply the IMAGINE process to agency policy change.

B.   Objectives
Students will:
1.   Examine a case example in macro practice involving agency policy change.
2.   Formulate a plan of action following the IMAGINE process.

C. Procedure
   1.   Review the content on the IMAGINE process.
   2.   Read the case example presented below.
   3.   Using a small group format or a full class discussion, ask students to answer the questions following the case scenario that follow IMAGINE.

D. Instructions for Students
   1.   Apply IMAGINE to the following case example by responding to the subsequent questions.[3]

Hsi-ping is a worker for the Comeasyouare County Department of Human Services. She and most other staff disagree with many policies initiated by Marcus, the agency director. Workers commonly refer to Marcus as Mr. Scrooge. They frequently question his decisions, which they believe are based on financial variables rather than clients' welfare.

The latest problem is Marcus's decision to stop sending letters to clients without telephones. These letters announce that a particular worker will visit a client's home at a designated time. If that time is inconvenient, the client is asked to contact the worker to reschedule the visit. The letter then adds that the worker is looking forward to talking with the client. These letters have traditionally been sent out far enough in advance to allow clients to accommodate their own schedules or let the worker know beforehand that the time is inconvenient. Apparently, Marcus and his Chief Financial Manager, Millicent (often referred to as Ms. Scrooge), have figured out these letters cost the agency about five dollars apiece to send—including worker time, secretarial time, paper, postage, and any other agency efforts expended. Hsi-ping thinks Millicent read the five-dollar figure somewhere in a financial magazine and magically transformed it into a fact. She has a number of problems with the policy even if the figure is accurate.

- First, it ignores clients' right to privacy, respect, and dignity. Dropping in on people unannounced is inconsiderate and simply rude.
- Second, it violates clients' right to self-determination because it does not allow them any input in setting meeting times.
- Third, it complicates both workers' and clients' lives. There is no guarantee that workers will arrive at convenient times for clients or that clients will even be at home.

Hsi-Ping thinks about who might agree with her that this policy is unacceptable. She knows other staff in her own unit agree with her, but many of them are fairly new and would probably be hesitant to speak up. Hsi-Ping's supervisor Sphinctera follows regulations to the letter—even to the comma—without question. Nevertheless, Hsi-Ping likes Sphinctera, so she decides to share her feelings about the problem and see what reaction she gets.

Much to Hsi-Ping's amazement, Sphinctera is very supportive of Hsi-Ping's position. Apparently, Sphinctera is tired of the agency's many policy changes and has difficulty keeping up with them. This no-letter policy is just too much. Sphinctera even comes up with an idea. Why not send out postcards announcing home visits? The cards could be preprinted for a nominal cost, workers could then address them, fill in the proposed visiting time, sign them, and send them out themselves.

---

[3] The idea and some details presented in this case example are taken from "The Appointment Letters," by G. H. Hull, Jr. In R. F. Rivas & G. H. Hull, Jr., *Case Studies in Generalist Practice* (Pacific Grove, CA: Brooks/Cole, 1996, pp. 150-53.)

It's a fine compromise—but Sphinctera hesitates to make waves and wants more information and more support before she will propose her idea to Marcus. Hsi-Ping volunteers to talk to her other colleagues in the unit, and verifies that they generally agree with her. One worker, Ruana, emphasizes her relief that someone else is addressing the problem.   She tells Hsi-Ping about a home visit she made the day before, an unannounced visit because of the no-letter policy. It took her about an hour to get to the client's home and back. Since the client wasn't there, Ruana's time was wasted—at a cost to the agency of about $11 in salary for Ruana's wasted time and about $12 in mileage reimbursement. Even if Millicent and Marcus are correct that letters cost the agency $5, Ruana's useless trip cost $23, so the agency lost $18 under the new procedure. Imagine multiplying this by the hundreds of home visits workers regularly make.

Hsi-Ping reports her findings to Sphinctera. Together they decide to address the issue with Marcus. Sphinctera suggests doing so at one of the agency's regular staff meetings when staff are encouraged to voice their ideas and concerns (whether or not administrators are paying attention). She encourages Hsi-Ping to raise the issue because it was originally Hsi-Ping's idea. Hsi-Ping thinks Sphinctera is really afraid to initiate it herself, but she agrees to do the talking and thanks Sphinctera for her support.

At the next staff meeting, Hsi-Ping expresses her concern about the no-letter policy. She takes a deep breath and is careful to speak with little emotion and no hostility. She presents the financial facts that support her proposal and emphasizes that she shares Marcus's concerns about the agency's finances. She then offers her suggestion and its rationale, adding that sending postcards was really Sphinctera's idea. Hsi-Ping adds that the postcards would not violate clients' confidentiality or privacy rights because they would carry no identifying information.

When she finishes, the eighty staff members in the room are dead silent for a few painful moments that seem like an eternity. Finally, six hands shoot up at once. One after another, staff support the idea. Hsi-Ping watches Marcus for some reaction. He looks straight ahead, says nothing, and pulls at his chin in his usual thoughtful gesture. Finally, he says, "You know, I think you just might have something here. Let's give it a try."

Hsi-Ping is overjoyed. She did it! She actually did it. She effected a substantive change in agency policy. Two days later Marcus sends a memo around the agency informing workers of the new change. Workers are generally pleased (although some old-timers still grumble that the letters were better). Marcus continues to seek new ways to cut costs—and, Hsi-Ping sometimes thinks, to make workers' lives miserable. However, the no-letter battle has been won and Hsi-Ping certainly is proud of that accomplishment.

2.   Follow the seven steps in IMAGINE and respond to the questions below:

Step 1: **IMAGINE**—Start with an Innovative *Idea.*

   A.   Summarize the problem presented above and describe the innovative idea for a
           solution. Explain the pros and cons of this idea.

   B.   Describe the innovative idea for a solution.

   C.   Explain the pros and cons of this idea.

Step 2:   IMAGINE—*Muster* Support and Formulate an Action System. Identify the
following systems portrayed in the case scenario above.

       Macro client system:

       Change agent:

Target system:

Action system:

Step 3: IMAGINE—Identify *Assets.* Identify the assets in Hsi-Ping's favor and explain why each is important.

Step 4: IMAGINE—Specify *Goals* and Objectives. Identify the major goal Hsi-Ping wished to accomplish.

4a.   Identify specific objectives necessary for leading up to this goal. Use the *who* did *what* by *when* format.

Step 5: IMAGINE—*Implement* the Plan. Evaluate and discuss the effectiveness of Hsi-Ping's implementation of her plan.

Step 6: IMAGINE—*Neutralize* Opposition. Explain how Hsi-Ping determined who would assume which roles in the change effort.

6a.   Discuss the interpersonal dynamics determining who actually presented the issue and proposed recommendations.

6b.   Explain how Hsi-Ping used persuasion to pursue her goal. What specific techniques did she use?

6c.   How might Hsi-Ping have used pressuring to attain her goal? What effects might pressuring have had?

Exercise 6.7: Assessing an Organization's Cultural Competence

---

A.   Brief Description
Students interview a social worker or administrator at a social services agency and write a paper summarizing their findings.

B.   Objectives
Students will:
1.   Identify the qualities of a culturally competent organization.
2.   Assess the cultural competence manifested by a social services agency.

C.   Procedure
1.   Review the material on culturally competent organizations.
2.   Instruct students to interview a worker or administrator at a social services agency (by phone or in person), ask the questions posed below, and summarize their findings in a 2 to 4 page paper.

D.   Instructions for Students
Make an appointment with a worker or administrator at a social services agency in your area. (If necessary, you can conduct this interview by phone.) Solicit answers to the following five questions aimed at assessing an organization's cultural competence. Examples of questions you might use for further clarification are presented in parenthesis following each question.

1. *How responsible is the organization in responding effectively and efficiently to the needs of the culturally diverse people it serves* (Coggins & Fresquez, 2007; Hyde, 2003; Nybell & Gray, 2004)? (Does the agency have a good grasp of its clientele's cultural diversity? Must further research be performed to identify target client groups? To what extent does the agency create a "welcoming" climate for clients [Hyde, 2003, p. 51]?)

2. *In what ways is the agency empowering its staff so that staff may, in turn, empower clients from diverse backgrounds* (Gutierrez & Lewis, 1999)? (To what extent do agency staff understand the needs, issues, and strengths of their diverse client population? Does the agency recruit, support, and retain leadership and direct service staff that reflect the client population's diversity? To what extent does the organization maintain values that reflect cultural competence and empowerment? To what degree does the agency provide multicultural training to enhance "knowledge about different racial and ethnic groups" and conduct "culturally sensitive client assessments" [Hyde, 2003, p. 53]?)

3. *In what ways could services be administered differently in response to the needs of the agency's culturally diverse client population* (Coggins & Fresquez, 2007; Mason, 1994)? (Are services readily accessible to culturally diverse client groups? If not, how might the agency make such services more accessible? Is the communication between staff and clients as effective as it could be? Should workers offer services in different languages? Can agency personnel solicit information from significant community leaders or from clients to identify and pursue better service provision?)

4. *What is the "organizational vision" with respect to the culturally diverse community* (Gutierrez & Lewis, 1999, p. 83)? (How might you best "envision the system as it should be and . . . identify ways of funding such a system" [Mason, 1994, p. 5]? How could you maximize the involvement of people who represent the diverse cultures your agency serves? How might you empower community residents? Can you and others helping you identify new potential resources for the community and the agency? Such resources might include "assisting with staff and board recruitment, encouraging . . . donations, identifying advocacy resources, and promoting parent or community education and support groups" [Mason, 1994, p. 5].)

5. *How might you determine that the goal of cultural competence has been achieved* (Coggins & Fresquez, 2007; Mason, 1994)? (What specific objectives and action steps might you identify to provide clear proof that your purpose has been actualized? What task groups might you and the agency establish to review progress, refine recommendations, and keep efforts on target?)

I.   **Introduction**

II.   **Initiating and Implementing a Project**

    A.   **I**MAGINE: Develop an innovative **Idea**

        1.   Highlight 7.1: Examples of Projects in Macro Practice

            a.   Meeting clients' special needs

            b.   Fundraising projects

            c.   Evaluating effects of agency or community changes

            d.   Evaluating new intervention approaches

            e.   Implementing internal agency changes

            f.   Providing internal services to your agency staff

    B.   I**M**AGINE: **Muster** support

    C.   IM**A**GINE: Identify **Assets**

    D.   IMA**G**INE: Specify **Goals**, objectives, and action steps to attain them

    E.   IMAG**I**NE: **Implement** the plan

        1.   PERT chart (Program Evaluation and Review Technique)—a flow chart or time chart that depicts a series of tasks or activities in the order that such tasks should be done to achieve project goals

        2.   Figure 7.1: Examples of Amended PERT Chart Formats

        3.   PERT charts illustrate objectives and action steps

        4.   PERT charts portray specific tasks

        5.   PERT charts depict task sequence

            a.   Make sure that the sequence makes sense

            b.   Note to yourself what activities should be given top priority

            c.   Think about potential barriers and problems you might face when implementing the activities

            d.   Force-field analysis—analysis of anticipated problems before they occur

6.   PERT charts and necessary resources

7.   PERT charts establish a time frame

8.   Advantages of PERT charts

9.   Case Example: A PERT chart for developing an inservice training project

10.   Figure 7.2: An Example of a PERT Chart for Developing an In-service Training Program

F.   IMAGI**NE**: **Neutralize** opposition

G.   IMAGIN**E**: **Evaluate** progress

     1.   Projects and diversity

     2.   Highlight 7.2: A Project Example: Substance Abuse Prevention for Puerto Rican Adolescents

         a.   Nuevo Puente (New Bridges)

         b.   Resilience—the strength and ability to resist risk-taking behavior

         c.   Self-esteem—one's inner sense of one's own value

         d.   Coping strategies—behaviors and choices used to contend with and survive stress

         e.   Three Kings' Day—Puerto Rican holiday

         f.   Community assets assessment—a systematic appraisal of the community's strengths

III.   Developing a Program

A.   Program/Social program—an ongoing configuration of services and service provision procedures intended to meet a designated group of clients' needs

B.   Highlight 7.3: Why Program Development Is Relevant to You

C.   **I**MAGINE: Develop an Innovative **Idea**

     1.   Work with your client system

     2.   Articulate the proposed program's purpose

         a.   Clearly define and document the unmet client needs

b.   Identify the clientele who will receive services

c.   State the services the program would provide

3.   Highlight 7.4: Ethical Questions and Critical Thinking about Public Assistance: Empowerment or Oppression for Women?

      a.   Personal Responsibility and Work Opportunity Reconciliation Act (1996)

      b.   Temporary Assistance for Needy Families (TANF)—replaced Aid to Families with Dependent Children (AFDC)

      c.   TANF and Work

           1)   Caroline Center—a career and learning resource center for women founded by the School Sisters of Notre Dame

           2)   Enabling women to leave welfare and become self-sufficient

      d.   TANF and Health

      e.   TANF and Family Structure

           1)   Family structure—the nuclear family as well as alternatives to nuclear family which are adopted by persons in committed relationships and the people they consider to be family

           2)   How ethical is it for government to regulate the childbearing behavior of poor women?

      f.   TANF and Child Care

      g.   Child Care in Denmark Versus Wisconsin: An International Perspective

           1)   In Denmark new mothers get 26 weeks of paid leave to care for their infants. In Wisconsin the state allows up to six weeks of unpaid leave (the federal government allows up to 12 weeks of unpaid leave)

           2)   In Denmark parents pay up to 30 percent of day care costs. In Wisconsin parents pay an average of 60 percent of their day care costs

           3)   In Denmark child care workers are paid 14 percent more than the personal median income; early childhood teachers 33 percent, and family day care providers 20 percent. In Wisconsin child care workers are paid an average of 28 to 48 percent, early childhood teachers 28 percent, and family day care providers 48 percent less than the median personal income

D.   IM**A**GINE: **Muster** support

    1.   Allocate responsibilities to a designated task group or advisory council

    2.   Advisory councils/boards—committees created outside of the organization's formal power structure that meet to provide information and feedback

E.   IM**A**GINE: Identify **Assets**

    1.   Prepare the agency for change

    2.   Consider implementing a feasibility study—a systematic evaluation of the resources necessary to achieve your program development goals

    3.   Solicit the financial resources you need to initiate the program

F.   IMA**G**INE: Specify **Goals**, objectives, and action steps to attain them

    1.   Consider developing a PERT chart—a tool for plotting your intervention plan in a linear manner

    2.   Describe how the program will provide services

G.   IMAG**I**NE: **Implement** the plan

    1.   Get the program going

        a.   Nurture participating staff's support

        b.   How about a trial run?

        c.   Consider starting out small

        d.   Formalize any contracts that might be needed (purchase-of-service contracts—formal agreements between one or more organizations where one organization purchases some specified service within a designated time period from one or more other agencies)

H.   IMAGI**NE**: **Neutralize** opposition

    1.   Anticipate a "honeymoon period"

    2.   Maintain administrative support

I.   IMAGIN**E**: **Evaluate** progress and effectiveness

    1.   Monitor daily activities and evaluate program impact

        a.   Monitor your program

        b.   Perform an impact evaluation (investigates outcomes and determines whether program goals have been met)

2.   Establish how services will be provided on an ongoing basis

      a.   Standardized procedures for continued implementation of the program should be clearly defined

      b.   The new program should be linked as much as possible with other units and aspects of the organization

      c.   The program's importance should be established within the context of other programs and services in the community

      d.   Develop an intelligence and feedback system

IV.   **Program Development: A Case Example**

    A.   Highlight 7.5: Program Development Ideas are Endless

      1.   Sanctuary for young homeless new mothers

      2.   Housing development for non-heterosexual seniors

    B.   IMAGINE: Develop an innovative **Idea**

      1.   Highlight 7.6 What is Sexual Harassment?

        a.   Title VII of the Civil Rights Act of 1964 covers discrimination on the basis of sex, along with discrimination on the basis of race; in 1991 this act permitted compensatory and punitive damages to be awarded

        b.   Two major dimensions to the definition

          1)   The concept of *quid pro quo* (I'll scratch your back if you scratch mine)

          2)   Creation of a hostile environment (where offensive gender-related physical or verbal behavior interferes with people's ability to complete their work)

        c.   Equal Employment Opportunity Commission, in 1993, expanded the definition of sexual harassment to include gender harassment, which is harassment directed against women as a class, which may not be specifically sexual in nature

    C.   IMAGINE: **Muster** support

    D.   IMAGINE: Identify **Assets**

E.   IMAGINE: Specify **Goals**, objectives, and action steps to attain them

    1.   Establishing a Sexual Harassment Awareness Program for Employees (SHAPE)

    2.   Figure 7.3: A PERT Chart for the Sexual Harassment Awareness Program for Employees (SHAPE)

    3.   Description of SHAPE

    4.   The SHAPE coordinator's role

        a.   Educational programming

        b.   Providing support for victims

        c.   Counseling

        d.   Formal grievance procedure

        e.   Informal indirect action

        f.   No action

    5.   Planning the program: Development of a PERT chart

        a.   Figure 7.4: A Budget Summary for SHAPE

        b.   Initial planning

        c.   Education

        d.   Public relations

        e.   Counseling

        f.   Evaluation of SHAPE functioning

F.   IMAGINE: **Implement** the plan

G.   IMAGINE: **Neutralize** opposition

H.   IMAGINE: **Evaluate** progress and effectiveness

Exercise 7.1: Imagine A Program

A.   Brief Description
Using a small group format, students discuss how the first three steps of the IMAGINE process might be applied a series of agency vignettes where program development might be required.

B.   Objectives
Students will:
1.   Review the IMAGINE process for pursuing program development.
2.   Discuss how the first three steps of the process might be applied to program development in response to vignettes describing a macro scenarios.

C.   Procedure
1.   Review the material in the text on using the IMAGINE process to develop a program.
2.   Read each vignette below that describes a programmatic need in the macro context.
3.   Divide the class into small groups of four to six.
4.   Ask the groups to discuss the first three steps of the IMAGINE process to begin program development in the vignette described below under "Instructions for Students." Instruct them to follow the instructions and address the questions provided after each vignette. Indicate that they should select a group representative who should be prepared to report to the entire class the small group's findings.
5.   After about 20 minutes, ask the small groups to terminate their discussions and participate in a full class discussion regarding their findings.
6.   Ask the representative from each group to share her or his summary of the discussion. Encourage participation from all class members.

D.   Instructions for Students
Read each vignette below. Respond to the subsequent instructions and questions concerning the application of the first three steps of the IMAGINE process to program development as it might apply to the vignette.

VIGNETTE A: You are a social worker in a Veteran's Administration (VA) Hospital in East LA. The VA, a federal organization initially established in 1920, provides a wide range of services to people who have served in the military in order to enhance their overall health and welfare; services include those directed at physical and mental illness, vocational training, financial assistance, and a host of others (Barker, 1999). Specifically, you work in a unit that provides short-term housing and alcohol and other drug (AODA) treatment for homeless veterans. The problem is that you're finding that more and more of your clients come to you and tell you they simply can't find any full-time jobs, even for minimum wage. You find yourself thinking more and more frequently to yourself, "Even a full-time minimum wage job is pretty much a bummer in terms of taking care of yourself."

    The issue you really feel boils down to adequate job training. Why can't the VA provide educational and vocational training, or else finance its purchase through some other agency? You have looked and looked for resources for your clients. They need to get back on their feet again. They need work that is relatively permanent, provides an adequate standard of living, and enhances their self esteem. What you and your clients really need is a job-training program with a strong educational component. But there isn't one. Now what?

1.	**IMAGINE Step 1:** Develop an innovative **idea.**

Propose and describe a program that you feel would meet clients' identified needs.

2.	**IMAGINE Step 2: Muster** support.

Who might be appropriate action system members from the agency and community in this situation? Explain why.

3.	**IMAGINE Step 3:** Identify **assets.**

a.	What variables might exist that could support your change efforts?
b.	Who else in the agency might be called upon for support (other than action system members)?
c.	How might you work to enhance your own power?
d.	What potential funding sources might you pursue?

Vignette B: You are an intake worker for the Sheboygan County Department of Social Services. The county is primarily rural with a smattering of small towns. Your primary job is to take calls from people requesting services, gather initial information about them and their problems, provide them with some information about county services, and make appropriate referrals to the agencies whose services they need.

You are alarmed at the growing number of calls concerning older adults having difficulty maintaining themselves in their own homes. Most are calls from neighbors, relatives, or the older adults themselves. Examples of concerns include: worries about falling and remaining stranded for days; forgetfulness (such as leaving the stove's gas burner on); lack of transportation to get to a critical doctor's appointment; difficulties in understanding complicated health insurance and Medicare reimbursements; and depression due to loneliness and isolation.

After you receive such calls, you typically refer the callers to the Department's Protective Services for Older Adults unit. However, you know all the unit can usually do is make an assessment home visit and either refer the client to a local nursing home or terminate the case. That's depressing. Many of these people just need company and supportive help to maintain their independent living conditions. You have heard of such programs in other parts of the state. It would be great to have a program through which staff could visit similar clients, help them with daily tasks, transport them to recreational activities, and generally provide friendly support. Such a program would help these older adults remain in their own homes. Can you initiate such a program?

IMAGINE Step 1: Develop an innovative **idea.**

Propose and describe a program that you feel would meet clients' identified needs.

IMAGINE Step 2: Muster support.

Who in your agency and/or community might be appropriate action system members for this macro change? Explain why.

160

IMAGINE Step 3: Identify **assets**.

     a.   What variables might exist that could support your change efforts?

     b.   Who else in the agency might be called upon for support (other than action system members)?

     c.   How might you work to enhance your own power?

     d.   What potential funding sources might you pursue?

Vignette C*:* You are a state probation officer. You notice a significant increase in your caseload (that is, the clients assigned to you) of men repeatedly committing acts that in your state are considered misdemeanors. A misdemeanor is a minor crime—less serious than a felony—that generally results in incarceration of less than six months (Barker, 1991, p. 146). These men, for example, are speeding while driving under the influence, shoplifting items such as CDs, and even urinating when driving a car. (This last incident actually happened, although it's hard to picture.) As their probation officer, you see these "dumb" things getting them several-hundred-dollar fines and several-month jail sentences. You think this is senseless. There must be a better way to deal with this problem and to make these men more responsible for their behavior.

    At a conference you hear about a "deferred prosecution" approach in an adjoining state. This program provides men arrested for such misdemeanors with alternatives to fines and jail terms. They can opt to participate in a 12-week group run by two social workers. Group sessions focus on enhancing self-esteem, raising self-awareness, improving decision-making skills, developing better communication skills, and encouraging the analysis of responsible versus irresponsible behavior. The program was initially funded by a grant (often referred to as "soft money," meaning temporary and limited funding), but it was so successful that the state now implements and pays for it in several designated counties with "hard money." ("Hard money" means relatively permanent funding that becomes part of an organization's regular annual budget.)

    Men who participated in the program had a significantly reduced recidivism rate. *Recidivism rates* in this context refer to the proportion of offenders who continue to commit misdemeanors. A recidivism rate of 25 percent, then, would mean that of 100 men, 25 committed additional misdemeanors and 75 did not.

    You think, "What a wonderful idea!" You begin to investigate how you can initiate such a program in your agency.

IMAGINE Step 1: Develop an innovative *idea.*

Propose and describe a program that you feel would meet clients' identified needs.

IMAGINE Step 2: *Muster* support.

Who in your agency and/or community might be appropriate action system members for this macro change? Explain why.

IMAGINE Step 3: Identify *assets.*

     a.   What variables might exist that could support your change efforts?

     b.   Who else in the agency might be called upon for support (other than action system members)?

     c.   How might you work to enhance your own power?

     d.   What potential funding sources might you pursue?

E.   Commentary
         This activity may also be conducted by holding a full class discussion without breaking students down into small groups. Depending on the time available, groups might address only one or two of the case vignettes.

Exercise 7.2: Identify an Innovative Program

A.   Brief Description
         Students identify an innovative program and examine its functioning.

B.   Objectives
         Students will:
         1.   Identify an innovative program operating in their macro environment.
         2.   Assess various aspects of its functioning and usefulness.

C.   Procedure
         1.   Give students the assignment of identifying a local, state, or national innovative social services program.
         2.   Read the assignment as it is discussed below under "Instructions for Students."
         3.   The assignment may be used in any of five ways:
                  a.   Have students bring their findings to class to participate in a full class discussion.
                  b.   Have students bring their findings to class for participation in small group discussions.
                  c.   Have students turn in a written assignment for a grade.
                  d.   Have students present brief oral reports to the class regarding their findings.
                  e.   Assign students to small groups who complete the assignment together.

D.   Instructions for Students
         Identify a program providing some kind of social services which you feel is innovative and especially useful. You may select a local, state, or national program. You may find your information in newspapers or news magazines, from public documents, on the Internet, or directly from agencies.

         Answer the following questions and be prepared to share your findings with the rest of the class.

         1.   What is the program's name?
         2.   What is the program's purpose?
         3.   Whom does the program serve?
         4.   What client needs does it meet or problems does it address?
         5.   How large is the program?
         6.   How is the program structured regarding staffing, internal organization, and power structure?
         7.   Who provides funding for the program?
         8.   What are your reasons for identifying it as an innovative program?
         9.   How useful is the program?
         10.   How is the program's effectiveness evaluated?

Exercise 7.3: Creative Projects

A. Brief Description
Students respond to case vignettes by suggesting creative projects to solve problems.

B. Objectives
Students will:
1. Examine problematic macro scenarios.
2. Propose creative solutions to these problems.

C. Procedure
1. Review content on examples of projects in macro practice.
2. Ask students to read the macro case vignettes presented below and respond to the following questions. (This may involve students doing a paper summarizing their ideas, or discussing their answers in a small group context or during a full class discussion.)

D. Instructions for Students
Read the following case vignettes and respond to the questions about potential project implementation.

Vignette #1: Manuela is a Protective Services Worker who helps "legal authorities with investigations to determine if children are in need of such services, help[s] children get services when needed," and provides family counseling (Barker, 1995, p. 56). Most of her clients are very poor, and since Thanksgiving is approaching, Manuela worries that many of them will be unable to have much food at all, let alone a grand turkey celebration.

What types of projects could Manuela initiate? Specifically, how might she go about doing so?

Vignette #2: Dougal is a counselor at a large urban YMCA. He organizes and runs recreational and educational programs for youth, functions as a positive role model, and provides informal counseling. Recently, he learned that the county social services agency had contracted with an expert on gang intervention to run a four-day in-service program for its staff. Dougal thinks it would be extremely helpful to the staff at the "Y" if they could somehow participate in such a program.

What sort of project might Dougal initiate to get in-service training for the "Y" staff? Specifically, how might he go about doing so?

Vignette #3: Jarita works at a Planned Parenthood organization where she does contraception and pregnancy counseling. She is also invited to give educational presentations to large groups of people. She finds that over the years her job has significantly changed: Whereas she once dealt primarily with contraception counseling, she now spends more time providing sex education, especially with respect to AIDS. Along with the changes in her job, many other changes have occurred in the agency over the past ten years. For one thing, it is much larger than it was when Jarita began working there. More restrictive state legislation has affected the referral process for abortions. Much more emphasis is now placed on sex education. Jarita observes that the agency policy manual has simply not kept up with the agency's progress and development. Even some personnel policies such as insurance coverage have changed significantly over time. Simply put, the policy manual is colossally out of date.

What sort of project might Jarita pursue in dealing with this concern? Specifically, how might she go about doing so?

Exercise 7.4: Developing a PERT Chart

A.   Brief Description
Students select a campus issue and develop a PERT chart regarding how to address it.

B.   Objectives
Students will:
1.   Identify a macro issue related to the campus community.
2.   Propose a solution following the PERT chart process.

C.   Procedure
1.   Review the material on PERT charts.
2.   Using a small group format or full class discussion, ask students to identify a problematic issue on campus.
3.   Help students develop a PERT chart concerning how they might address this issue and solve the problem.

D.   Instructions for Students
1.   Select a campus issue (for example, lack of adequate, inexpensive campus parking; difficulties getting into required course sections; or problems in the field placement assignment process) that you feel is significant. Think carefully about how you might implement a macro level change if you had the time and energy. Would you develop and conduct a survey to establish the significance of the issue and gain support? Which administrators would you approach about the issue? How would you present your position and your plan? Would fundraising or grant writing be necessary to achieve your goal?
2.   Develop a PERT chart to address this issue. Be sure to identify the primary goal, establish a sequence of tasks, and propose a time frame for task completion. You may choose to establish a PERT chart with concurrent task sequences for each individual involved.

Exercise 7.5: PERT Role Play

A.   Brief Description
Students participate in a role play where they develop a PERT chart to establish a new agency program.

B.   Objectives
Students will:
1.   Demonstrate skills involved in program development.
2.   Formulate a plan to solve the identified problem by using a PERT chart.

C.   Procedure
1.   Review the content on PERT charts.
2.   Review the following description regarding how the role play will proceed.
3.   Ask for volunteers to play the five roles described below or assign the roles to specific students (Giving extra credit to volunteers usually works well.) The role play requires five characters: two unit counselors (change agents); the school's principal; a social work therapist; and the unit counselors' supervisor. In order to reflect real professional

life, each character has a professional and individual personality, and a personal agenda. The practice setting is Getalife, a residential treatment center for male adolescents with severe behavioral and emotional problems.

4. Remaining students should observe the role play and record their impressions on the Feedback Form included here. Role players should *not* record observations on Feedback Forms because that distracts from their role enactment.

5. Each role player should then read out loud his or her respective lines.

6. Review the organizational chart included below to understand the agency's chain of command. (Note that in the organizational chart the positions of people involved in the role play are highlighted in **boldface italics**.)

7. Begin the role play and allow it to continue for approximately 20 minutes. The instructor should be responsible for halting the role play after the time has elapsed.

8. After the role play is halted, the entire class should discuss critical points, constructive techniques, and suggestions for improvement concerning what occurred. Use the feedback forms to aid in discussion. Role players may share their perceptions concerning their roles and what transpired.

Unit Counselor #1: Your job is to supervise daily living and recreational activities for Getalife's residents, to implement individual residents' behavioral programming, to keep records, and to participate in the residents' group counseling sessions. You also periodically attend staffings where individual case plans are established, implemented, and updated. You work in the Box Elder Unit which includes fourteen boys ages 13 to 15. You have worked for the agency for two years, like your job, and feel you can make valuable contributions to residents' well-being. You are especially concerned about residents' need for sex education. Many—perhaps most—of the center's residents have been sexually active. You know this from talking with residents, reading records, and attending treatment conferences where such information is shared and addressed.

You can't think of anyone in the residential center—including child-care workers, teachers, social workers, or administrators—who has an expertise in this area. You set up a meeting with the head child-care worker (your direct supervisor), the residential unit's social work therapist, and the school's principal to establish a plan. You have already explained to them your general idea so that they will have time to think about the issues prior to the meeting. You have discussed your ideas in greater depth with Unit Counselor #2 who seems to agree strongly with you and is willing to help you conduct the meeting. Together you hope to convince this group of the usefulness of your plan. You intend to establish a PERT chart for how to go about setting up a series of sex education sessions for your unit's residents.

You feel that sex education is tremendously important. You have a 14-year-old sister who is pregnant, and that adds to the significance of this issue for you. You are happy that Worker #2 agrees with you and is willing to help you pursue a sex education program for the Box Elder Unit. However, you believe that you are more committed to the issue than Worker #2, and you would like to apply some pressure on Worker #2 to take on more responsibility for planning and implementing the program.

Unit Counselor #2: You work in the Box Elder Unit with Worker #1 who has talked to you about the sex education proposal. You think that sex education is a very important need for the boys in the Box Elder Unit, but you are pretty busy with your job and you are going to school part-time. You'd like to get the sex education program going, but you don't have much extra time for planning or implementation. You like and respect Worker #1, and you realize that Worker #1 is extremely committed to the issue. It seems logical to you that Worker #1 should take on the most responsibility for planning and implementation. You are willing to expend substantial energy to get a PERT plan in place, but you would then like to minimize your involvement in the plan's implementation.

The Center's School Principal: You supervise six special education teachers and their six respective assistants in Getalife's on-grounds school. You have been with the center for three years, and you believe that anything related to education comes under the school's responsibility. Right now, the school is pressed for resources, and you consider sex education a frill that the school can't afford to address. What's more, in your opinion none of the current educational staff has any expertise in this area, and you wonder whether they would feel comfortable teaching about sexuality. All in all, you resent having to attend this meeting. You wish that the two workers would just drop the subject and mind their own business. You also don't much like the Box Elder Unit's social work therapist. You see the therapist as an ineffective employee in a cushy job. You believe that a good education will offer the adolescent residents more hope for their futures than is likely to come from talking about their feelings with some social worker in hocus-pocus, psychobabble therapy. In short, you have very little confidence that the social workers can accomplish much.

You don't plan to support this "sex plan," and you're coming up with a list of reasons that it's a dumb idea. If in the end the group decides to implement it anyway, you definitely want the programming to be provided by an expert from outside the agency. On this point you do not intend to budge.

The Box Elder Unit's Social Work Therapist: You are an MSW charged with providing the adolescents in your unit with one hour of individual therapy and two hours of group therapy each week, in addition to any family counseling that is deemed necessary. You also assist staff in developing behavioral programming, coordinate residents' individual plans through periodic staffings, write staffing summary reports, coordinate staff activity in implementing treatment recommendations, and monitor residents' progress. You have been with the agency for almost six months.

You are a relatively new "gung-ho" social worker, anxious to do your job and do it well. You have finally been able to get your bearings after six months of struggling to figure out how the agency operates and what you're doing with your clients. You have had some difficulty working with both the school principal and the head child-care supervisor. Both seem to resent any suggestions you make for treatment and your efforts to implement treatment plans in the unit and in the school. Without consistency and follow-through, it's hard to get your clients' behavioral programming to work. The principal is especially difficult to work with and very protective of school turf. The head child-care supervisor is more easy-going but appears to "know everything." You feel the supervisor treats you rather condescendingly and doesn't always come through after promising that something will get done. You think the supervisor is pretty passive-aggressive.

You really like the idea of implementing the sexuality programming. You took a sexuality course in college and have had some subsequent training, so with some brushing up on the content you think you could present a really good program. You also feel it would enhance your relationship with your clients.

The Unit Counselors' Supervisor: You supervise all the counselors (child-care) for the residential center's six units—a total of 58 full-time and part-time staff. You are responsible for scheduling their shifts, supervising their work, and arranging for training to meet ongoing treatment needs. You have an associate's degree from a local community college and have been in your current position for the past 17 years.

Since you have been at the agency an awfully long time, you believe that you really know what's going on. These young whippersnappers on the staff come and go, but you maintain continuity for ongoing treatment and care. You also feel that you're pretty much "a natural" with the kids. You don't need a lot of fancy degrees to work effectively with the residents and develop caring and consistent programs for them. You feel you've helped many, many young people get their acts together. You haven't as yet developed confidence in the social work therapist's ability to work effectively with the residents. The social worker seems to you to have promise, but still needs more experience. You think the school principal is rather cocky, but then you've seen half a dozen principals come and go. You're pretty easy-going and are willing to work with the principal's "eccentric" behaviors and needs.

You attend this meeting out of respect for your two Potawatomi Unit Counselors. You like to encourage your staff to develop new ideas. You also like to present opportunities for them to do so. You feel that it would be best for the agency if some in-house staff did the programming. After all, this idea is basically a fad or frill. Why should the agency expend its scarce resources to pay some expert to come in? Why not have some volunteer staff do the sex ed programming and, essentially, get it over with?

PERT Role Play Organizational Chart

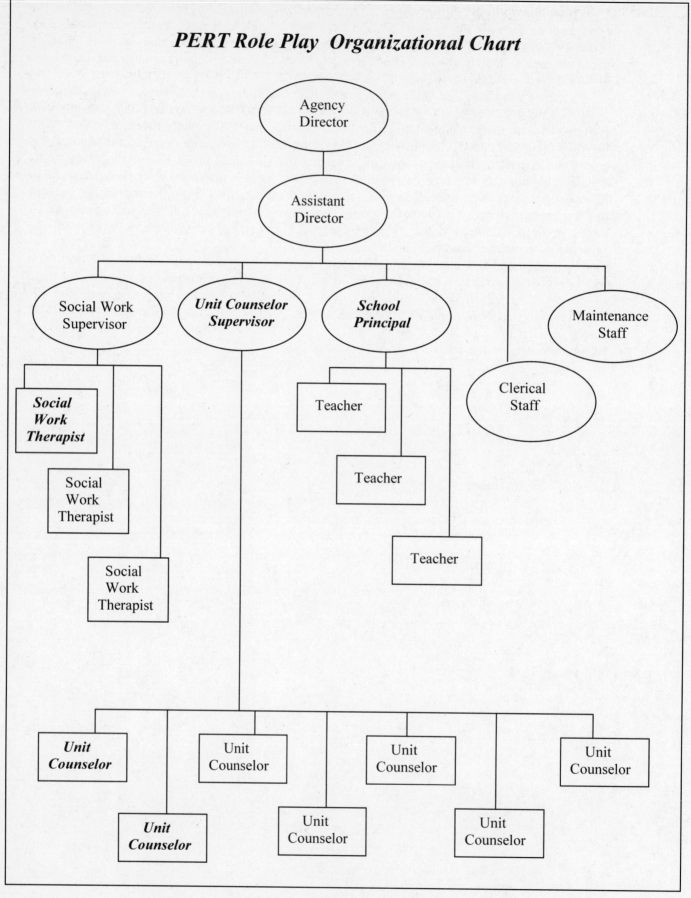

Role Play Feedback Form

1. What were the critical points or major issues addressed in the role play?

2. What especially helpful techniques and approaches were used? Please be specific.

3. What specific suggestions for improvement can you make? For example, how could issues have been addressed more effectively? What alternative responses might have solicited more information or cooperation? Please be specific.

I.   **Introduction**

II.   **The Role of Social Workers in Neighborhoods and Communities**

   A.   National Association of Social Workers Code of Ethics

   1.   Enhance human well-being and help meet the basic needs of all people, with particular attention to the needs and empowerment of people who are vulnerable, oppressed, and living in poverty

   2.   Attend to the environmental forces that create, contribute to, and address problems in living

   3.   Promote social justice and social change with and on behalf of clients

   4.   Be sensitive to cultural and ethnic diversity, and strive to end discrimination, oppression, poverty, and other forms of social injustice

   5.   Focus on individual well-being in a social context and the well-being of society

   B.   Council on Social Work Education

   1.   To enhance human well-being and alleviate poverty, oppression, and other forms of social injustice

   2.   To enhance the social functioning and interactions of individuals, families, groups, organizations, and communities by involving them in accomplishing goals, developing resources, and preventing and alleviating distress

   3.   To formulate and implement social policies, services, and programs that meet basic human needs and support the development of human capacities

   4.   To pursue policies, services, and resources through advocacy and social or political actions that promote social and economic justice

   5.   To develop and use research, knowledge, and skills that advance social work practice

   6.   To develop and apply practice in the context of diverse cultures

   C.   Guest worker program

   D.   Generalist practitioners' typical activities

   1.   Assessing needs through use of interagency committees

   2.   Identifying service gaps, and recommending new programs

3.   Advocating for policy changes in response to needs identified by grassroots community organizations

4.   Participating in professional association action groups

III.   Defining Community and Neighborhood

A.   Traditional communities—encompass places like cities, towns, and villages, identifiable geographical entities

B.   Nontraditional communities—nonplace or nongeographic communities (i.e. legal community), also known as identificational communities

C.   Common components of traditional definitions of communities

1.   Community occupies a shared physical space

2.   Community members interact with each other differently than they interact with people outside the community

3.   Community members often form a strong affiliation and identity with their community

D.   Neighborhood—a region or locality whose inhabitants share certain characteristics, values, mutual interests, or styles of living

1.   A community is composed of many neighborhoods

2.   The degree of neighborhood identity is often even greater than the sense of identity found in the larger community

E.   Functions of communities

1.   Socialization—transmission of values, culture, beliefs, and norms to new community members

a.   Values—those principles a group considers important

b.   Culture—includes customs and ways of doing things

c.   Beliefs—ideas that members assume are true, but may not be verifiable

d.   Norms—a community's expectations for how its members should act

2.   Production, distribution, and consumption of goods and services

3.   Social control, which involves setting limits on behavior by creating and enforcing laws via police and other official bodies

4.   Mutual support, meaning that community members take care of one another

5.   Providing for the participation of its residents

6.   Highlight 8.1: Examples of Two Communities

F.   Types of communities

1.   Most common classification system is size

    a.   Metropolitan communities—vary in size from about 50 thousand to several million residents, they are large cities that serve as the surrounding area's business and economic center

    b.   Nonmetropolitan communities differ from metropolitan communities mainly in terms of size

        1)   Small cities (15,000-50,000)

        2)   Small towns (8,000-20,000)

        3)   Rural communities (under 10,000)

        4)   Reservation communities—located on Native American reservations recognized by the federal government

        5)   Bedroom communities—predominantly residential in nature

        6)   Institutional communities—one major employer that may overshadow the whole surrounding area (company towns)

2.   Communities may be classified by ethnic composition or degree of homogeneity/heterogeneity

3.   Boundaries of cities are easily identified; community boundaries may be more diffuse

IV.   Using the Systems Perspective

A.   Figure 8.1: A Social Systems Model

B.   Change agent system—refers to worker or agency to whom a "problem" is reported

C.   Target system—includes those individuals, organizations, or community elements that need changing

D.   Client system—consists of those who will benefit directly or indirectly from the change

E.   Action system—those individuals, groups, or other entities that will carry out the effort to cause change

V. The Community as an Ecological and Social System

    A.   Ecological perspective

        1.   Ecosystems or ecological theory emphasizes the importance of the transactions between systems within an environment

        2.   Intervening at the macro level requires a solid recognition of the community as an ecological system

    B.   Social systems perspective

        1.   Every community can be viewed as a social system with all the associated characteristics

            a.   Boundaries—borders or dividing lines

            b.   Homeostasis—equilibrium or relative balance and an attempt to maintain the status quo

            c.   Stressors—forces that disrupt the homoeostasis of a system

            d.   Task and maintenance functions—communities seek to maintain a range of services, attend to the needs of multiple audiences, and respond to special-interest groups

            e.   Primary groups, self-help groups, and service clubs help the community function

            f.   Subsystems—communities may be viewed as a collection of these smaller, internal systems

    C.   Social structural perspective

        1.   Focuses on understanding how various subsystems affect the individual and group

        2.   Attention is directed to how some social structures empower clients and others oppress them

    D.   Human behavior perspective

        1.   Human behavior theories—the roles of adaptation and stress are useful in understanding how and why individuals behave in a certain manner when dealing with larger systems such as communities

        2.   Rational theories—actions and feelings arise from our thinking process

VI. Additional Perspectives on the Community

A. Highlight 8.2: Key Concepts for Understanding Communities

    1. Competition—the struggle within a community by various groups, all seeking to have their interests and needs considered more important than others' needs

    2. Centralization—the practice of clustering business services and institutions in one area of a city

    3. Concentration—the tendency of certain groups (particularly ethnic groups) to cluster in a particular section of a neighborhood or a community

    4. Gentrification—a pattern whereby upper-middle-class families move back into downtown and near-downtown residential areas, turning second floors of businesses into lofts and rehabilitating large older homes

    5. Invasion—a tendency of each new group of in-migrants to force out or replace existing groups previously living in a neighborhood

    6. Succession—the replacement of the original occupants or residents of a community or neighborhood by new groups

B. Competition

    1. Communities are often battlegrounds for groups and organizations competing for resources

    2. Competition is essentially a political activity in which many valid needs vie with other equally valid needs

C. Centralization

    1. Communities, through zoning and other land-use restrictions, frequently attempt to centralize certain businesses in specific areas

    2. Zoning laws are why subdivisions of expensive homes are approved and rules established excluding less-expensive homes

D. Concentration

    1. Housing in an area may cost less

    2. Oppression and discrimination often results in housing segregation

E. Invasion—primarily affects housing

F. Gentrification—those forced out are often lower- or fixed-income elderly

G. Succession—can continue indefinitely in some areas of a community

H. Concepts characterize real life

VII. Community Resource Systems

    A.   Informal—include family members, coworkers, friends, neighbors, and others who provide emotional, social, or more tangible types of support

    B.   Formal—membership organizations including social or fraternal organizations

    C.   Societal—institutionalized organizations or services, such as private and public social service agencies

    D.   Figure 8.2: Community Resource Systems

        1.   Government units

        2.   Spiritual/religious groups

        3.   Professional groups

        4.   Social service agencies

        5.   Business/trade groups

        6.   Civic groups

        7.   Consumer groups

        8.   Educational organizations

VIII. Demographic Development of Communities

    A.   Urbanization and Suburbanization

        1.   Urbanization—the trend in which multitudes of people move to large metropolitan areas and away from rural, outlying areas

        2.   Suburbanization—residents deserted large cities and moved to smaller communities nearby

        3.   White flight—the most upwardly mobile members of our society, composed disproportionately of white, middle-class Americans, moving out of the central city

        4.   Blockbusting—a form of social and economic injustice in which realtors tamper with the natural buying and selling trends in a community or neighborhood

B.   Gentrification

    1.   Rehabilitation of rundown buildings improves the quality of life in a community and prevents further deterioration

    2.   The process eventually hurts low-income families and individuals who may have few other housing choices

C.   Rural communities

    1.   Rural communities often have many of the same problems that urban areas have, but fewer of the services needed to cope

    2.   Strong value systems in rural areas and the pressure to conform to longstanding traditions may make it more difficult for newcomers to fit in

    3.   Rural residents are often more willing to help each other in times of need

    4.   A community belief in self-reliance may result in opposition to development of new societal resources

    5.   Highlight 8.3: Social Work in Rural Areas

        a.   Rural areas frequently suffer from a variety of problems including few resources, no public transportation systems, isolation of resource providers, and a loss of anonymity usually available in more urban areas

        b.   Rural residents tend to rely on themselves for problem solving, value high levels of autonomy, and prefer informal to formal resource systems when help is needed

        c.   In times of crisis, rural dwellers are more likely to consult their spiritual advisor than a mental health professional

        d.   About one-third of social workers in rural areas tend to be engaged in advocacy, program development, management, education, and training

        e.   Generalist practice, with its broad range of skills, is especially appropriate and practical for rural environments

D.   Where is the best place to live?

IX.   **Social Stratification**

A.   Social stratification—the division of a society into categories (e.g., income or social class)

    1.   Used for needs assessments and to better understand our society and the vast disparities within it

2. Can be used to discriminate against groups who differ by gender, race, sexual orientation, or other characteristics

3. Underclass—a term that refers to the poorest of the poor

X. Community Economic Systems

A. Economic systems—whether at the national, state, or local level, are concerned with the production, distribution, and consumption of goods and services

1. Underground economic system—consists of off-the-books businesses (such as some child- and lawn-care enterprises), bartering, and even gambling

2. Underclass—refers to members of a community who feel alienated from the community and hopeless about the future

3. Many Mexicans lost their livelihood as a result of the North American Free Trade Agreement (NAFTA)

4. The enormous emphasis communities place on recruiting new businesses is testimony to the importance of the economic system on the local level

5. There is often tension and competition in the community between the goals of a healthy economy and concerns about the environmental impact of new industries

6. An environmental justice issue is the tendency for urban growth to occur through development of farmland, green areas, and previously undeveloped rural areas while ignoring deteriorating inner cities or neighborhoods where new jobs and housing rehabilitation are badly needed

7. You cannot overestimate the importance of the economic system

XI. Community Political Systems

A. Formal organizations and informal political processes

1. Federal government—funds many social programs, maintains the U.S. monetary system, oversees interstate commerce, provides for the national defense, and protects the civil rights of U.S. citizens

2. State governments—fund a significant portion of the health and mental health services provided by social workers and others, and play a role in education, providing financial support for local school districts, and enforcing rules regarding how this financial support is spent

3. Local governments (county or city)—often provide health and social services, fire and police services

B.   Formal structure of the community political system

    1.   Official governance structure, consisting of elected officials, the city bureaucracy, the staff who carry out the city functions, and appointed committees

        a.   Highlight 8.4: Governmental Activities in the Community

            1)   Designing community programs

            2)   Allocating funds

            3)   Providing services for citizens

            4)   Building projects

            5)   Awarding and supervising contracts

            6)   Determining and enforcing laws

            7)   Making and enforcing regulations

            8)   Negotiating agreements

            9)   Mediating disputes

            10)   Planning for the community

    2.   Citizen participation

        a.   Formal citizen involvement through organizations such as the Chamber of Commerce

        b.   Informal involvement through the personal power and influence of individual community members and through the power structure

XII.   Power in the Community

A.   Defining power

    1.   Power—the capacity to move people in a desired direction to accomplish some end; also the ability to prevent someone from doing something they want to do

    2.   Highlight 8.5: Power at Work

B.   Types of power

    1.   Potential power—power that has not yet been exercised, it exists when we can influence others but have not done so

    2.   Actual power—the *use* of power to influence others

C.   Sources of power

1.   Financial asset

2.   Business ownership

3.   Community status

4.   Possession of information

5.   Links to other individuals, groups, or organizations with power

6.   Methods of detecting power

a.   Reputational approach—involves simply asking others about who has power

b.   Issues approach—assumes that there are always important community issues under consideration and that those who are influential in addressing these issues are powerful people

c.   Positional approach—assumes that those who hold various important positions in a community also have power

D.   Power and conflict

1.   Power becomes more visible in times of community conflict

2.   During conflicts you are most likely to observe those with power influencing the outcome

XIII.   Neighborhoods

A.   Functions of neighborhoods

1.   Social functions—include providing friendships, status, socialization, mutual assistance, and informal helping networks

2.   Institutional functions—include providing employment, connecting new residents to older residents, providing access to specific services, and otherwise helping neighborhood members integrate

3.   Political function—allowing members to become involved in the political process to influence elected and appointed decision makers

4.   Economic functions—include provision of housing and places to shop. These are the functions most threatened by technology, changing demographics, and changes in the nature of businesses

5.   Highlight 8.6: Goodbye to Geneva

B. Types of neighborhoods

    1. Composed of highly mobile residents who will be there for only a short time

    2. Consisting of residents who have lived there all or most of their lives

    3. Characterized by the lack of integrating mechanisms, they are almost disorganized in a social sense

    4. Transient neighborhoods with little cohesion are less likely to function as informal resource systems

    5. Ghetto—used to describe a section in which a specific ethnic group or people of color must live

    6. Slums—indicates they are run-down, deteriorating, or otherwise blighted

    7. Ethnic neighborhoods—where ethnic similarity among the residents is great. The degree of residential segregation that occurs in these neighborhoods challenges the image of the melting pot

C. Neighborhoods as helping networks

D. Neighborhood organizations

    1. It is estimated that there are over 100,000 neighborhood organizations in this country

    2. The Neighborhood Watch program

    3. Empowerment for both members and their organizations

    4. Highlight 8.7: Two Effective Neighborhood Associations

    5. Highlight 8.8: Neighborhood Organizations

    6. Highlight 8.9: Neighborhood Resources

E. Community and neighborhood resources

XIV. Putting It All Together: Assessing Communities and Neighborhoods

A. Useful sources of information for community assessment

    1. Census records, planning agency documents, and business development plans

    2. Newspapers, libraries, books about the community's history, and information from the Internet

        3.   United Way and other existing data sources

        4.   Database of important officials and individuals (key informants—knowledgeable persons in the community with special expertise in your area of interest)

B.   Highlight 8.10: A Model for Community Assessment

C.   Community capacity—the link between the operation of formal and informal networks of social care in the community and the actual results achieved by these networks

        1.   Evaluation of two factors

              a.   The extent to which community residents, leaders, and agencies have a shared sense of responsibility for the welfare of the community's members

              b.   The collective competence of the community in addressing the identified challenges, making the most of change opportunities, and attacking the problem

D.   Highlight 8.11: KidsPlace

Experiential Exercises and Classroom Simulations

Exercise 8.1: Nontraditional Communities

A.   Brief Description
Students differentiate between traditional and nontraditional communities.

B.   Objectives
Students will:
1.   Identify traditional and nontraditional communities of which they are a part.

C.   Procedure
1.   Ask students to list any communities of which they are a part.
2.   Ask them to indicate which of the communities are traditional and which are nontraditional.
3.   Lead a discussion about the differences and similarities of traditional and nontraditional communities in terms of their functions for members.
4.   Allow about 10 minutes for the first two steps and another 10 minutes for the discussion.

D.   Instructions for Students
List all communities of which you are a member. Make a note next to each community as to whether it is a traditional community or a nontraditional community.

E.   Commentary
Students can also complete this assignment in small groups.

Exercise 8.2: Assessing Community Effectiveness

A. Brief Description
Students discuss the effectiveness of their own community with respect to traditional community functions.

B. Objectives
Students will:
1. Apply community concepts to their own community.
2. Assess the extent to which their community performs specific functions.

C. Procedure
1. Discuss in class the traditional functions of communities.
2. Divide class into groups of four to six.
3. Ask each group member to look at his/her hometown and to assess how well that community performed the functions expected of a community. Share this information within the group.
4. Ask each group to record the functions which members believed were well performed and those which were less well performed. Ask them to suggest ways in which a less well-performed function could be enhanced.

Exercise 8.3: Context vs. Target

A. Brief Description
Students consider situations in which the community may be both a context for change as well as a target for change.

B. Objectives
Students will:
1. Identify situations in which a community can be either a context for change or the target of change or both.

C. Procedure
1. Divide the class into about 5 groups.
2. Ask them to read the scenario and answer each of the questions that follow.
3. Ask each group to report back their decisions to the class.
4. Answer any questions about topic.

D. Instructions for Students
In each of the boxes below is a scenario involving a community. Read each case and answer the two following questions.

> A. Your first job out of school is in the foster care unit of a county social service agency. You work with adolescents placed in various community group homes. Lately several group home residents have commented on the rude treatment they receive from certain neighborhood residents. In the section below, give an example in which the community is the context for your practice and another in which the community is the target of change.

1.	Community as Context:
2.	Community as Target:

B.   Now you are the Director of Social Services for a nursing home. You recruit, orient, and serve clients for your facility (a for-profit organization). You are new to this position and wish you had someone to talk to about your work. A former professor suggests that you join the nursing home social workers association. You inquire about this group and learn that the nursing home social worker organization used to hold monthly meetings but has not met for a couple of years. Now what? Considering this situation, give an example in which the community is both the context for your practice and the target of change.

    1.   Community as Context:

    2.   Community as Target:

E.   Commentary
This assignment can also be completed using the entire class rather than break the class into small groups.

Exercise 8.4: Identifying Systems

A.   Brief Description
Students will apply the concepts of client, action, change agent, and target system to a case example.

B.   Objectives
Students will:
1.   Identify client, action, change agent, and target systems within a community.

C.   Procedure
1.   Review material on using the system perspective within a community.
2.   Ask students to read the following case illustration, thinking about the various systems that are evident.
3.   Ask students to identify and write down the client, action, change agent, and target systems in this community.
4.   Ask students to report on their decisions.

D.   Instructions to Students.
Read the following case illustration and identify the client, change agent, target, and action systems.

Livermore is a small East Coast city with a big problem. Situated along a major interstate highway, it has become a haven for street gangs and drug dealers because it has only a small police force and is less able than the nearby large city of St. Trump to arrest and prosecute these criminals. Mary Mercado moved to Livermore to escape the violence and crime in St. Trump. As a hospital social worker, she knew first-hand the effects of violence. Worried that her new city is going to end up like her old one, Mary talks with a few of her friends who suggest that she bring her concerns to the attention of her city council representative. Mary meets with Paul Hernandez and together they ask the city council to fund a small task force.

The task force (composed of Mary, Paul, another city council member, the city attorney, a probation and parole officer—a social worker—and the police chief) prepares a report recommending that the city take seven steps to reduce or eliminate the drug and gang problem in Livermore.

Identify the following systems:

client system

action system

change agent system

target system

E.   Commentary
This assignment can be used both with the class as a whole or with small groups.

Exercise 8.5: Which Theory Is Most Helpful?

A.   Brief Description
Students will utilize various theories to better understand events that occur in a community.

B.   Objectives
Students will:
1.   Recognize the differences among various theories used to help understand community life.
2.   Apply a theory to events in a particular community.

C.   Procedure
1.   Divide the class into subgroups.
2.   Ask each group to read each of the community situations listed and select which theory (ecological, human behavior, social systems, social structural, or organizational) best explains the particular community event.
3.   Ask each group to report their decisions back to the class.

D.   Instructions for Students
Using your understanding of the following theories (ecological, human behavior, social systems, social structural, or organizational), decide which theory or theories best explain the community situation.

Which theory is most useful in understanding each of these community situations?

A. The largest employer in a community goes out of business, throwing hundreds of people out of work.

B. A large community attempts to annex (take over) an adjacent smaller community.

C. The business sector in a community is deteriorating. Business owners are resisting community attempts to revitalize the downtown area and are failing to improve their own businesses.

D. The city council has passed a resolution calling for the city building inspector and the police department to work together to target deteriorated buildings and fine landlords who fail to keep up their properties. This is the first attempt to get these two bodies working together.

E. Maria Hatcher no longer calls the police when shots ring out in her neighborhood. After all, the police have been unable to stop the violence since it began three years ago.

E. Commentary
This exercise may be expanded to include additional examples. It can also be used as part of a quiz or examination.

Exercise 8.6: Identifying Resource Systems

A. Brief Description
Students will learn to identify and differentiate informal, formal, and societal resource systems within their own experience.

B. Objectives
Students will:
1. Correctly identify informal, formal, and societal resource systems with which they are personally familiar.

C. Procedure
1. Review in class or ask the class to review the descriptions of resource systems in the community described below.
2. Ask students to answer the questions listed.

D. Instructions for Students
You likely have some experience with informal, formal, and societal resource systems. Read the brief description of each below and then answer the questions that follow.

Resource Systems in Communities

Social workers and community residents depend upon the availability of resource systems to meet a variety of needs. Most such systems can be classified as informal, formal, or societal.

186

Informal systems develop naturally and include family members, friends, and neighbors. The resources available from such a system might include emotional support, financial assistance, or both.

Formal resource systems (also called membership systems) are groups we have joined or of which we are members. They include service clubs (Junior League, Moose), unions (Teamsters, or American Federation of State, County, and Municipal Employees), professional organizations (Bar Association or NASW), and churches. Each of these resources can provide a variety of support and assistance to its members and sometimes to nonmembers. Any such group should be considered a possible source of help at the micro, mezzo, or macro levels.

Societal resources are the institutions, agencies, and organizations established to provide help to residents of the community. Among these are social service agencies (both public and private) in which most social workers are employed. While the resources of these societal systems may be great, it is often more appropriate to help clients (whether individuals, groups, or larger systems) use the other resource systems.

1.   List two people who are part of your own informal resource system. What kinds of assistance could they provide you in an emergency?

2.   Identify two formal resource systems of which you are a member. List the kinds of assistance you might expect from them if you were in desperate need.

3.   Identify at least three public and three private societal resource systems with which you are acquainted. These agencies can be drawn from any community.

E.   Commentary
This exercise can be used with students in small groups or with the entire class.

Exercise 8.7: Hometown Demographic Factors

A.   Brief Description
Students will use their own hometowns to illustrate the ways in which urbanization, suburbanization, white flight, and/or gentrification have impacted that community.

B.   Objectives
Students will:
1.   Identify and describe the role that concepts such as urbanization, suburbanization, white flight, and/or gentrification have impacted their home communities.

C.   Procedure
1.   Review the definitions of urbanization, suburbanization, white flight, and/or gentrification.
2.   Ask students to think about either their home community or the community with which they are most familiar.
3.   Have students provide examples of how these concepts have impacted their community.

D.   Instructions to Students
Using the concepts of urbanization, suburbanization, white flight, and/or gentrification, identify how they have impacted your community. Give specific examples.

E.   Commentary
It may be necessary to help students differentiate among the different concepts and provide examples from their own experience.

Exercise 8.8 Assessing Communities

A.   Brief Description
Students will begin to identify important aspects of a community assessment.

B.   Objectives
Students will:
1.   Identify sources of information that will be useful in a community assessment.
2.   Describe data that may be needed to better understand a community or neighborhood.

C.   Procedure
1.   Review the process of doing a community assessment including the types and sources of data that would be helpful.
2.   Ask students to read the brief statement about assessing communities and neighborhoods and then answer the questions below.

D.   Instructions for Students
Using your home community as an example, identify how well it carried out the functions of socialization, social control and mutual support.

Socialization:
Social Control:
Mutual Support:
Identify how the functioning of your community could have been improved.

E.   Commentary
This exercise can be conducted in a large group with students reporting back to the entire group or be completed in a smaller group.

Exercise 8.9: Involvement In Political Systems

A.   Brief Description
Students discuss the extent of their and their family's involvement in their hometown political system.

B.   Objectives
Students will:
Recognize various mechanisms for involvement in the political process.
Assess their own and their family's contribution to political decision-making.

C.   Procedure
1.   Review the ways in which social workers can participate in the political process.
2.   Ask students to look at their own level of political activity and that of their family with respect to their hometown.
3.   Have students share their observations with the entire class.
4.   After all students have shared, lead a discussion on why there are differences among the level of participation of different families/individuals.

D.   Instructions for Students
List and describe any involvement you or your family have had in your hometown political system. Please consider all possible levels of activity from voting to running for office.

E.   Commentary
This exercise can be done in small groups by asking the group to identity common themes explaining why some families/individuals are more politically involved than others.

Chapter 9
Macro Practice in Communities

I.   **Introduction**

II.   **Change in Communities**

    A.   Highlight 9.1: Community Change Activities

    B.   Highlight 9.2: Social Workers in the Community

    C.   Philosophical perspective on macro practice: Pursuit of social and economic justice

    D.   Philosophical perspective on macro practice: Empowerment

        1.   Five competencies needed to engage in effective empowerment

            a.   Informational competence—includes knowledge and awareness social workers possess regarding the groups with whom they are working

            b.   Intellectual competence—requires that the social worker consider how informational knowledge can be used to work with the client system

            c.   Intrapersonal competency—involves the social worker's genuine affinity for the individual or community with whom he or she is working

            d.   Interpersonal competency—the ability to communicate with genuineness and warmth

            e.   Interventional competency—requires that the social worker be able to utilize knowledge and various skills in pursuit of empowerment

        2.   Highlight 9.3: Empowering Clients' Participation in Decision Making

III.   **Perspectives on the Community**

    A.   The community is the context in which we practice

    B.   The community is the target of our change efforts

    C.   The community is the mechanism for change

    D.   Approaches to community change

        1.   Working with the power structure in a consensual, gradual way that focuses on service delivery

2. Focusing on conflict, mediation, and challenges to the power structure

3. Neighborhood maintenance, which combines a consensual, peer pressure system with legal action and political lobbying to improve property values, maintain neighborhoods, and deliver services

IV. Beginning the Change Process

A. Engagement in the community

B. PREPARE: Assessing potential for community change

    1. Figure 9.1: PREPARE—An Assessment of Community Change Potential

    2. Step 1: PREPARE—Identify **Problems** to address

        a. Identification by news media reports

            1) Sometimes the news media reports a sensational event that underscores the existence of a community problem

            2) Highlight 9.4: Gang Graffiti

        b. Identification by social service providers

        c. Identification by beneficiaries

        d. Describe problems clearly

        e. Research the problem carefully

        f. Community capacity building

            1) A neighborhood-based approach to improving conditions in an area

            2) Consistent with the strength approach, and is based on the premise that neighborhood residents should establish the priorities that will be pursued

            3) Characteristics include the following efforts

                a) Focused around specific improvement initiatives in a manner that reinforces values and builds social and human capital

                b) Community-driven with broad resident involvement

                c) Comprehensive, strategic and entrepreneurial

                d) Asset-based

e)   Tailored to neighborhood scale and conditions

f)   Collaboratively linked to the broader society to strengthen community institutions and enhance outside opportunities for residents

g)   Consciously changing institutional barriers and racism

3.   Step 2: **PREPARE**—Assess your macro and personal **Reality**

a.   Force field analysis—a review of the barriers to accomplishing your goal and the factors likely to help you achieve it

b.   Community asset mapping (CAM)—looks at potential resources, whether they are human, financial, or material, in an attempt to accurately predict the likelihood of a successful change effort

     1)   Benefits of asset mapping—unites residents and helps them think about their own communities and develop a shared sense of what makes them a good place to live

     2)   Community asset categories

         a)   Built assets—physical structures or public areas

         b)   Natural assets—include a community's environment

         c)   Social assets—the friendliness of residents, resources that bring people together

         d)   Economic assets—the availability of jobs, economic conditions in the community

         e)   Service assets—health, educational, and welfare services available to community members

     3)   Sources of information

     4)   Types of resources

     5)   Cataloging skills

         a)   Figure 9.2: Individual Capacity Inventory

         b)   Figure 9.3: Community Asset Map

     6)   Potential barriers to community asset mapping

     7)   Pursuing community change

	c.	Assessing target systems

d. Highlight 9.5: Geri's Force Field Analysis

4. Step 3: PREPARE—**Establish** primary goals

5. Step 4: PREPARE—Identify relevant **People** of influence

    a. Highlight 9.6: Identifying People of Influence

        1) People who get things done

        2) People to whom others look for guidance

        3) People who will become leaders in your organization

        4) People who can motivate their peers

        5) People who have connections with other important people or resources

        6) People who have particular skills

    b. Highlight 9.7: Gathering People of Influence

6. Step 5: PREPARE—**Assess** potential financial costs and benefits

7. Step 6: PREPARE—Review professional and personal **Risk**

8. Step 7: PREPARE—**Evaluate** the potential success of a macro change process

    a. Collaborative approaches carry much less risk than conflict tactics, but they may not be as effective in getting you where you want to go

    b. Highlight 9.8: Evaluating Potential Success

C. IMAGINE: A process for community change

1. Figure 9.4: IMAGINE—A Process for Initiating and Implementing Macro Change

2. IMAGINE: Start with an innovative **Idea**

    a. The innovative idea you will begin with is the plan you identified for effecting change

    b. Highlight 9.9: An Innovative Idea

3. IMAGINE: **Muster** support and formulate an action system

4. IMAGINE: Identify **Assets**

5.   IMAGINE: Specify **Goals**, objectives, and action steps to attain them

    a.   Highlight 9.10: Goals, Objectives, and Action Steps: Reducing Gang Activity

    b.   Highlight 9.11: Getting Things Done

        1)   Holding meetings

        2)   Mass mailings

        3)   Leafleting

    c.   Highlight 9.12: Goal, Objective, and Action Step: Obtaining a Permanent Shelter

6.   IMAGINE: **Implement** the plan

    a.   It is important to recognize the strengths of everyone involved in the implementation process

    b.   Holding meetings is one of the most frequent activities in the implementation phase

    c.   Highlight 9.13: Implementing the Plan

7.   IMAGINE: **Neutralize** opposition

    a.   Highlight 9.14: Confronting a Bad Idea

    b.   Social action: Confrontation and conflict approaches

        1)   Clashes of position

            a)   Actions such as debate, legal disputes, written statements of intent, public speeches, and bargaining and negotiating

            b)   Highlight 9.15: Bargaining and Negotiating

        2)   Violations of normative behavior

        3)   Violations of legal norms

    c.   Choose goals wisely

8.   IMAGINE: **Evaluate** progress

    a.   Stabilizing change

    b.   Highlight 9.16: Evaluating Progress and a Follow-up

    c.   Termination and follow-up

Exercise 9.1: Community as Client, Target, Context or Mechanism of Change

A.   Brief Description
Students look at the community from several different perspectives.

B.   Objectives
Students will:
1.   Recognize different perspectives on the community.
2.   Identify a particular perspective appropriate to a given community.

C.   Procedures
1.   Present an overview of the community as a potential client, target, context, or mechanism of change.
2.   Divide the class into groups of four to six.
3.   Ask each group to discuss the scenario shown in the box below and to arrive at a solution with which most members agree.
4.   Ask each group to report on their findings and their reasoning.

D.   Instructions for Students
Read the scenario shown in the box below. Share with members of your group your opinion about the appropriate answer and your reasoning.

> As the director of social services at a local hospital in Muddy Hills, you often use community services to help clients when they are discharged. These include programs such as Meals on Wheels, homemaking services, and chore services. Each service is designed to help clients who cannot take care of their own needs for food or household maintenance. Generally, the existing services are satisfactory, but they could be improved. You decide that the Meals on Wheels program in particular could be operated with greater sensitivity to the needs of Hispanic clients. You set up an appointment with the program's director to discuss your ideas. Do you consider Muddy Hills the context, target, client, or mechanism for your practice? Explain your reasons.

E.   Commentary
This activity can be done in the class as a whole rather than in small groups.

Exercise 9.2: People of Influence

A.   Brief Description
Students discuss the concept of influence in a community.

B.   Objectives
Students will:
1.   Recognize their own potential for community influence.
2.   Identify areas of the community where their influence can be exercised.

C.   Procedure
1.   Lead a discussion on the concept of influence in a community.

2.   Ask students to identify people of influence known to them or to members of their family. Ask them to identify the sphere of influence that is evident.

D.   Instructions for Students
1.   Consider all the people of influence in your community that you know or that members of your family know.
2.   Identify in which areas of the community they are most likely to have influence.
3.   Share this information with the class.

E.   Commentary
This exercise may be done with small groups or with the entire class.

Exercise 9.3: An Innovative Idea

A.   Brief Description
Students consider innovative ideas and possible obstacles.

B.   Objectives
Students will:
1.   Develop one innovative idea for community change.
2.   Identify potential obstacles to achieving change.

C.   Procedure
1.   Ask students to look at their hometown and to identify one innovative idea that could improve the quality of life in the community.
2.   Once this step is accomplished ask them to identify individuals, organizations, or groups who might oppose this idea.
3.   Lead a discussion and help categorize the possible reasons for opposition to an innovative idea.

D.   Instructions for Students
Look at your hometown and identify one innovative idea that could improve the quality of life in that community. Also identify any individuals, groups, or organizations that might oppose your idea. Why do you think this opposition might occur?

E.   Commentary
This exercise can be done in small groups by asking the groups to categorize the reasons for opposition to an innovative idea.

Exercise 9.4: Community as Client, Target, Context, and Mechanism of Change

A.   Brief Description
Students will study a community scenario and decide whether the community is a potential client, target, context or mechanism of change.

B.   Objectives
Students will:
1.   Apply concepts of the community as client, target, context or mechanism of change to selected scenarios.

C. Procedure
1. Provide a brief description of how a community may be viewed from four different perspectives.
2. Ask students to read each scenario and match each with the corresponding view of the community.

D. Instructions for Students

Below are four community scenarios. Read each and decide whether the community appears to be a potential client, target for change, context for change, a mechanism for change or some combination.

Scenario 1:

San Garcia is a community with many problems, primary among which is the absence of shelter for the homeless. The city council has repeatedly turned down a state grant that would help establish a homeless shelter. Julio Ruiz, the shelter's major opponent on the city council, is a very conservative individual who opposes all social programs. He faces reelection in a month and his opponent is a progressive former mayor of San Garcia, Miguel Gonzales. Mr. Gonzales has asked you to help him get elected because you are well known in the community, especially among the Spanish-speaking population. You both believe that residents will support a homeless shelter if for no other reason than to assure that the homeless will not begin sleeping on the streets of residential areas. If you decide to help in this campaign, would you consider the city of San Garcia the client, the target, the context, or the mechanism of change? Explain your answer.

Scenario 2:

Franco City is a poor community on the edge of a mid-sized city, Beltville. Beltville has taken over most of the neighboring cities by annexation, a process of legally incorporating adjacent communities. A Franco City citizens' group is very concerned about this trend and wants the community to remain an independent community. At a community meeting they suggest that a task force be formed to plan a campaign against the loss of their independent status. You agree to serve on the task force. Is Franco City the target, client, context, or mechanism for change in this case? Defend your choice.

Scenario 3:

Munchhausen Vale has been a wonderful community in which to live. Lately, several events have challenged the status quo in the town. The influx of immigrants from Southeast Asia has created tensions among many residents who have no experience with the benefits of community diversity. Residents have begun to lose the sense of community that once made living in "the Vale" so attractive. You live in the community and serve as an at-large member of the city council. The council decides to hold a series of community meetings to which all residents will be invited. The meeting will look at ways of recreating the positive feeling that previously characterized citizens' views of their town. You will serve as the convener for several of these meetings. Do you think that Munchhausen Vale is the mechanism, target, client, or context for your practice? Why?

Scenario 4:
As the director of social services at a local hospital in Muddy Hills, you often use community services to help clients when they are discharged. These include programs such as Meals on Wheels, homemaking services, and chore services. Each service is designed to help clients who cannot take care of their own needs for food or household maintenance. Generally, the existing services are satisfactory, but they could be improved. You decide that the Meals on Wheels program in particular could be operated with greater sensitivity to the needs of Hispanic clients. You set up an appointment with the program's director to discuss your ideas. Do you consider Muddy Hills the context, target, client, or mechanism for your practice? Explain your reasons.

E.   Commentary
This also can be used as a small group exercise or a quiz to test student understanding of the concepts involved.

Exercise 9.5: Reality Check—A Force Field Analysis

A.   Brief Description
Students will work through a community challenge applying a force-field analysis to the situation.

B.   Objectives
Students will:
1.   Identify individuals, groups, and organizations that support or oppose a given proposal.
2.   Describe beneficiaries and those who will suffer from the proposal.
3.   Assess the power and influence of proponents and opponents.
4.   Discuss the potential for successfully opposing the proposal.

C.   Procedure
1.   Review the salient components of a force field analysis.
2.   Form students into work groups.
3.   Ask each group to read the scenario and to answer the questions that follow.

D.   Instructions for Students
Read the scenario below, discuss within your group the situation, and answer each of the questions listed below.

Your social work program is considering raising the grade point average needed at the time of graduation from a 2.5 to a 3.5 because some faculty members believe that grade inflation has made the 2.5 meaningless. The social work program is your community. You spend considerable time in social work classes, many of your friends are in social work, and the social work program has become the context of your sense of who you are. You have a field placement set up for next fall, and you know that your own GPA of 3.1 will probably keep you from graduating if this new change is made. (The remaining exercises in this chapter will also focus on this example.)

As a social work student in this community, do a force field analysis. Review those variables that may help or impede your attempts to stop the implementation of this proposal. Answer the following questions:

1. Who is likely to oppose this proposal?

2. Who is likely to benefit from it?

3. Who is unlikely to see the proposed change as a problem?

4. Assess the power and influence of those who support the proposal.

5. Assess the power and influence of those who oppose the proposal.

6. Who is the potential target in this situation?

7. Do you think the target shares your aspirations, values, and goals? Why?

8. How susceptible is the target to outside pressure?

Exercise 9.6: Asset Identification

A. Brief Description
    Students will practice identifying assets that might be useful in opposing the above proposal.

B. Objectives
    Students will:
    1. Identify prospective assets that might be employed in opposition to a proposal.

C. Procedure
    1. Review with students the concept of identifying assets.
    2. Ask students to work individually or in small groups to identify assets that they might use
        to help defeat the proposed grade point policy described in Exercise 9.5.

D. Instructions for Students
    Refer to the situation described in Exercise 9.5 involving a proposal to increase the minimum
    grade point average needed to graduate. Take a position in opposition to the proposal and
    identify the types of assets available to you in your effort to kill this policy change. Consider the
    following four categories of assets:

    1. Finances

    2. People

    3. Time

    4. Other

E. Commentary
    Students can be asked to follow the complete PREPARE and IMAGINE process in responding to
    the proposed grade point policy.

Chapter 10
Evaluating Macro Practice

I.   **Introduction**

II. **Overview of Evaluation**

    A.   Evaluation research has a rich history at the macro level

    B.   Two perspectives of evaluation of macro practice

        1.   Determining effectiveness of specific programs (program evaluation)

        2.   Evaluation of success as macro-level change agents

III. **Purposes of Program Evaluation: A Summary**

    A.   Help us save time and money or avoid wasting precious resources on approaches that either don't work or don't work very well

    B.   Allow us to spend our resources on unmet needs as we discover gaps among those being served

    C.   Allow us to change our programs to make them more effective, identifying areas of strength and weakness

    D.   Assure us that planned programs provide the services we intended

    E.   Build support for continuing effective programs

    F.   Distinguish which services produce the more favorable outcomes

    G.   Identify side effects that were not intended or planned for

    H.   Help us gain personal satisfaction from knowing that our programs work and work well

IV. **Key Concepts in Evaluations**

    A.   Control group—the group used for comparison purposes that is not receiving the intervention

    B.   Experimental group—the group that receives an intervention

    C.   Dependent variable—that which we are most interested in understanding, measuring, or predicting

    D.   Independent variable—that which we believe is likely to influence, cause, or contribute to a particular phenomenon

    E.   Sampling—a sample or subset of the total group rather than the entire group

F.   Random sample—one in which every element in a population has an equal chance of being selected for inclusion in the sample

G.   Experimental design—involves attempts to manipulate the intervention to determine whether change occurs in a target group. Experimental designs cannot be followed in practice because we are not able to randomly assign clients to groups

H.   Quasi-experimental design—use some, but not all, elements found in the typical experimental design

I.   Baseline—tells us how often a problem or behavior occurred either at a specific point in time or during a specified period

   1.   Retrospective baseline—used when there is no data about something because no records were kept and is composed of data collected after the fact from people's memories

   2.   Concurrent baseline—used when there is no data about something because no records were kept and is data gathering simultaneously with the intervention

J.   Mean—an arithmetical average derived from adding all the entries and dividing by the number of entries

K.   Median—the centermost figure in a distribution of figures listed from highest to lowest or vice versa

L.   Mode—the most frequently observed score in a group of scores

M.   Standard deviation—a measure of the amount of variability of observations around a mean

N.   Reliability—the likelihood that a measurement will yield the same results at subsequent times

O.   Validity—the ability of an instrument to measure what it is supposed to measure

   1.   Face validity—means that a common-sense view of the instrument suggests that it measures what it's supposed to measure

   2.   Predictive validity—a measure of validity based upon the ability of an instrument to predict future performance

P.   Descriptive statistics—statistics that describe a phenomenon

Q.   Inferential statistics—any set of statistics used to make an inference (or draw a conclusion) about a population based upon a sample of that population

R.   Outcome—a quality-of-life change resulting from social work interventions

S.   Outcome measure—the means by which we determine the actual outcome of an intervention

    1.   Practice outcomes—those that can be observed by either the client system or the social worker

    2.   Functional outcomes—focus on changes in the client's quality of life

    3.   Process of care outcomes—those that relate directly to how a service was provided

T.   Statistical significance—a measure of the risk that exists when we generalize from a sample to the population

U.   Chi-square test—a statistical procedure to compare the expected frequencies in a study to observed frequencies

    1.   Expected frequencies—the outcomes that are expected to occur

    2.   Observed frequencies—the actual results you get from your study

V.   Problems and Barriers in Program Evaluation

A.   Failure to plan for evaluation—without a built-in plan for evaluation, including decisions on what information to gather and for what purposes, evaluators are at a loss for ways to proceed

B.   Lack of program stability—it is likely that the program you started evaluating several years ago is not quite the same program now

C.   Relationships between evaluators and practitioners—practitioners are usually concerned primarily with delivering a service; evaluators are interested in measuring the effectiveness of that service

    1.   Practitioners may feel like their worth is under examination. Administrators need to involve practitioners in designing the evaluation, use measures that don't place undue record-keeping burdens on staff, and reduce disruptions in service

    2.   Give practitioners feedback during the process so that they see the importance of the evaluation to their practice

D.   When evaluation results are unclear—when well-planned evaluation produces equivocal or unclear results, perhaps the most logical solution is to conduct multiple evaluations so that no one explanation can rule out all your findings

E.   When evaluation results are not accepted—sometimes evaluations demonstrate things that the people involved do not or cannot accept

F.   When evaluation is not worth the effort—a special event that occurs only once does not necessarily merit evaluation

VI. **Kinds of Evaluation**

    A.   Formative (or monitoring) evaluations

        1.   Focus more on the process than on the outcome of an intervention

        2.   Occur during the implementation stage and are designed to improve the change effort

        3.   Focus on describing what the program does and what is happening during the service delivery process

        4.   Data to assist with monitoring is usually available through treatment manuals, minutes of board or committee meetings, monthly and annual reports, and case records

    B.   Summative evaluations

        1.   They are sometimes called impact evaluations, and they measure the consequences of services provided

        2.   They are normally conducted following an intervention and focus on changes occurring in the target population

    C.   Effectiveness and efficiency evaluations

        1.   To be effective, an intervention should produce a desirable end product

        2.   Efficiency evaluations are concerned with whether a program achieves outcomes in the least expensive manner

VII. **Evaluative Approaches**

    A.   Quantitative methods

        1.   Use objective (numerical) criteria (such as scores on a test, number of arrests, or frequency of temper tantrums) to learn whether change has taken place following an intervention

        2.   Meta-analysis—the combining of the results of several smaller studies, and statistically analyzing the overall findings

    B.   Qualitative methods

        1.   Designed to seek to understand human experiences from the perspective of those who experience them

        2.   Typically involve in-depth review of a small number of cases, and their goal is to describe or explore the experiences of clients or others involved in the process

        3.   Tend to focus more on the human experience and to provide substantial amounts of information that is then categorized, sorted, and analyzed to determine patterns

C.   One group post-test designs—evaluations that look at a single target group, focusing only on changes that have occurred following intervention. They are sometimes called A-B designs

D.   Pre-test/post-test designs—sometimes called A-B designs, they are more useful than post-test-only designs because they allow us to show changes over time

E.   Client satisfaction surveys

      1.   Client or consumer satisfaction inventories or surveys measure general satisfaction with a service or with achievement of specific goals

      2.   One of the major drawbacks to client satisfaction surveys is that the results are almost invariably positive, regardless of the client population, services provided, or other variables

      3.   Figure 10.1 Client Satisfaction Survey

F.   Goal attainment scaling

      1.   Design used to monitor the progress of individual clients and then to aggregate the data on a weekly, monthly, or yearly basis

      2.   It is often, but not always, a qualitative design and is very flexible

      3.   It generally has good face validity and usually does not interfere with the intervention

      4.   Figure 10.2: Goal Attainment Scaling

G.   Target problem scaling

      1.   A method of monitoring changes in a client's behavior, is primarily a qualitative design used in simple evaluations

      2.   Figure 10.3: Target Problem Change Scale

      3.   Advantages are that you can use it to assess changes in a macro-level problem in a single area or neighborhood, and you can also combine it with ratings from other neighborhoods to provide a more comprehensive view of residents' opinions

H.   Case studies

      1.   Qualitative measurement designs allowing the use of a single case or a small group of cases

      2.   Allows the use of unstructured interviews and asking whatever questions that may help understand a situation

I.   Group comparisons

      1.   Compares outcomes between two or more groups—one of which is the treatment group and the other the control group

      2.   Quasi-experimental designs use comparison rather than control groups

J.   Quality assurance reviews

      1.   Involve determining compliance with an established set of standards and using the findings to correct shortcomings or deficiencies

      2.   Focus on finding defects in service and enhancing uniform quality of service

      3.   Figure 10.4: Quality Assurance Review

K.   Summary of evaluation designs

VIII.   Stages in Evaluation

A.   Stage 1: Conceptualization and goal setting

      1.   Begins with agreement upon the goals to be achieved and the indicators of goal achievement to be employed

      2.   Goal—a statement of observable effects that are expected from a set of actions

      3.   One common problem involves goals that are so poorly defined they cannot be measured

      4.   Feedback systems—methods employed to help us know whether goals were achieved

      5.   Benchmarks—short-term indicators of progress that show how things are going

      6.   Highlight 10.1: Guidelines for Planning an Evaluation

B.   Stage 2: Measurement

      1.   In this stage you refine the measures you will use to learn whether the stated goals have been accomplished

      2.   The more objective the measures, the higher the agreement rate about what they mean

      3.   Figure 10.5: Possible Outcome Measures

      4.   Quantitative evaluations offer certain kinds of information, and qualitative measures gather other information

      5.   Unanticipated consequences have been well documented in the research and can have a very negative impact on clients

C.   Stage 3: Sampling

      1.   The stage where we decide whether to gather data from all participants or sample part of the population

      2.   Statistical Package for the Social Sciences (SPSS)—software package that is an effective means for deciding appropriate sample size

      3   Systematic random sampling—simply divides the population by the desired sample size

      4.   Stratified random sampling—used to ensure that clients are proportionately represented in the sample. You assign numbers using a table of random numbers (a table of random numbers is a list of numbers produced by a computer and is used for selection of random sample members)

D.   Stage 4: Design

      1.   Concerned with selecting an appropriate design and eliminating other possible explanations for the observed outcomes

      2.   Creaming—selecting the "cream of the crop" for evaluation

      3.   Maturation—an internal process in which time itself affects the client

      4   Highlight 10.2: Six Common Evaluation Designs

          a.   Pre-experimental designs

              1)   One-group post-test only design—involves a single group in which progress is measured only at the end of the intervention

              2)   Post-test only design with non-equivalent groups—employs a comparison group that we hope will be similar to our experimental group

              3)   One-group pre-test/post-test design—assesses change over time using the same test, or a variation of the same test, at two points

          b.   Quasi-experimental designs

              1)   Nonequivalent control group designs—use two groups, both of which are given pre-tests and post-tests. The groups are similar on important variables, but there is no random assignment

              2)   Time series designs—use a series of observations before and after an intervention to gather longitudinal data to help spot patterns occurring over time

              3)   Multiple time series designs—are essentially the time series design with an added control group

c. Experimental designs—an ideal model, most are difficult to use in actual practice. They require both random assignment of subjects and a control group that receives no (or different) treatment to compare with the treatment group

E. Stage 5: Data gathering

   1. Data gathered for evaluating, whether goals are achieved or not, can come from several sources

   2. Figure 10.6: Sources of Data

   3. Instruments, tests, and scales

      a. Evaluating a program's effectiveness is often facilitated when the agency already uses standardized instruments for the quantitative analysis of clients' progress

      b. Figure 10.7: Sources of Measurement Instruments and Tests

      c. Important factors in instrument selection—validity, reliability, the sensitivity of the instrument to any changes caused by the intervention, length of the instrument, difficulty level for the client, and ease of use

      d. CES-D Scale

         1) Developed to help measure depression and its symptoms

         2) Figure 10.8: CES-D Scale

      e. Rosenberg Self-Esteem Scale

         1) A normed instrument that allows comparisons of those who complete it with a broader population

         2) Figure 10.9: Rosenberg Self-Esteem Scale

F. Stage 6: Data analysis

   1. Data analysis is the actual process of assessing the nature and significance of the results obtained

   2. Univariate analysis—used if you are only interested in explaining single variables and descriptive statistics

   3. Bivariate analysis—used to determine the degree of association between two variables (software packages such as SPSS and SASS [Statistical Analysis for the Social Sciences] make computations much easier)

4.   Multivariate analysis—used when examining three or more variables in relation to one another

      a.   Multivariate analysis generally requires use of a computer and statistical software designed specifically for this level of analysis

      b.   Regression analysis—a statistical procedure to determine how much of a change is due to the event under your control (independent variables) and how much to other factors

G.   Stage 7: Presentation of data—must communicate clearly to your intended audience the evaluation's results. A final evaluation report will likely contain six sections

1.   Part 1: Introduction

      a.   The introductory section reviews the situation that prompted the evaluation in the first place

      b.   Here you describe the research questions you want answered

2.   Part 2: Literature review

      a.   The literature review should provide a thorough summary of existing research on the topic under consideration

      b.   Because of the potential wealth of material available, you may have to be very specific about what ends up in your literature review

      c.   If relatively little information is available on a topic, that point should be included in your literature review

3.   Part 3: Methodology

      a.   The methodology section describes the evaluation design and the data collection methods used

      b.   Discuss the data analysis system selected

4.   Part 4: Results

      a.   The results component describes your findings with appropriate graphics (charts, graphs) and reports on the findings' importance

      b.   Figure 10.10: Pie Charts

      c.   Figure 10.11: Line Graph, Bar Chart, and a Three-Dimensional Bar Chart

5.   Part 5: Discussion

    a.   The discussion section briefly summarizes your findings, describes any unexpected findings, and describes any practice implications

    b.   Describe any limitations of the research

6.   Part 6: References and appendices

    a.   References include any sources (books, journal articles, and similar items) you consulted in preparing and conducting your evaluation

    b.   Appendices might include any documents too large to fit into the study itself

7.   Summary of data presentation

    a.   Always present data as clearly as possible

    b.   Use headings, titles and numbers to delineate data

    c.   Public presentation of data requires more use of graphics than might be required for a written report

IX.   Ethics and Values in Evaluation

A.   Whenever you contemplate using subjects as part of the evaluation (such as when interviewing or testing), those subjects must be volunteers, and they should know the risks associated with participation

B.   The privacy of participants should be zealously protected

C.   NASW Code of Ethics

D.   Human subjects committees now routinely review research proposals that may expose people to emotional or physical danger

E.   Clients must give permission before audio- or videotaping contact with them or before letting a third party observe sessions

F.   Sometimes values can become a barrier to effective action following an evaluation

G.   Perhaps the most important ethical consideration for doing evaluation is our obligation to clients

Exercise 10.1: Evaluating Your Practice

A. Brief Description
Students will identify primary reasons for evaluation of practice.

B. Objectives
Students will:
1. Identify primary reasons for evaluating their own practice.

C. Procedure
1. Divide the class into groups of four to six students.
2. Ask each group to identify as many possible reasons for evaluating their own practice as possible.
3. Have each group list their reasons on the board.
4. Discuss any reasons that students have not touched on.

D. Instructions for Students
With other members of your group, list as many reasons as you can for evaluating your own practice as a social worker.

E. Commentary
The exercise can be done in a larger class.

Exercise 10.2: Measures of Central Tendency

A. Brief Description
Students practice calculating measures of central tendency.

B. Objectives
Students will:
1. Calculate the mean, median, and mode of a group of scores.
2. Recognize the advantages of one measure over another.

C. Procedure
1. Have each person in the class write down their age on a piece of paper, fold it in half, and pass it to the front of the class.
2. List all age figures on the board in order from lowest to highest.
3. Ask students to calculate the mean, median, and mode for the age figures.
4. Lead a discussion about which measure of central tendency would be most useful in describing this class of students.

D. Instructions for Students
Write your age on a piece of paper, fold the paper and pass it to the instructor. After the instructor has placed all age figures on the board, calculate the mean, median, and mode for the ages listed.

E. Commentary
Any set of figures can be used for this exercise including income.

Exercise 10.3: Key Concepts

A.   Brief Description
Students will become more familiar with various key concepts from the chapter.

B.   Objectives
Students will:
1.   Recognize the difference between descriptive and inferential statistics.
2.   Become sensitive to the concept of statistical significance.
3.   Identify characteristics of random sampling.

C.   Procedure
1.   Divide class into small groups of four to six.
2.   Give the class the three problems listed in the box below and ask them to answer each question posed.
3.   Have each group report back to the larger group.

D.   Instructions for Students
In small groups, read the questions contained in the box and answer each question. Discuss answers within the group until you arrive at a consensus.

Questions to Consider:

A recent report said that the average age of residents in a small nursing home was 72 and most residents were women. Are the statistics used here likely to be descriptive or inferential? Why?

The community of Plantwart has an average per capita income of $15,000 while the neighboring community of Nosegay has a per capita income of $16,000. A friend says there is a real difference of $1000 between the two communities but the difference is not statistically significant. What does she mean by this?

A polling organization is using sampling to gather opinions about voting preferences from members of your community. If every person in your community has an equal chance of being selected to participate in the study, what type of sampling is being used?

E.   Commentary
This exercise may be accomplished in the larger class or with any other set of questions from the chapter.

Exercise: 10.4: Evaluation of Practice

A.   Brief Description
Students will consider ways to improve objectives to enhance evaluation.

B.   Objectives
Students will:
1.   Recognize problematic program objectives.
2.   Identify ways to improve the evaluation of program objectives.

C.   Procedure
      1.   Divide the class into small groups of four to six.
      2.   Assign all groups the task of responding to the questions shown in the box below.
      3.   Ask each group to report back on their answers.

D.   Instructions for Students
      In your small group, discuss the questions posed in the box below. Come up with as many possible responses as possible.

Exercise 10.5: Program Objectives

A.   Brief Description
      Students will evaluate a program objective and identify how to improve it using information from the chapter.

B.   Objectives
      Students will:
      1.   Evaluate a program objective using recommendations contained in the chapter.
      2.   Identify possible improvements in wording of the objective.

C.   Procedure
      1.   Review material on designing measurable objectives.
      2.   Divide the class into small workgroups of 5-6.
      3.   Ask each group to read the information in the following box and to answer both of the following questions.

Your field agency has a stated objective for its family enrichment program that reads as follows:
      "We will help each client improve his or her life."

1.   What potential problems might the agency have in evaluating its effectiveness in meeting this objective?

2.   How would you improve the objective? Write out your suggestion.

E.   Commentary
      This exercise can be done with either large or small groups using these or similar questions from the chapter. It can also be incorporated into a quiz or exam.

Exercise 10.6: Keeping It All Straight

A.   Brief Description
      Students will test their familiarity with a variety of evaluation concepts.

B.   Objectives
      Students will:
      1.   Test their familiarity with various evaluation and research concepts.
      2.   Identify concepts to which they need further exposure.

C.   Procedure
1.   Ask students to review the major concepts of the chapter
2.   Have students take the following quiz to identify any terms with which they are not yet sufficiently familiar.

D.   Instructions to Students
1.   Match the following concepts with the corresponding description.
2.   Identify any concepts with which you are still unfamiliar.

---

1. Baseline   _____   11. Median   _____
2. Control Group   _____   12. Mode   _____
3. Experimental Group _____   13. Standard Deviation   _____
4. Dependent Variable _____   14. Reliability   _____
5. Independent Variable _____   15. Validity   _____
6. Sampling   _____   16. Descriptive Statistics _____
7. Random Sample   _____   17. Inferential Statistics _____
8. Experimental Design _____   18. Outcome   _____
9. Quasi-Experimental Design _____ 19. Statistical Significance _____
10. Mean   _____   20. Chi-Square Test   _____

A.   A statistical procedure for comparing expected and observed frequencies.
B.   The most frequently observed score in a group of scores.
C.   A group used for comparison purposes.
D.   Using a subset of all clients seen by an agency rather than surveying the entire group.
E.   The group receiving an intervention.
F.   A design using control and experimental groups but not random assignment.
G.   The original amount or occurrence of a behavior or event.
H.   The behavior intervention is intended to change.
I.   The ability of an instrument to measure what it is supposed to measure.
J.   The arithmetic average of a group of numbers.
K.   A measure of the variability of a group of scores around a mean.
L.   A quality of life change resulting from social work intervention.
M.   The risk involved generalizing from a sample to the population as a whole.
N.   Statistics used to draw a conclusion about a population based on a sample of that population.
O.   The middle figure in a distribution of figures listed from highest to lowest or vice versa.
P.   The likelihood that a measurement will yield the same results at subsequent times.
Q.   The average age of a group of delinquent youth, for example.
R.   A social work intervention is an example of this type of variable.
S.   A subset chosen so that all members of the population have an equal chance of being selected.
T.   An elaborate method for evaluating an intervention; includes control groups, experimental groups, and random assignment of clients to one group or the other.

Exercise 10.7: Which Interventions Should You Evaluate?

A.   Brief Description
Students will be asked to decide the extent to which an intervention can be implemented given the available information.

B.   Objectives
Students will:
1.   Identify interventions that can be effectively evaluated using the tools described in this chapter.

C.   Procedure
1.   Divide the class into several small groups.
2.   Ask the groups to read the introductory statement and the four vignettes.
3.   Identify those situations (vignettes) that can be evaluated.
4.   Identify any vignettes where evaluation is not possible.
5.   Provide reasons for your decisions.

You will often have the opportunity to evaluate, but you may decide that some efforts simply are not necessary. Look at the following four vignettes, then decide which you would evaluate and explain why or why not.

Vignette 1: Nathan House Renovation
Nathan House is a shelter for runaways that is operated by your agency. A local service organization has offered to renovate Nathan House over a six-month period. Renovations will include paint, new carpeting and furniture, and new lighting. Would you evaluate this intervention? Explain your answer.

Vignette 2: Nathan House Legal Education Program
Runaways at Nathan House are expected to participate in a legal education program designed to make them aware of their rights and obligations under the law. The program is founded on the idea that residents will be less likely to get into further trouble if they understand the law. Should you attempt to evaluate this program? Why or why not?

Vignette 3: Drug Abuse Community Education Program
Nathan House is one of several agencies offering all residents an opportunity to learn about drugs and thus to help reduce the levels of drug abuse in the community. The program is based on a national model in use in other states and will begin in about six weeks. Would you recommend evaluating this program? Give your reasons.

Vignette 4: Council of Agency Executives Group
Your agency director is part of a new group composed of executives of all agencies serving adolescents in the community. The group meets once a month to share information and discuss community-wide problems. The director asks you if you think this group should be evaluated. Should this group's efforts be evaluated? Discuss your reasons.

A.   Brief Description
Students will identify appropriate program evaluation approaches for several different types of programs.

B.   Objectives
Students will:
1.   Test their understanding of several program evaluation approaches.
2.   Match evaluation methods with the needs of agency and types of programs being evaluated.

C.   Procedure
1.   Review the section on program evaluation approaches.
2.   Break the class into small groups.
3.   Ask the groups to respond to the scenarios contained in the following box.

D.   Instructions to Students
Since different types of programs may require different evaluation methods, it is important to know what methods work best with each intervention that we wish to assess. Read each of the scenarios below and discuss how you would evaluate the program.

> A: Evaluating Hospital Discharge Planning: You are the Director of Social Services at Our Lady of Perpetual Misery Hospital. Your unit is primarily involved in doing discharge planning, with three BSW social workers assigned to this function. Discharge planning involves working with the hospital medical staff to facilitate patients' transition following discharge. Typically, your unit helps clients return to their own homes, go to nursing homes for temporary care or on a permanent basis, or go to live with relatives. Your unit uses a variety of community services including transportation, medical equipment for use in the home, visiting nurses, home health care, and similar services. The hospital administrator has asked all directors to begin to consider how they might evaluate the effectiveness of their units. You want to develop an evaluation program that can be done with existing staff, does not intrude on your work with patients, and is relatively simple to implement. Explain the methods you will use to evaluate your unit's effectiveness.
>
> B: Evaluation of a Hospice Care Program: Your hospice program has been funded by the county for its first year of operation. As a condition of continued funding, you must develop an evaluation component that will allow the funding source to determine whether to continue your program next year. Patients come to you from area hospitals, nursing homes, and from their own homes. All are suffering from terminal illnesses ranging from AIDS to cancer to other life-ending diseases. Your hospice provides services to in-patients and to people in their own homes. Your evaluation plan should provide the county with data to justify your continued funding.
>
> C: Evaluating an Assertiveness Training Group: Your agency operates assertiveness training groups for women who are survivors of domestic violence. Each group lasts four weeks and consists of 6-8 women per group. You lead this group and are curious about whether members really become more assertive after leaving the group. Design an evaluation system that would help you answer this question.

D: Evaluating a Neighborhood Watch Program: You have helped the Green Oak neighborhood develop a neighborhood watch program to combat the many burglaries and auto thefts suffered by area residents. The police department was very cooperative in helping you establish this program, but your agency director isn't convinced that these kinds of programs are worthwhile. He questions why you spend your time on such activities. How would you design an evaluation program to show whether this type of program is effective in reducing crime?

Chapter 11
Advocacy and Social Action with Populations-at-Risk

I. **Introduction**

II. **Defining Advocacy, Social Action, Empowerment, and Populations-at-Risk**

    A.   Highlight 11.1: Key Terms

          1.   Advocacy—representing, championing, or defending the rights of others

          2.   Case advocacy—work on behalf of individuals and families

          3.   Cause advocacy—work on behalf of groups of people

          4.   Discrimination—negative treatment of individuals, often based upon their membership in some group (such as women) or upon some characteristic they share with others (such as a disability)

          5.   Empowerment—ensuring that others have the right to power, ability, and authority to achieve self-determination

          6.   Oppressed populations—refers to groups that experience serious limitations because others in power exploit them

          7.   Populations-at-risk—those groups in society most likely to suffer the consequences of, or be at risk for, discrimination, economic hardship, and oppression

          8.   Social action—a coordinated effort to achieve institutional change to meet a need, solve a social problem, correct an injustice, or enhance the quality of human life

          9.   Social and economic justice—exists when every individual has opportunities, rights, and responsibilities equal to those of all other members of a society

    B.   Defining advocacy

          1.   Advocacy—representing, championing, or defending the rights of others

          2.   Macro practice, in particular, often involves cause advocacy, which is work on behalf of groups of people who lack the ability to advocate for themselves

          3.   You are likely to pursue case advocacy in micro and mezzo practice with individuals and families

          4.   Social workers have a rich history of cause advocacy, including working for civil rights legislation and fighting for the rights of people with physical and emotional disabilities and for other populations-at-risk

          5.   Highlight 11.2: Advocacy Produces System Change

C. Defining social action

    1. Social action is a method of practice designed to place demands on a community to obtain needed resources, attain social and economic justice, enhance quality of life, and address social problems affecting disenfranchised and disadvantaged populations

    2. Highlight 11.3: Coordinated Social Action Efforts

D. Defining empowerment

    1. Empowerment is the use of strategies that increase the personal, interpersonal, or political power of people so that they can improve their own life situations

    2. Believing that people have both the right and capacity to achieve their goals is consistent with social work values, particularly self-determination

    3. Highlight 11.4: Caveats in Empowerment

E. Defining populations-at-risk

    1. Populations-at-risk are those groups in society most likely to experience and suffer the consequences of discrimination, economic hardship, and oppression

    2. Historically, among the groups most frequently experiencing these societal influences are women, lesbian and gay people, and persons of color

    3. Also includes elderly persons with physical, emotional, or developmental disabilities and those holding religious views significantly different from those of the rest of society

III. Populations-at-Risk

A. Factors contributing to populations being at-risk

    1. Physical differences

    2. Values and beliefs that differ from those of the dominant or more powerful segment of a society

    3. Preconceptions about the ability or competence of members of a group

    4. A result of our economic system

    5. Values are often behind other instances of discrimination and oppression

    6. Others in society may define a group as economically or socially insignificant

    7. When businesses decide to move away from communities where wages are considered too high

B.   Examples of populations-at-risk

1.   African Americans

a.   They are almost three times as likely to live below the poverty line as non-Hispanic whites

b.   Almost 20 percent have no health insurance; infant mortality rates are almost 80 percent higher than for whites; they are less likely to survive physical illnesses such as cancer and more likely to suffer from hypertension and strokes

c.   Black males are more than seven times more likely to die from homicides than are white males

d.   They constitute less than 13 percent of the total population; however, they make up more than 30 percent of those arrested in the U.S.

2.   Hispanic Americans

a.   They represent 31.5 percent of all federal prisoners in 2000; the percentage of juveniles incarcerated is increasing faster than other groups

b.   They are more likely to drop out of school and less likely to have completed four or more years of college than either blacks or whites

c.   Almost one-third lack health insurance

3.   Native Americans and Alaskan Natives

a.   They have some of the most serious health and social problems of all the groups in the nation

b.   In all categories of causes of death, they have a rate higher than that of the rest of the U.S. population

c.   The suicide rate is highest of all U.S. ethnic groups

d.   Twenty-nine percent have no health insurance

4.   Asian Americans and Pacific Islanders

a.   Many have great difficulty making the transition to an urban lifestyle due to their low proficiencies in the English language and agrarian and rural backgrounds

b.   Traditional customs and norms often clash with those of whites in America

c.   Reliance on family and clan for support often places them outside the usual formal networks of social service providers

221

5. Women

    a. They receive lower pay for the same jobs

    b. They are more likely to be subjected to sexual harassment in the workplace and maltreatment after surviving a sexual assault

    c. They are often denied the right to control her own body

6. Lesbian and gay persons

    a. They often experience discrimination in hiring for teaching and other jobs involving children

    b. Partners are denied the rights accorded other next of kin

    c. U.S. military still discriminates against them

7. Clients receiving public assistance

8. Other at-risk populations

    a. Homeless

    b. People with physical and mental disabilities

    c. Teenagers who have no plans for college

    d. Teens who have planned, or unplanned/unwanted pregnancies

C. The role of social workers with populations-at-risk

    1. Social workers are in an excellent position to help prevent populations from being placed at risk

    2. Social workers must be vigilant regarding how their agencies and other societal institutions interact with high-risk populations

    3. Social workers must alert themselves to the community's treatment of populations-at-risk

    4. Social workers will face some practical and ethical considerations with working to assist populations-at-risk

        a. Clients have the general right to self-determination

        b. Clients have the right to fail as well as to succeed

IV.   Advocacy

A.   Concerns about the use of advocacy

1.   Workers may be afraid of controversy, which is a natural consequence of advocating for an oppressed group or population-at-risk

2.   Workers may be unable to determine the outcomes of advocacy

3.   Workers may fear what will happen if they advocate for a change and the change actually occurs

B.   The value and limitations of advocacy

1.   The National Association of Social Workers' (NASW) and the Canadian Association of Social Workers' (CASW) ethical codes make it a worker's duty to engage in advocacy

2.   A major benefit of macro-level advocacy is that it can attack core problems rather than merely treat crisis situations

3.   Apathy is perhaps the most dangerous threat to progress in combating oppression and pursuing social and economic justice

C.   Agency commitment to advocacy

1.   Some agencies actively pursue outreach efforts to ensure that their services are available to populations-at-risk and groups underserved by existing agencies

2.   Some agencies do not see advocacy as an important part of their mission

D.   Opportunities for macro-level advocacy

1.   Highlight 11.5: Advocacy for Change—Thinking Big about Child Care

2.   Efforts to change policies and laws at the institutional, community, or other level

3.   Homophobia—irrational fear and loathing of homosexuals

E.   Principles of macro-level advocacy

1.   Advocates should work to increase accessibility of social services to clients

2.   Advocates must promote service delivery that does not detract from the dignity of the groups they serve

3.   Advocates should work to ensure equal access to all who are eligible

F. Guidelines for macro-level advocacy

 1. Be reasonable in what you undertake

 2. Teamwork often produces better outcomes

 3. Being an advocate sometimes requires being assertive

 4. Flexibility is a strength, not a weakness

 5. Accept that sometimes you win—sometimes you lose

 6. Be prepared to use a variety of strategies

G. Advocacy tactics

 1. Persuasion

  a. Questioning—asking the target system a series of questions designed to make them think about their original conclusion

  b. Objectivity or providing arguments on both sides of an issue—involves stating not only your opinions and facts, but also acknowledging the opinions, concerns, and facts of the other side

  c. Persistence—most people give up when they meet resistance

  d. Highlight 11.6: Advocacy in Action

 2. Fair hearings, grievances, and complaints—administrative procedures designed to ensure that clients or client groups, who have been denied benefits or rights to which they are entitled, get equitable treatment

  a. Fair hearings—an outside person (usually a state employee) is appointed to hear both sides of the argument

  b. Grievances—are usually a part of an agency's own policies

  c. Complaints—are similar to grievances but are provided for in certain laws

 3. Embarrassing the target of change

  a. Highlight 11.7: Embarrassing the Target

  b. Letters to the local newspaper, sit-ins, and demonstrations are tactics designed to embarrass (and inconvenience) the target

 4. Political pressure—public (tax-supported) organizations are more likely to be sensitive to the concerns of political figures who control them

5. Petitioning

    a. Petitioning is the act of collecting signatures on a piece of paper that asks an organization or agency to act in a specified manner

    b. Highlight 11.8: A Petition Form

V. Legislative Advocacy

A. Legislative advocacy—a macro-level intervention like other types of cause advocacy, specifically involves efforts to change legislation to benefit some category of clients

    1. Responsibility for legislative advocacy is part of being a social worker because so many decisions affecting social work programs, social workers, and clients are made in the legislative arena

    2. Realistic barriers reduce the likelihood of getting new legislation passed

    3. Even bills that seem to benefit everyone may not become law

    4. Even a legislator's agreement to support a bill may prove meaningless

B. Factors affecting legislative advocacy

    1. Financial or fiscal implications of a bill

    2. A bill's popularity

C. Steps in legislative advocacy

    1. Highlight 11.9: Steps in the Legislative Process

    2. Step 1: Developing and revising the draft bill

        a. Most ideas for laws are sent to an already established unit (sometimes called a legislative reference bureau)

        b. Because legislative reference bureaus work for the legislative body, it is difficult for social workers to have much direct impact on their work

        c. In the process of pursuing a macro intervention in the legislative arena, you will have to become something of an expert on the bill(s) in which you have an interest

    3. Step 2: Identifying, obtaining and maintaining the bill's supporters

        a. Every bill has some natural supporters

        b. It is equally important to predict who will be neutral or opposed to a bill

     c.   In many cases it is wise to meet with both supporters and opponents and go over actual copies of the draft bill

     d.   State and federal agencies are more likely to be successful in getting bills they support approved

4.   Step 3: Arrange for sponsorship of the bill

     a.   It is essential to identify legislators willing to introduce and work for passage of a bill

     b.   Legislators who easily win election or re-election (safe legislators) can often take riskier positions than those who worry that they may lose the next election

     c.   Whenever feasible, seek support from legislators in the majority party

5.   Step 4: Introducing the bill

     a.   Early bills give you more opportunity for lobbying and, if necessary, amending the bill to attract supporters

     b.   Lobbying—involves seeking direct access to lawmakers in order to influence legislation and public policy

6.   Step 5: Work with interest groups to broaden support for a bill

7.   Step 6: Educate the public

8.   Step 7: Influence legislative committee consideration

     a.   The specific committees that consider given bills are a potential focus of lobbying efforts

     b.   Suggestions for presenting testimony at public hearings

          1)   Identify those who will speak, in what order, and what they will say

          2)   Don't use professional terms that only those in your field will understand

          3)   It is permissible to use case examples to illustrate the impact of a specific bill

          4)   Use humor very carefully

          5)   Avoid hostility and focus testimony on the proposed legislation

        6)   Practice what you will say and dress professionally

        7)   Having the ability to get up in front of a group, describe a problem, propose a solution, and ask others to support the position is an important skill to macro practitioners

9.   Step 8: Influencing action on the floor

     a.   Most bills are modified by legislators once they reach the floor of the House or Senate

     b.   If at all possible, you and your supporters should be present for the debate on a bill

     c.   Do not become discouraged when a bill is amended

D.   Other ways to get involved

1.   An appropriate macro-level intervention is working for the election of candidates favorable to social work positions and issues

2.   Political Action for Candidate Election (PACE)—established by NASW to work for candidates who support social work values and ideals

3.   Highlight 11.10: Communicating with Elected Officials

4.   Some of the skills that social workers already possess, such as the ability to compromise and bargain, are particularly useful in the political arena

E.   Other political activities

1.   Registering voters

2.   Running for nonpartisan political office and seeking appointment to boards and commissions in their area of interest

3.   Becoming involved in local, state, and national campaigns as long as the activities take place outside the workplace

VI.   Social Action

A.   Alinsky's social action approach

1.   Power is essential to change the status quo

2.   Power is not the sum of what you actually have, but rather the sum of the appearance of what you have

3.   Power is not given to you; you acquire power by taking it from those who have it

4.   Use methods that are familiar to you (or the action system) and unfamiliar to the target system

5. All organizations have rules that they say they can live by

6. People should be organized around issues that are vital to them

7. Most people in power respond to political pressure

8. Successfully attacking a target requires a clear demarcation between good and evil, or haves and have-nots

9. Turn negatives into positives

10. Prepare yourself to propose an alternative

B. Concerns about social action

    1. Some of Alinsky's principles may be less useful today

        a. Enemies are harder to identify and the high-tech world of today makes the role of the media much more influential in affecting ideas, perceptions, and actions

        b. We need to connect people to existing sources of power both inside and outside the community

        c. The use of collaboration and coalitions are supported now to bring about change

        d. Reactive approaches do little to prevent them from occurring in the first place

    2. Social workers who violate rules and regulations end up putting themselves, their clients, and the profession at risk

    3. To be effective generalists, social workers must be flexible

    4. Highlight 11.11: Social Action on Behalf of the Homeless: Some Considerations

C. Legal action

    1. *Roe v. Wade* (1973)—women's right to an abortion

    2. *Brown v. Board of Education* (1954)—separate but equal school systems struck down

    3. First Nations Peoples—Court decisions have returned lands or required restitution to the plaintiff tribes

    4. The Americans with Disabilities Act has provided a means for courts to force an end to discrimination against people with disabilities

    5. Class action suits argue that an entire group has been hurt and needs the courts' help to remedy the problem

6.   Finding that the courts will help is an empowering experience for those long used to having no power

7.   Courts tend to be more immune to the political process

8.   Lawsuits can seemingly take forever to run their course, leaving you and your group waiting

9.   When you decide to use legal action to pursue your claim, others may brand you as a troublemaker

10.   Court injunctions are sought when immediate steps are needed to stop an impending action that, if allowed to proceed, could not be undone

D.   Participatory action research (PAR)

1.   This method involves people affected by a problem in efforts to study the issue, identify and carry out appropriate interventions, and evaluate the success of the effort

2.   The term action reflects the emphasis on members taking concrete steps to study, act, and evaluate

3.   PAR has found widespread acceptance in many countries

4.   The process is similar to the steps in any planned change project

5.   Figure 11.1: Model of Participatory Action Research

VII.   Empowerment

A.   Inherent in both social and legal action is a commitment to the principle of empowerment

B.   Oppression, exploitation, and the absence of alternatives all lower the opportunity to self-determine and can result in social and economic injustice

C.   Sharing power with clients may mean giving clients more role in deciding how agency resources are spent, organizing clients of the agency as a collective and dealing with them as a group, or creating alternative programs

D.   Your expert knowledge is a form of power that can further distance you from clients

E.   Demystifying what you do can empower clients

F.   Another source of power is the legitimate authority vested in you by the state

G.   The strengths perspective, so important to generalist practice, assumes that power resides in people and we should seek it through such things as refusing to label clients, avoiding paternalistic treatment of clients, and trusting clients to make appropriate decisions

Exercise 11.1: Populations-At-Risk

A.   Brief Description
Students discuss what places a population at risk.

B.   Objectives
Students will:
1.   Recognize factors that place a population at risk.
2.   Identify populations that are at risk.

C.   Procedure
1.   Divide class into small groups of 4-6.
2.   Ask the groups to respond to two questions: Identify at least 5 populations-at-risk served by social workers and what places the population at risk.
3.   Have each group report back to the larger group and list their responses on the board.

D.   Instructions for Students
In groups of 4-6, answer the following two questions:
1.   Identify at least 5 populations at risk served by social workers.
2.   What places these populations at risk?
3.   Report your responses back to the larger group.

E.   Commentary
This exercise can be done with any size group including using the entire class as a group.

Exercise 11.2: Advocacy

A.   Brief Description
Students discuss various aspects of advocacy.

B.   Objectives
Students will:
1.   Recognize the role of advocacy in improving services to clients.
2.   Examine advantages and disadvantages of certain forms of advocacy.

C.   Procedure
1.   Divide the class into three groups.
2.   Assign each group one of the following questions to discuss and decide.
3.   Ask each group to report their results to the rest of the class.

D.   Instructions for Students
Discuss one of the three questions below as assigned by the instructor. Be prepared to report your response back to the entire class.

1. What does it mean to say that advocacy should be designed to increase the accessibility of services for clients?
2. Discuss the advantages and disadvantages of two advocacy tactics: persuasion and embarrassing the target.
3. Under what circumstances would political pressure be an appropriate advocacy tactic?

E. Commentary
This exercise can be used with any number of small groups by adding more questions. It can also be used as a discussion starter with the entire class.

Exercise 11.3: Recalling Key Concepts

A. Brief Description
Students will connect key concepts to case examples and discuss their decisions.

B. Objectives
Students will:
1. Apply concepts from the chapter to case situations and provide the rationale for each decision.

C. Procedure
1. Divide class into small groups.
2. Ask students to review each case situation and respond to the questions following the case.

D. Instructions for Students
Review each of the case situations shown below. Using your knowledge of advocacy, answer each of the questions that follow the case illustration.

Miguel Gonzales is a social worker with A Family Affair, a counseling service for couples and families. During one of his sessions with the Chou Vang family, recent immigrants from Southeast Asia, he learns that the Vang children have been prevented from using the community swimming pool. According to Mrs. Vang, one of the lifeguards has called her children names and said they should go back to their own country. Miguel offers to help the family deal with this situation and agrees to talk to the city's recreation director who oversees the pool. Using the information given, answer each of the following queries.

1. Is Miguel engaged in cause advocacy or case advocacy as he seeks to help the Vang family? Explain your answer.

Miguel discovers that the director of recreation believes that the Vang children and other Hmong refugees should not be using the pool because they are not yet U.S. citizens. Miguel decides to challenge the director's decision by enlisting the help of the local Urban League. Together, they picket the swimming pool and invite the media to cover the event.

2. Does Miguel's strategy fall under the classification of social action? Why or why not?
3. What would be needed to empower the Vang family to solve this problem by themselves?
4. Do you consider the Vang family a population-at-risk? Explain your answer.

A.   Brief Description
Students will apply concepts related to populations-at-risk to their own living experiences.

B.   Objectives
Students will:
1.   Demonstrate awareness of populations-at-risk in various communities.

C.   Procedure
1.   Ask each student to work alone on the questions noted below.
2.   When students are finished, ask them to share their answers to each question.

D.   Instructions for Students
Read each of the questions listed below. Using your own experience and knowledge gained from this chapter, answer each question.

> 1.   Think about the place where you grew up. List any groups living in your community that you would classify as at-risk and give a brief explanation of why you listed them.
> 2.   Now think about where you are living today. List any groups in your present community that you would classify as at-risk. Again, give your reasons.
> 3.   Is every member of these groups at risk? Explain your answer.

Exercise 11.5: Assessing Your Experience as an Advocate

A.   Brief Description
Students will share experiences dealing with potential advocacy situations.

B.   Objectives
Students will:
1.   Think about advocacy situations they have encountered in their life.
2.   Identify different strategies that may have been more effective for these situations.

C.   Procedure
1.   Divide class into small groups.
2.   Ask each person in the group to read the following statement, share an advocacy experience they have had, and critique how it was handled.

D.   Instructions to Students
Read the following paragraph and respond to the questions listed.

> In the past you've probably come across situations when it was necessary to advocate for yourself or others. Describe such situation you encountered and list the actions you took. If you took no action, what considerations led you to decide not to act? What was the eventual outcome? Looking back, what do you think you should have done to increase your effectiveness?

E.   Commentary
This can also be used by calling on volunteers from the class, perhaps after the instructor has shared a similar experience.

Exercise 11.6: Using Advocacy Tactics

A.   Brief Description
Students will discuss four scenarios and decide which advocacy tactics are most appropriate for each.

B.   Objectives
Students will:
1.   Learn to apply appropriate advocacy tactics to different scenarios.

C.   Procedure
1.   Review five advocacy tactics that social workers might employ.
2.   Divide the class into groups.
3.   Ask each group to review each scenario indicating which advocacy tactic is likely to be most appropriate.
4.   Ask each group to share their decisions.

D.   Instructions to Students
Based on the information given in each of the scenarios below, indicate which advocacy tactics might be most appropriate.

Scenario 1: The state legislature is taking up the issue of property tax reform and is considering shifting financial responsibility for certain public assistance programs from the local community to the state. This would result in lower property taxes for everyone in the community but higher income taxes. You believe this would make the method of paying for welfare fairer and more progressive. Select the advocacy tactic that seems most appropriate for this situation and explain your choice.

Scenario 2: Neighbors in the Elm Terrace section of your community are upset by a proposal to widen their street to allow larger trucks into the area. Many residents are elderly, low-income, and politically inexperienced. Select the advocacy tactic you would use to oppose this proposal. Explain why you chose this tactic.

Scenario 3: Your agency director has been asked to hire at least one new Spanish-speaking worker to work with the growing Hispanic population served by your organization. He isn't convinced that there is sufficient justification for such a hire. He has kicked the issue down to you, his assistant director, for input. Assuming you support this proposal, what tactic would be most appropriate and why?

Scenario 4: Rosa Daniels has been suspended from school because she came to class wearing her hair in the braided fashion popular in Jamaica. Other teenagers are free to wear their hair in the latest fashion. However, the school's principal believes Rosa's hairdo is a sign of gang affiliation. If you were to advise the Daniels family, which advocacy tactic would you suggest and why?

Exercise 11.7: Understanding Alinsky

A.   Brief Description
Students will discuss some advocacy ideas proposed by Saul Alinsky.

B.   Objectives
Students will:
1.   Assess and evaluate the validity and appropriateness of ideas proposed by Saul Alinsky.
2.   Demonstrate critical thinking skills.

C.   Procedure
1.   Review material on Saul Alinsky.
2.   Read each of the statements listed below.
3.   Ask students to respond to each question and provide their rationale for each answer.

D.   Instructions for Students
Read each of the numbered items below and give your reasoned response to each.

---

1.   Saul Alinsky believed that power and the appearance of power are critical elements to the success of social action. Do you agree or disagree with his perspective? Give your reasons.
2.   Another Alinsky rule was that you always paint issues as a conflict between good and evil or the haves and have-nots. Do you agree with this argument in a current context? Give your reasons.

Chapter 12
Ethics and Ethical Dilemmas in Macro Practice

I.   **Introduction**

II.   **Professional Values and Ethics in Macro Contexts**

A.   Values are what you consider good or desirable

B.   Ethics are sets of principles that guide the behavior of professionals

C.   Five dimensions of ethical decision making (Cournoyer)

1.   Understand those legal duties that apply to all professional helpers

2.   Be familiar with the state, local, and federal laws and regulations that affect the profession and practice of social work in your locale

3.   Thoroughly comprehend the core social work values and be extremely familiar with the social work code of ethics

4.   Be able to identify those ethical principles and legal duties that pertain to specific social work practice situations

5.   When several competing obligations apply, you need to be able to decide which take precedence

D.   Ethical dilemmas

III. **The NASW Code of Ethics**

A.   Highlight 12.1: A Summary of the Ethical Standards in the NASW Code of Ethics

B.   The social workers' ethical responsibilities to clients

1.   1.01: Commitment to clients—the client should come first

2.   1.02: Self-determination—requires that clients know what the resources and choices are and the consequences of selecting any of them

3.   1.03: Informed consent—means that clients know the risks of social work services or other interventions, limitations imposed by managed care, costs of service, alternatives that are available, and their right to refuse to participate

4.   1.04: Competence—you must use interventions for which you have appropriate training or education

5.   1.05: Cultural competence and social diversity—strive to identify and appreciate the strengths inherent in any particular culture and recognize differences among cultures

   a.   Highlight 12.2: Ethical Boundaries and Spirituality

      1)   Religion—involves people's spiritual beliefs concerning the origin, character, and reason for being, usually based on the existence of some higher power or powers. These beliefs often include designated rituals and provide direction for what is considered moral or right

      2)   Spirituality—the individual search for meaning, purpose, and values that typically rises above everyday physical limitations and connects one to something greater than oneself

      3)   Social workers must develop sensitivity and competence in dealing with spiritual diversity, just as in dealing with cultural diversity

6.   1.06: Conflicts of interest—situations where the client's benefit is actually or potentially compromised by an action of the social worker

   a.   Dual or multiple relationships—occur when professionals assume two or more roles at the same time or sequentially with a client (such as blending a professional and nonprofessional relationship)

   b.   Examples of dual relationships include providing counseling to a relative or a friend's relative, socializing with clients, becoming emotionally or sexually involved with a client or former client

   c.   One of the more problematic areas of dual relationships is when a social worker is providing services to multiple people who have relationships with each other

7.   1.07: Privacy and confidentiality

   a.   Privacy—people's right to be free from other people's intrusion in their personal affairs

      1)   Information a social worker seeks should be clearly related to providing service, not information sought out of pure curiosity

      2)   Information learned from a client must be maintained in confidence

   b.   Confidentiality—the ethical principle that workers should not share information provided by or about a client unless that worker has the client's explicit permission to do so. This confidentiality is not absolute

236

       c.   New NASW Code of Ethics' references concerning how clients should be reported under certain circumstances: *"However, social workers' responsibility to the larger society or specific legal obligations may on limited occasions supersede the loyalty owed clients, and clients should be so advised. (Examples include when a social worker is required by law to report that a client has abused a child or has threatened to harm self or others) (NASW, 1999, 1.01)"*

       d.   The use of computers for maintaining records has opened up other possibilities for breaching confidentiality

8.   1.08: Access to records—clients should have reasonable access to records that concern them

9.   1.09: Sexual relationships—explicitly prohibits sexual activities or contact between current or former clients and workers, regardless of whether it is consensual. The prohibition extends to client's relatives or others with whom the client has a close relationship. It is also inappropriate to provide professional services to a client with whom one has had a prior sexual relationship

10.   1.10: Physical contact—it is prohibited; appropriate "culturally sensitive" physical contact is permitted as long as the worker sets clear boundaries for such contact

11.   1.11: Sexual harassment—explicitly prohibited and includes such actions as solicitation for sexual favors, verbal or physical sexually tinged contact, and advances

12.   1.12: Derogatory language—social workers are not to use derogatory language in any of their communication about or with clients

13.   1.13: Payment for services—social workers are responsible for establishing fair and reasonable fees that reflect accurately the services provided

14.   1.14: Clients who lack decision-making capacity—when you must act on behalf of clients with diminished capacities, it is critical that you take all reasonable actions to protect the clients' interests

15.   1.15: Interruption of services—continuity of service is an obligation of the worker that requires that appropriate efforts be made to ensure clients get services they need

16.   1.16: Termination of services—should occur when the professional relationship is no longer necessary or when it no longer is beneficial

C.   Social workers' ethical responsibilities to colleagues

1.   2.01: Respect—required to treat colleagues with respect and never to misrepresent the competence and views of their coworkers

2.   2.02: Confidentiality—obligated to maintain in confidence information provided by colleagues in their professional capacity

3.   2.03: Interdisciplinary collaboration—the well-being of clients is the primary basis for collaboration among professionals on an interdisciplinary team

4.   2.04: Disputes involving colleagues—never take advantage of a dispute involving colleagues and their employers for their own interests nor exploit clients in disputes with colleagues

5.   2.05: Consultation—the act of seeking help from someone with expertise in a subject to devise a plan or solve a problem should involve only a colleague, administrator, or another person who has the appropriate competence or experience

6.   2.06: Referral for services—requires that the worker take steps to ensure an effective referral including, with clients' permission, providing all appropriate information

7.   2.07: Sexual relationships—between supervisors and supervisees are prohibited, as are such activities between students and field supervisors or in any other situation where one worker exercises authority over another. Sexual relationships between colleagues in other situations that may create a conflict of interest should be avoided

8.   2.08: Sexual harassment—workers are not to engage in sexual harassment of supervisees, students, or colleagues

9.   2.09: Impairment of colleagues—if you are aware of a colleague's impairment or incompetence, you must consult with that individual (if possible) and help the person seek help

10.   2.10: Incompetence of colleagues—if you are aware of a colleague's impairment or incompetence, you must consult with that individual (if possible) and help the person seek help

11.   2.11: Unethical conduct of colleagues—whenever possible you are obligated to prevent, expose, or otherwise discourage the unethical behavior of colleagues

D.   Social workers' ethical responsibilities in practice settings

1.   3.01: Supervision and consultation—no one should purport to provide either without the requisite knowledge and skill, and both consultants and supervisors should operate only within their specific areas of knowledge and competence

2.   3.02: Education and training—teachers, trainers, and field instructors are required to base their instruction on the most up-to-date information available, and only operate within their areas of competence

3.   3.03: Performance evaluation—evaluators are obliged to conduct their evaluations in a fair manner, based upon clear performance criteria, and in a way that is considerate of the person being evaluated

4.   3.04: Client records—ensure that documentation in records is accurate and clearly identifies the services given

5.   3.05: Billing—ensure accurate representation of the type and extent of services provided and clearly identify the service provider

6.   3.06: Client transfer—prior to accepting a client for service, the social worker should determine whether the client has an on-going professional relationship with another service provider

7.   3.07: Administration—social work administrators are responsible for advocating for sufficient resources to meet client needs and to ensure adequate staff supervision, and that the employing environment supports compliance with the code

8.   3.08: Continuing education and staff development—both administrators and supervisors are responsible for providing or arranging continuing education and staff development for those they supervise

9.   3.09: Commitment to employers—adhere to commitments to employing organizations and to do our best to improve agency policy, procedures, and services provided to clients

    a.   Help make employers aware of our obligations under the code of ethics and of the code's impact on social work practice

    b.   When there is a conflict between policies and the code, the worker is obliged to seek changes in the former

    c.   It is the social worker's responsibility to prevent or end discrimination in employment practices or work assignments

    d.   The social worker is expected to make appropriate use of agency resources, conserve funds when possible, and never to employ funds for unintended purposes

10.   3.10: Labor-management disputes—the code of ethics specifically allows social workers to participate in labor unions to improve both services to clients and working conditions

E.   Social workers' ethical responsibilities as professionals

1.   4.01: Competence—it is imperative that we accept employment or professional responsibilities only when we have the ability to perform those duties satisfactorily

2.   4.02: Discrimination

    a.   Social workers are expressly forbidden to engage in any form of discrimination based upon race, ethnicity, religion, age, sex, disability, marital status, national origin, color, sexual orientation, or political belief

b.   Highlight 12.3 Combating Your Own Stereotypes and Prejudices

      1)   Carefully observe and monitor your thoughts when interacting with anyone belonging to a group with characteristics significantly different from your own

      2)   Identify exactly how you treat this person differently

      3)   Gradually change your behavior toward the identified person, bringing it more in line with your behavior toward "nondifferent" people

      4)   Monitor your progress in combating your stereotypes and prejudices

      5)   Maintain a perspective that appreciates and respects both individual and cultural differences

3.   4.03: Private conduct—social workers must not allow their private conduct to interfere with their professional responsibilities

4.   4.04: Dishonesty, fraud, and deception—these have no place in the practice of social work

5.   4.05: Impairment—social workers must not let these difficulties interfere with their professional performance or harm those to whom they have a professional obligation

6.   4.06: Misrepresentation—social workers must be careful to not allow statements or actions as private citizens to be misconstrued as representing the social work profession or one's employing agency

7.   4.07: Solicitations—social workers should not solicit clients in any way that takes advantage of their vulnerability nor should they ask clients to provide testimonials of their service to them

8.   4.08: Acknowledging credit—social workers claiming credit for work that they have not done, or submitting as their own work done by others, is a violation of the code

F.   Social workers' ethical responsibilities to the social work profession

1.   5.01: Integrity of the profession—social workers seek to promote and maintain the highest practice standards

2.   5.02: Evaluation and research—social workers ensure that their own practice reflects the best practices of their profession

240

G.   Social workers' ethical responsibilities to the broader society

1.   6.01: Social welfare—social workers are expected to act to benefit the general welfare of society at all levels

2.   6.02: Public participation—social workers should encourage the public's involvement in the development and improvement of public policy

3.   6.03: Public emergencies—social workers should offer their professional services to the extent possible and with consideration of the needs of the public

4.   6.04: Social and political action—the goals of providing people equal access to all critical societal resources require that social workers pursue appropriate political and social action

IV.   Personal Values

A.   It is important to separate your personal values from professional, objective judgments in the macro context

B.   When confronted with any macro situation, you must carefully identify your personal values and distinguish them from what is in your client system's best interest from that system's own perspective

V.   Types of Ethical Issues Confronting Agency Workers

VI.   Ethical Absolutism versus Ethical Relativism

A.   Ethical absolutism—assumes that moral laws exist to govern ethical decision making in virtually any situation

B.   Ethical relativism—requires the evaluation of any particular action on the basis of its potential consequences. The emphasis is on *results* rather than on *principles*

VII.   Ethical Dilemmas

A.   Ethical dilemmas—problematic situations whose possible solutions all offer imperfect and unsatisfactory answers

B.   In an ethical dilemma, we are faced with a situation in which a decision must be made under circumstances that set two or more ethical principles in conflict

VIII.   Facing an Ethical Dilemma: Decision-Making Steps

A.   Figure 12.1: Conceptualizing an Ethical Dilemma

B.   Step 1: Recognize the problem

C.   Step 2: Investigate the variables

D.   Step 3: Get feedback from others

E. Step 4: Appraise the values that apply to the dilemma

F. Step 5: Evaluate the dilemma

G. Step 6: Identify and think about possible alternatives

H. Step 7: Weigh the pros and cons of each alternative

I. Step 8: Make your decision

IX. Ranking Ethical Principles

A. Reamer's guide to ethical decision-making

    1. Rules about basic survival supersede rules governing lesser actions

    2. One person's right to well-being supersedes another person's right to self-determination

    3. One person's right to self-determination supersedes that same person's right to well-being

    4. Obeying rules you have agreed to support supersedes the right to freely break these rules

    5. People's right to well-being supersedes adherence to rules you have agreed to support

    6. Preventing harm and fulfilling basic needs supersedes withholding your own property

    7. Postscript

B. Dolgoff, Loewenberg, and Harrington's "Ethical Principles Screen"

    1. Figure 12.2: A Hierarchy of Ethical Rights: ETHICS for U

        a. **E—Exist** with their basic needs met (Life)

        b. **T—Treatment** that is fair and equal (Equality)

        c. **H—Have** free choice and freedom (Autonomy)

        d. **I—Injury** that is minimal or nonexistent (Least harm)

        e. **C—Cultivate** a good quality of life (Quality of life)

        f. **S—Secure** their privacy and confidentiality (Privacy)

        g. **U—Understand** the truth and receive available information (Truthfulness)

2. Principle 1: People have the right to *Exist* with their basic needs met (life)

3. Principle 2: People have the right to *Treatment* that is fair and equal (equality)

4. Principle 3: People have the right to *Have* free choice and freedom (autonomy)

5. Principle 4: People have the right to *Injury* that is minimal or nonexistent (least harm)

6. Principle 5: People have a right to *Cultivate* a good quality of life (quality of life)

7. Principle 6: People have the right to *Secure* their privacy and confidentiality (privacy)

8. Principle 7: People have the right to *Understand* the truth and receive available information (truthfulness)

X. Ethical Dilemmas in Macro Contexts

A. Distributing limited resources (four variables to consider when trying to make the right distribution of scarce resources)

1. Equality

2. Need

3. Compensation

4. Contribution

B. Community support (or the lack thereof) for service provision

C. Relationships with colleagues

1. Choices when dealing with colleagues' unethical behavior

a. You can simply ignore the behavior, the "out of sight, out of mind" attitude

b. Approach the colleague yourself and share your concerns with him or her informally

c. You can inform your supervisor about the situation

d. In the event that the colleague is an NASW member, you can bring the unethical behavior to the attention of the local NASW chapter for censure

e. You can bring it to the attention of the state licensing board for professional social workers

f. Consider whistle-blowing

2.   Highlight 12.4: Whistle Blowing

  a. Whistle-blowing—the act of informing on another or making public an individual's, group's, or organization's corrupt, wrong, illegal, inefficient, or hazardous behavior

  b. The choice of whether to blow the whistle should be based upon the seriousness and the harm involved, the quality of the evidence of wrongdoing, the impact on both the agency and the perpetrator, the motivation of the whistle-blower and other options available

  c. Before blowing the whistle on agency or colleagues, consider four questions

    1) How great is the threat to the potential victims?

    2) What type and quality of proof do you have available that the wrongdoing has occurred or is going on?

    3) Will less severe alternative measures remedy the problem?

    4) Can you assume the burden of risk?

  d. Recommendations to consider before blowing the whistle

    1) Be certain that you clearly define the variables and issues involved

    2) Know what your rights are

    3) Be prepared for the consequences

    4) Follow the chain of command

    5) Establish a clearly defined plan of action

D. Engaging in sexual activities with clients

E. Neglecting child maltreatment

F. Highlight 12.5: Negative Responsibility

  1. Positive responsibility—responsibility for your own behavior

  2. Negative responsibility—responsibility for those actions you choose *not* to take

G. Incompetence due to personal problems

H. Conforming to agency policy

I. Highlight 12.6: Agency Policy and Ethics in a Multicultural Context

    1. Recommendations for applying ethical principles in multicultural contexts

        a. Anticipate potential conflict

        b. Assess the cultural sensitivity of your ethical code

        c. Balance culture and the ethical code

    2. Cultural encapsulation—the perspective characterized by defining reality according to one set of cultural assumptions, insensitivity to cultural variations, irrational adherence to one's own beliefs as being the only right ones, and an overly simplified view of both reality and problem resolution

    3. Ten conditions that tend to characterize cultural encapsulation in agencies and their staffs

        a. All persons are measured according to the same hypothetical "normal" standards of behavior, irrespective of their culturally different contexts

        b. Individualism is presumed to be more appropriate than a collectivist perspective in all settings

        c. Professional boundaries are narrowly defined, and interdisciplinary cooperation is discouraged

        d. Psychological health is described primarily in abstractions [using technical jargon and vague labels], with little or no attention to [how people effectively function in their unique] cultural context

        e. Dependency [on others including family or community members] is always considered to be an undesirable or even a neurotic condition

        f. A person's support system is not normally considered relevant to any analysis of the person's psychological health

        g. Only linear, "cause-effect" thinking is accepted as scientific and appropriate

        h. The individual is usually or always expected to adjust to fit the system

        i. The historical roots of a person's background are disregarded or minimalized

        j. The [social worker] presumes her- or himself to be free of racism and cultural bias

J.   Breaching confidentiality in a macro context

1.   Absolute confidentiality—the clients' confidence will not be broken no matter what

2.   Relative confidentiality—professional practitioners may have to break confidentiality under compelling circumstances

3.   Eight common reasons for breaking confidentiality

   a.   When a court appoints a social worker to evaluate a person, that worker is obligated to provide the court with information about the client

   b.   In the event that a worker determines that a client is a potential suicide risk, that worker should inform the appropriate helping body

   c.   When a client sues a social worker, such as for malpractice, the worker may have to share information about the client

   d.   When a client introduces "mental condition" as a claim or defense in a court action, the worker may be forced to respond to this claim

   e.   Workers must report confidential information in the event that a minor is being maltreated

   f.   A worker must report information and get help for a client who the worker suspects has such a severe mental condition that the client requires hospitalization

   g.   When otherwise confidential information is made an issue in court, a worker must respond

   h.   Social workers must report to the appropriate authorities when a client reveals that she is going to harm someone else

4.   Communication with other professionals

5.   Administrative record-keeping

6.   Insurance company requirements

7.   Police concerns

K.   Co-optation versus cooperation

1.   Co-optation—refers to eliminating opposition to a cause, plan, or organization by assimilating opponents into the group favoring the cause, plan, or organization

2.   Cooperation—involves different factions working together to achieve some mutually agreed-upon goal without either faction losing its own identity

L.   Conflict of interest

M.   Potential harm to participants

N.   Stigmatization tactics

      1.   Stigmatization—identifying or describing someone or something in disgraceful, contemptuous, or reproachful terms

      2.   Recognize realistically that there are few permanent friends, allies, or enemies in a professional context

O.   Furthering ethical practice in agency settings

Experiential Exercises and Classroom Simulations

Exercise 12.1: NASW Code of Ethics

A.   Brief Description
Students discuss core values of the Code of Ethics and relate the Dolgoff, Loewenberg, and Harrington's (2005) hierarchy of ethical principles to the Code.

B.   Objectives
Students will:
      1.   Recognize core values undergirding the NASW Code of Ethics.
      2.   Relate the work of Dolgoff and his colleagues (2005) to the Code.

C.   Procedure
      1.   Use this exercise with the entire class as a discussion starter.
      2.   Ask students to identify each of the six core values underpinning the Code of Ethics.
      3.   Place these core values on the board and ask the students to define each of them using their own words.
      4.   Ask students how the hierarchy of ethical principles can be used by a social worker adhering to the Code of Ethics.

D.   Instructions for Students
      1.   The six core values in the NASW Code of Ethics include: (1) service, (2) social justice, (3) dignity and worth of the person, (4) the importance of human relationships, (5) integrity, and (6) competence. Define each of these concepts in your own words.
      2.   How does each relate to the Dolgoff et al. (2005) hierarchy of ethical principles?

E.   Commentary
This exercise can also be conducted using small groups of 4 to 6 students.

Exercise 12.2: Using an Ethical Principles Screen

A.   Brief Description
Students discuss the use of the Dolgoff et al. (2005) Ethical Principles Screen for making appropriate practice decisions.

B.   Objectives
Students will:
1.   Utilize an ethical screen for making an appropriate practice decision.
2.   Identify situations where organizational guidelines clash with ethical principles.

C.   Procedure
1.   Review the Dolgoff et al. (2005) Ethical Principles Screen.
2.   Divide the class into groups of 4-6 students.
3.   Give each group the scenario noted in the box below and ask them to decide as a group what action is appropriate.
4.   Ask each group to report back to the entire class.

D.   Instructions for Students
In your groups, review the case situation below. Discuss your response to the case and what you would advise Manny and his social worker to do.

Using Ethical Screens
Manny H. has told his social worker that he intends to hurt his ex-girlfriend who he says "dumped him" for another guy. According to the Dolgoff et al. (2005) Ethical Principles Screen, a client has a right to autonomy and self-determination, confidentiality and privacy. Yet the social worker is concerned about possible harm to Manny's ex-girlfriend. What principles from the ethical screen would apply here? Manny's agency has a policy that attempts to ensure absolute confidentiality to clients and discourages workers from talking about cases with other agencies without a written release of information from the client. What should Manny and the social worker do?

E.   Commentary
The exercise can be used with a large group to get discussion going. Additional scenarios can also be created by the instructor with a different one being given to each group of students.

Exercise 12.3: Addressing Ethical Dilemmas

A.   Brief Description
Students address a range of ethical dilemmas, apply the Ethical Principles Screen, and propose solutions.

B.   Objectives
Students will:
1.   Discuss a range of ethical dilemmas that may occur in macro practice contexts.
2.   Apply the Ethical Principles Screen (Ethics for U) for each.
3.   Propose courses of action.

C. Procedure
   1. Review the Ethical Principles Screen (Ethics for U) in the text and the various ethical dilemmas in macro contexts that social workers might encounter.
   2. Using either a small group format or a full class discussion, instruct students to apply Ethics for U to each problematic vignette and propose a viable solution.

CASE SCENARIO A (Distributing Limited Resources): The family services agency where you work counseling survivors of domestic violence has suffered significant budget cuts. The agency administration has indicated that it will eliminate some services in order to stay afloat. Potentially targeted programs include day-care for working parents, sex education and contraception counseling for teens, or the thriving but expensive foreign adoptions program. The agency's other alternatives might include elimination of your own domestic violence program, decreasing staff for all programs including your own, or significantly cutting workers' salaries (including your own) across the board.

The community has depended on your agency's provision of its various services for many years. Thus, adequate alternate services do not exist in your community.

---

   1. Which principles in *ETHICS for U* might apply to this situation?
   2. How can you use the Ethical Principles Screen in deciding how best to cut expenses?
   3. As a social worker, what would *you* do in this situation?

CASE SCENARIO B (Colleagues' Sexual Involvement with Clients): You see a professional colleague engaging in what you consider unethical behavior. Twice you have seen him out in the community on dates with women you know to be his clients. It would be very uncomfortable for you to confront him about this behavior. Informing your supervisor seems like tattling.

---

   1. Which ethical principles in *ETHICS for U* might apply to this situation?
   2. How can you use the principles' ranking in deciding what to do in this situation?
   3. As a social worker, what would *you* do in this situation?

CASE SCENARIO C (Whistle-blowing): (*Whistle-blowing* is the act of informing on another or making public an individual's, group's or organization's corrupt, wrong, illegal, inefficient, or hazardous behavior.) You are a public assistance worker facing an ethical dilemma concerning whether or not to blow the whistle on a newly promoted supervisor (Reamer, 1990). You have worked at the agency for almost two years, and you are increasingly frustrated by the attitudes and work habits of a number of your immediate colleagues. They seem to spend as little time as possible with clients, even denying them necessary and appropriate assistance if the worker doesn't have time to complete all the necessary paperwork. In other cases, workers bend the rules to give clients benefits to which they are not entitled. For instance, many clients work as domestic help and are paid in cash, and workers do not always report all the clients' income. Workers simply make decisions according to their own discretion. Additionally, you note that workers consistently pad their travel expense accounts.

You are appalled by this behavior, and although you don't like the thought of "making waves," you finally confide your concerns to your friend and colleague Zenda. Zenda "pooh-poohs" your concerns condescendingly, remarking that such violations bend rules that aren't very good to begin with. She explains that such worker discretion is really an informal agency policy and adds that padding travel expense accounts is universally accepted as a means of increasing workers' relatively meager salaries. Zenda tries to soothe you and arrest your concerns, but it doesn't work. You decide that from now on you had best keep your concerns to yourself until you can figure out what to do about them.

Abruptly you find out that Zenda has been promoted and is your new unit supervisor. You are stunned. How can Zenda maintain order and help supervisees follow agency and other regulations when Zenda herself typically violates them?

What can you do? Ignore the whole situation? Confront your colleagues about their behavior? Confront Zenda again, even though it did no good the first time? Report your concerns to someone higher up in the administration? If you do and Zenda considers you a traitor, how miserable can Zenda make your life as an employee? Should you report the problem to NASW or the State Licensing Board? Should you blow the whistle to the press? How long do you think you'll keep your job if you take the problem outside established agency channels? Should you quit?

1. Discuss which principles in *ETHICS for U* might apply to this situation?
2. How can you use the principles' ranking to come to a decision?
3. As a social worker, what would *you* do in this situation?

CASE SCENARIO D (Racist Individual and Organizational Behavior): The private social service agency you work for does not have a formal affirmative action policy for hiring personnel. You have heard the agency director make several lewd racial remarks and jokes. You cannot believe he has gotten away with it. You have only worked for the agency for three months of your six-month probationary period, so you could be dismissed in the blink of an eye. The agency has no minorities of color on staff though it has clients who are minorities of color.[1] You believe that recruiting staff who are minorities of color is essential to the agency's ability to perform its functions. You also think the staff and the agency director need feedback in order to change their prejudicial and discriminatory behavior.

What is your role? Should you look away and pretend you don't know anything is wrong? Should you charge into the Director's office like a bull in a china shop and complain? Can you talk to other staff to see what they think? Should you contact the agency's board of directors? Should you contact the press or some external regulatory agency and blow the whistle? Should you quit your job?

1. Which principles in *ETHICS for U* might apply to this situation?
2. How can you use the principles' ranking to come to a decision?
3. As a social worker, what would *you* do in this situation?

CASE SCENARIO E (Initiating Community Action "Against the Flow"): The community in which you live and work provides no services for homeless people, despite the fact that their numbers are escalating. Every day on your way to and from work you pass at least a half dozen people roaming the urban streets. Many times you see children with them, dirty, probably hungry, and obviously not in school. Most people at your agency don't really want to talk about it. You get the feeling that colleagues, supervisors, and administrators think they have enough to do already. Work demands continue to increase while funding resources shrink.

---

[1] *Minority* is "one term for a group, or a member of a group, of people of a distinct racial, religious, ethnic, or political identity that is smaller or less powerful than the community's controlling group" (Barker, 2003, p. 274). The term *minorities of color* concerns "people who have minority status because their skin color differs from that of the community's predominant group. In the United States, the term usually refers to African Americans, Asian Americans, American Indians, and certain other minority groups" (Barker, 2003, p. 274).

1. Which ethical principles in *ETHICS for U* might apply to this situation?
2. How can you use the principles' ranking to come to a decision?
3. As a social worker, what would *you* do in this situation?

CASE SCENARIO F (Lack of Community Support): You are a worker at a rural county social services agency. You, other colleagues, and agency administration have identified a significant lesbian and gay population in the area. You and the other professionals would like to implement a new program providing support groups for lesbian and gay people dealing with several issues, including single parenthood, legal difficulties such as housing discrimination, and other issues. Several relatively powerful members of the County Board get wind of your idea and react with almost violent frenzy. They band together with a number of citizens who adamantly refuse to allow expenditure of public resources on lesbian and gay people.

---

1. Which principles in *ETHICS for U* might apply to this situation?
2. How can you use the principles' ranking in coming to a decision?
3. As a social worker, what would you do in this situation?

Chapter 13
Working with the Courts

I.   **The Significance of the Legal System**

    A.   Social workers and others serving as advocates for those denied social and economic justice have repeatedly asked the court system to intervene

    B.   Seven areas basic to all social work practice and its relationship to the legal system

        1.   Confidentiality

        2.   Clients' consent to intervention

        3.   Legal rights of clients

        4.   Documentation of evidence in the case record

        5.   Legal authority for practice

        6.   Testimony in court

        7.   Legal duties implicit in professional practice

II.   **Functions of Professional Terminology**

    A.   To shorten communication and ensure shared meaning

    B.   To establish boundaries between users of such terms, such as the designated professional and those who do not belong to these professions

III.   **Important Legal Terms**

    A.   Highlight 13.1: Legal Terminology in Your Area of Practice

    B.   Laws—those standards, principles, processes, and rules that are adopted, administered, and enforced by a governmental authority and that regulate behavior by setting forth what people may and may not do and how they may do what they can do

    C.   Criminal laws—those that govern the operation of state and federal criminal justice systems

    D.   Civil laws—those that govern the behavior of individuals or organizations; however, they are materially different from criminal law in that it is usually private citizens who exercise the power to punish the person who has broken a civil law

E.   Violations—offenses that involve the breaking of a law or rule. Violation and offense can be used interchangeably

    1.   Criminal violations—offenses penalized by fine and/or imprisonment or probation

        a.   Felonies—crimes considered serious enough to be punishable by imprisonment for a term of one or more years

        b.   Misdemeanors—less serious crimes punishable by confinement in a city or county jail for a period of less than one year

    2.   Civil offenses—the sole penalty is forfeiture of money or goods

    3.   Ordinance offenses—violation of civil (noncriminal) laws enacted by a local unit of municipal government. Conviction for a noncriminal offense can draw a fine but not incarceration of the offender

F.   Jurisdiction—authority to act

    1.   Juvenile court has jurisdiction over most illegal acts committed by children (people under age 18); however, there are exceptions

        a.   Delinquency—definitions typically include the following factors: age and the identified behavior, often defined as a behavior that would be a law violation if committed by an adult

        b.   Children in need of services—is often defined using incorporation of status offenses (acts that if committed by an adult would not be illegal, such as truancy or curfew violations)

        c.   Children referred to as dependent, neglected, or abused

    2.   Initially established in the early 1900s as family courts, such legal arrangements were organized and run on a more informal, often paternalistic model, where there was legal recourse to appeal for rights similar to those of an adult

    3.   Social workers involved in jurisdictional disputes over procedures are well advised to consult with their supervisors or corporation counsel

G.   Allegation—the assertion of one side in a lawsuit setting out what that party expects to prove at the trial

H.   Court process

    1.   Adjudication—phase where facts are presented, and the charge is determined by a judge or a jury

    2.   Disposition—occurs after adjudication and refers to the sentence determination

I. Due process

  1. The 14th Amendment to the U.S. Constitution mandates that courts must document that it guarantees the protection of a fair trial (innocent until proven guilty)

  2. *In re Gault*, 1967—due process rights protect juveniles as well as adults

  3. "Best interest of the child" concept—decision making by any authority figure should reflect the adult's judgment as to the best alternative for the child

J. Stipulation—both parties agreeing on the point of information or fact

K. Burden of proof—rests on the prosecution or plaintiff (the party making the complaint)

L. Standards of proof—level or degree of certainty needed to prove an allegation in court

  1. Beyond a reasonable doubt—used in criminal or delinquency cases (*In re Winship*, 1970). It necessitates evidence that is entirely convincing to a moral certainty (sometimes referred to as 90 percent sure)

  2. Clear and convincing evidence—refers to approximately a 70 percent degree of certainty. Such a degree may be used in cases of child abuse or neglect

  3. Preponderance of the evidence—51 percent minimum certainty; it is the standard of proof applied in civil (as opposed to criminal) cases; some states also use this standard for child abuse and neglect cases

M. Evidence

  1. Real evidence—consists of tangible objects, such as weapons or photographs

  2. Documentary evidence—pertains to certified documents usually identified and authenticated by proper authorities

  3. Testimony—refers to the actual interviewing of a witness by the defendant or, more typically, his or her attorney

  4. Hearsay evidence—refers to testimony about a statement made outside the courtroom

  5. Quality of evidence

    a. The source must be competent (qualified) to make the observation

    b. Information must be relevant, meaning it must bear on the proceeding at hand

    c. Information must be material and thus have important consequences for the case

N.   Witnesses

   1.   Lay (factual)—refers to one who is limited in testimony to what she or he saw, heard, smelled, or touched

   2.   Expert—is rendered "qualified" by the judge to give opinions in a particular area of expertise. Judges vary greatly in admissibility of social workers as expert witnesses

O.   Guardian *Ad Litem*—appointed by the court to represent the individual's best interests; to be determined by the guardian *ad litem*, not by what the client might identify as his or her preferences

P.   Confidentiality and privileged communication

   1.   Confidentiality—refers to the principle that information shared between the client and social worker is intended to be kept private. As both a professional and a legal term, it is seldom as pure as inexperienced social workers or clients might expect

   2.   Privileged communication—refers to information shared between the client and another party that is protected by statute

   3.   Contempt of court—refers to willful disobedience to or open disrespect for the rules of the court

   4.   *Jaffee v. Redmond*, 518 U.S. 1 (1996) recognized that, like psychologists and psychiatrists, communications between clients and social workers should remain confidential and that this is essential to psychiatric treatment

Q.   Subpoena—required to appear in court

   1.   Often the subpoena requires that the professional bring any and all paperwork, files, reports, and informal notes as well

   2.   The NASW's Code of Ethics notes that the professional maintains client confidences "except for compelling professional reasons"

   3.   The social worker should keep a detailed record on what steps were taken to ensure compliance with the order but still protect the client as much as possible

   4.   The area of subpoenaed documents often creates a potential conflict between legal requirements and professional ethics

IV. **Differences Between Courtroom Protocol and Social Work Practice**

    A.   Figure 13.1: Social Work Practice versus Courtroom Protocol

    B.   Adversarial versus conjoint problem solving

           1.   For the duration of the proceedings in court, plaintiff and defendant become adversaries

           2.   Social work practice is much more likely to be based on a model of planned change that stresses a conjoint solution

           3.   Highlight 13.2: Court is Like a Stage

    C.   Formal versus informal atmosphere

           1.   A court of law is conducted according to historical precedents that dictate the setting, appearance of the participants, and rules of conduct

           2.   Practitioners are advised to prepare themselves for the differences in formality and to dress much more formally than usual for a court appearance

    D.   Legal due process versus client rights

           1.   In a court of law in this country, the defendant is assumed to be the one most in need of safeguards protecting his or her rights

           2.   Common client rights include foreknowledge of confidentiality and its constraint, self-determination, and informed consent for treatment

    E.   Outcome: Determination of the charge versus rehabilitation

           1.   The end result in the courtroom is clear and unambiguous

           2.   Social work practice is much more ambiguous in process and, often, in outcome

V. **Presentation in Court**

    A.   Highlight 13.3: Summary: Your Role in Court

           1.   The primary mission of a professional social worker testifying in court is to inform or educate the finder of fact

           2.   Social workers are generally advised to present themselves as "friends of the court"

VI. Preparation for Testimony

A. Documentation

    1. Often the credibility or believability of testimony is directly related to the amount and accuracy of detail the worker has put into the case record

    2. Documentation typically includes acknowledgment of all contacts the worker has had with the client and others involved in the case

    3. Avoid value-laden terms and use more neutral terms plus one or two behaviorally specific descriptions to enhance the record's and the worker's credibility

    4. Positive, as well as negative, observations should be included in the record

B. Review of other documents

C. Establishment of expert witness status

D. Review of testimony with attorney

    1. Petition—essentially a complaint that specifies the reasons for a case being brought to court and usually identifies a remedy sought by the petitioner

    2. Highlight 13.4: A Court Petition

E. Preparation of witnesses

VII. Phases in the Adjudication Process

A. Direct examination of witnesses

    1. The purpose of direct testimony is to communicate as persuasively as possible the truthful facts pertinent to a case

    2. The social worker as a witness is allowed to use notes during testimony

    3. Language is more lively and forceful if the active voice is used

    4. Exhibits are tangible articles, such as weapons or copies of documents that have been collected, identified, and made available to the court for a particular case

    5. Highlight 13.5 Questions for Direct Examination

B. Cross-examination of witnesses

    1. Cross-examination is the step in the courtroom process that is most likely to show the adversarial nature of the proceedings

    2. Highlight 13.6 Cross-Examination

VIII. Strategies in Cross-Examination

A. Attacking direct examination testimony

B. Attacking credentials

C. Attacking you as a person

D. Attacking the profession

E. Other confrontational tactics

F. Suggestions for cross-examination testimony

1. It is generally advisable not to answer questions that are ambiguous or unclear

2. Use your listening skills

IX. Stages in the Juvenile Court Process

A. Figure 13.2 The Temporary Custody Stage of the Juvenile Court Process

B. Figure 13.3 The Jurisdictional Stage of the Juvenile Court Process

C. Figure 13.4 The Dispositional Stage of the Juvenile Court Process

D. Figure 13.5 The Post-Dispositional Stage of the Juvenile Court Process

X. Developing Issues in Social Work and the Law

A. Social workers in hospitals and nursing homes must have a working knowledge of patient rights, advanced medical directives, and legal guidelines regarding the appointment of any interactions with guardians and protective payees

B. Confidentiality and privacy of client information and the type of storage of documents relating to any given case are new and developing issues

C. Many states, in an attempt to deal with an increase in the seriousness of juvenile crimes, have lowered the age at which a juvenile is automatically transferred into adult court

D. Forensic social work will continue to expand as society asks the courts to decide complicated moral and ethical issues

E. In child abuse and neglect cases, an emerging issue is "fetal abuse": drug use by the mother and the resultant damage to the fetus

F. Social workers are also working alone and with others in doing life history research for capital cases

G. Forensic social work has grown and now there is a national organization entitled the National Organization of Forensic Social Work, as well as many new books devoted to the topic

Exercise 13.1: Understanding Court Terminology

A.   Brief Description
Students match various concepts of court terminology with their respective meanings.

B.   Objectives
Students will identify and discuss various concepts of court terminology.

C.   Procedure
1.   Provide students with copies of the matching exercise under "Instructions for Students."
2.   After allowing students a few minutes to complete the exercise, initiate a discussion with the class regarding the importance and relevance of each of these concepts.

D.   Instructions for Students
Match the following concepts concerning goals with their respective meanings.

1.	Criminal violation	_____
2.	Jurisdiction	_____
3.	Allegation	_____
4.	Disposition	_____
5.	Due process	_____
6.	Stipulation	_____
7.	Burden of proof	_____
8.	Standards of proof	_____
9.	Real evidence	_____
10.	Documentary evidence	_____
11.	Testimony	_____
12.	Hearsay evidence	_____
13.	Civil offense	_____
14.	Misdemeanor	_____
15.	Felony	_____
16.	Confidentiality	_____
17.	Privileged communication	_____
18.	Subpoena	_____

a.   An agreement by both parties on a point of information or fact that pertains to the proceedings or trial.

b.   The principle that information shared between the client and social worker is intended to be kept private.

c.   A legal writ ordering an individual to appear in court to testify regarding a client, often requiring that written documents be brought along as well.

d.   An offense penalized by fine and/or imprisonment.

e.   A violation for which the sole penalty is forfeiture of money or goods.

f.   A less serious crime considered serious enough to be punishable by imprisonment for a term of one or more years.

g.   Authority to act.

h.   The requirement that law in its regular course of administration must document that it guarantees the protection of a fair trial.

i. Testimony about a statement made outside the courtroom.
j. The condition that it is the responsibility of the party making the complaint to prove the allegations set out in the petition filed before the court.
k. Information shared between the client and another party that is protected by state statute.
l. The assertion of one side in a lawsuit setting out what that party expects to prove at the trial.
m. Evidence consisting of tangible objects such as weapons or photographs.
n. The second phase of the court process where the sentence is determined.
o. The level or degree of certainty needed to prove an allegation in court.
p. The actual interviewing of a witness by the defendant or, more typically, his or her attorney.
q. Certified documents usually identified and authenticated by proper authorities.
r. A crime considered serious enough to be punishable by imprisonment for a term of one or more years.

E. Commentary
Answers are: 1d; 2f; 3l; 4n; 5h; 6a; 7j; 8o; 9m; 10q; 11p; 12i; 13e; 14f; 15r; 16b; 17k; 18c.
This exercise may also be conducted using the small group format described in earlier exercises.

Exercise 13.2: Courtroom Protocol and Social Work Practice

A. Brief Description
Using a small group format, students appraise a vignette describing a social worker's behavior in court and make suggestions for improvement.

B. Objectives
Students will:
1. Appraise a vignette describing the behavior of a social worker in a courtroom setting.
2. Identify inappropriate courtroom behavior.
3. Compare and contrast behavior patterns commonly characterizing social work practice and those patterns deemed appropriate in court.
4. Recommend improved behavior coinciding with formal courtroom protocol.

C. Procedure
1. Review the material on the differences between courtroom protocol and social work practice.
2. Read the vignette presented below under "Instructions for Students" and initiate a discussion for each regarding which functions the vignettes indicate are being fulfilled and how.
3. Divide the class into small groups of four to six.
4. Ask the groups to discuss the first three steps of the IMAGINE process to begin program development in the vignette described below under "Instructions for Students." Instruct them to address the questions provided after the vignette. Indicate that they should select a group representative who should be prepared to report to the entire class the small group's findings.
5. After about 10 minutes, ask the small groups to terminate their discussions and participate in a full class discussion regarding their findings.
6. Ask the representative from each group to share her or his summary of the discussion. Encourage participation from all class members.

D.   Instructions for Students
Read the following vignette and answer the subsequent questions.

> Vignette: Larry is a social worker at a residential treatment center for adolescents who have serious behavioral and emotional problems. He attends a courtroom proceeding to speak on the behalf of Archibald (nicknamed Archy), one of his clients at the center. Archy was caught shoplifting and faces a possible return to a juvenile correctional facility. Larry feels Archy has made significant progress at the center and hates the thought of Archy returning to "jail" and backsliding concerning the treatment progress he's made. Wearing blue jeans and an orange T-shirt, Larry is called to the stand.
>
>   Larry is an outgoing person who tends to act in a friendly manner with most people with whom he comes into contact. On his way up to the stand, he smiles, waves, and says, "Hi, Judge." His intent is to develop rapport with the judge. As Larry answers questions, he leans towards the bench and the judge. He speaks using his most sincere tone. At times he raises his voice to make his point. He hopes he doesn't sound like he's whining, but is committed to helping Archy.
>
>   When asked to make his recommendations regarding Archy's treatment for the next six months, Larry states, "It seems to me that Archy will be capable of making much more progress at the treatment center than in the residential facility." Larry is then asked to submit his progress reports for the judge's perusal. Larry indicates that he isn't quite finished with them yet, but will get them to court by tomorrow.
>
> 1.   What behavior might be ineffective and inappropriate in a courtroom setting?
> 2.   What are the differences between common behavior patterns in social work practice and the appropriate behavior patterns in a formal courtroom setting?
> 3.   What are recommendations for improved courtroom protocol?

E.   Commentary
1.   Note that some of the behavior described above may not be allowed in a real courtroom setting. It is presented here simply as fuel for discussion.
2.   This exercise may also be conducted using a full class discussion format without breaking students into small groups.

Exercise 13.3: Evidence, Evidence, Evidence

A.   Brief Description
Students will assess their knowledge of different kinds of evidence used in court.

B.   Objectives
Students will:
1.   Match definitions of various types of evidence with the legal descriptions.

C.   Procedure
1.   Review the different types of evidence discussed in the chapter.
2.   Ask students to match the definitions of each with the legal description.

D.   Instructions to Students
After reviewing the different types of evidence discussed in the chapter, test your understanding by completing the matching items shown below.

Match each example to the appropriate type of evidence.

1.	Documentary	_____	5.	Relevant	_____
2.	Testimonial	_____	6.	Material	_____
3.	Real	_____	7.	Competent	_____
4.	Hearsay	_____			

A.   Statements made to a witness by a person who is not present in the courtroom.
B.   Evidence considered consequential to the outcome of the trial.
C.   Evidence provided by a qualified witness.
D.   Testimony by a crime victim about his injuries.
E.   A gun used in a robbery.
F.   Testimony with a direct bearing on a case.
G.   Medical records authenticated by a hospital records clerk.

E.   Commentary
This exercise can be done in small groups or used as a graded quiz.

Chapter 14
Developing and Managing Agency Resources

I. **Introduction**

II. **Working with the Media**

    A.   Highlight 14.1 The Media's Influence

    B.   General guidelines for using the media

          1.   Maintain ongoing relationships with media personnel

          2.   Nurture a variety of contacts within the media

          3.   If you happen to be a local expert on a subject, let the media know this

          4.   Make sure you have sanction, or permission, to speak for your agency

          5.   Make it easy for the media representatives to contact you

          6.   Learn the media's time schedules

          7.   Avoid playing favorites among the news media

          8.   Recognize that the media can and do make mistakes

          9.   Don't be disappointed if a story you hoped would appear does not

          10.   Remember that anything you say to the media can, and often does, end up in print

    C.   Contacts with the media

          1.   The media may contact you

          2.   You can call the media yourself and explain that you have what you believe is a newsworthy item

          3.   You may contact the media through a news release

          4.   Highlight 14.2: Example of a News Release

    D.   Media interviews

E.   Letters to the editor and editorials

        1.   Letters to the editor

        2.   Editorials

        3.   Highlight 14.3: Example of a Newspaper Editorial

III.   Using Technology in Your Agency

A.   Understanding computer hardware

        1.   Central processing unit (CPU), monitor, keyboard, and printer

        2.   Bytes—each byte represents a character; a gigabyte holds over 1 billion characters

        3.   Hard drive (fixed disk)—the data storage device

        4.   Compact discs, DVDs, and USB flash memory devices are other storage systems

        5.   Apple Computer Company produces the Mac operating systems; Microsoft Corporation produces the Windows-based systems

        6.   Laptop computers are used in some agencies

B.   Understanding the software

        1.   Database software allows us to maintain extensive records and retrieve that data quickly

        2.   Spreadsheets allow us to calculate and maintain various kinds of financial or numerical information

        3.   Figure 14.1: Information in a Database

        4.   Figure 14.2: A Spreadsheet

C.   Agency software usage

        1.   Geographic information system (GIS)—allows agencies to produce maps showing areas where services are nonexistent or where transportation problems prevent clients from using available services

        2.   Management information systems (MIS)—methods for gathering, analyzing, and evaluating data in an agency or organization

        3.   Highlight 14.4: Management Information Systems

D.   Using the Internet

      1.   Increasingly, social workers are using the Internet for many purposes and provides a wealth of resources for macro practice

      2.   Figure 14.3: Other Potential Online Resources

E.   General observations about computers

IV.   Fund-Raising

A.   Highlight 14.5: Fund-Raising

B.   Sources of funds

      1.   Individual donors

            a.   Benefits

            b.   Benefit variations

            c.   Direct solicitation

            d.   Foundations—seeking group giving

            e.   Membership dues—creating your own organization

            f.   Other fundraising techniques

V.   Grants and Contracts

A.   Social work programs are almost always in need of additional resources, and macro change efforts often require funds not already in any agency budget

B.   Grant—a transfer of funds or assets from one government, organization, or individual to another for fulfilling some broadly specified function or purpose

C.   Contracts—agreements between two organizations or bodies that specify that one will provide certain services in exchange for payments from the other

VI.   Finding Out about Grants and Contracts: Where Are They?

A.   Government grants and contracts are often restrictive in nature, limiting funding to only those purposes approved by the particular legislative body

B.   Private foundations and corporate sources are often more flexible in what and when they may fund; they might be more willing to support creative new programs or to respond quickly to a funding request

C. Granting source references books and internet sites include: *Foundation Directory, Annual Register of Grant Support, Chronicle of Higher Education, Foundation News, Foundation Grants to Individuals, National Directory of Corporate Giving, Foundation Center Information Quarterly, Chronicle of Philanthropy,* The Foundation Center, the Grantsmanship Center, the *Catalog of Federal and Domestic Assistance, the Internet Prospector, Council on Foundations,* and *Independent Sector*

D. Government grants

    1. The largest source of grant funds in the United States is the federal government

    2. Federal programs are listed in the *Federal Register* and the *Catalog of Federal Domestic Assistance*

    3. State programs are often announced in the *State Contract Register*

    4. Granting agencies include the National Institute for Mental Health and the National Institute on Aging

    5. Agencies announce the availability of grants through requests for proposals (RFPs)

    6. Bidder's conferences—where government grantors provide more information to interested parties

    7. Highlight 14.6: My First Grant

E. Foundation grants

    1. All foundations are governed by boards of directors that often decide which grant applications to fund

    2. Most have identified specific areas where they concentrate their grant giving

    3. Getting information is not easy. Sources are the Foundation Center, the Donors' Forum, the *Foundation Directory*, the Foundation Research Service, and the Taft Information System

    4. Unsolicited proposals are ones in which the foundation has not previously indicated an interest

F. Business or corporation grants

    1. Many large businesses have established charitable divisions often called foundations to dispense funds for various purposes

    2. Nonprofit organizations are those that do not intend to produce revenue over their costs of operation

    3. Many business foundations exist to support research in areas that indirectly benefits the corporation; others fund areas not at all related to the needs of the particular company

4. There are no universally helpful resources identifying the purposes and grant-making history of corporate foundations

5. Unlike most government granting agencies, private foundations and corporations may make a site visit to your agency

VII. How to Apply for a Grant

A. Figure 14.4: Steps in Applying for a Grant

B. Pre-application phase

   1. You must identify potential grant sources

   2. Figure 14.5: Potential Grant Information Sources

C. Application phase

   1. Highlight 14.7: Critical Topics Regarding Grant Applications

   2. Writing a grant proposal

      a. Description of a grant proposal—characteristics

         1) The proposed activity must relate to the interests or purposes of the funding agency

         2) The proposed activity will, in some way, promote a desirable end

         3) It shows that the proposer knows the territory

         4) The people carrying out the project are competent to do so

         5) The expected results justify the costs involved

      b. Problems with proposals

         1) The proposal was poorly written

         2) The competence of those who would carry out the proposal was not clearly documented

         3) Inadequate planning was evident in the application

         4) The application itself was not carefully prepared

         5) The proposal was good but needed revisions, and there was insufficient time to modify it

         6) The problem being addressed is not significant

         7) The proposal does not make clear how funds will be used

8) The means proposed for dealing with a problem don't make sense

9) Objectives cannot be adequately assessed

10) The grant seeker has no past record of dealing with the proposed problem

11) Human subject concerns have not been addressed

3. Kinds of grant and contract proposals

a. Program proposals—designed to provide a particular service to a particular size system

b. Research proposals—typically involve studying a particular problem or testing a specific intervention approach

c. Training proposals—requests for funds to train or educate a specific group

d. Planning proposals—designed to allow an organization or agency to plan for a new program

e. Technical assistance proposals—provide for specialized help, allowing organizations or individuals to carry out a program

f. Contract for services—simply an agreement between two agencies or organizations for one to provide services to be paid for by the other

4. Parts of a grant proposal

a. Cover page

1) Cover page should include information about the agency and persons who are applying for the grant; the subject of the proposal; the starting and ending times for the project; the money requested; and the date of application

2) Highlight 14.8: Example of a Cover Page

b. Table of contents—a separate page identifying each distinct section of the proposal

c. Abstract or summary

    1) A 200- to 300-word summary makes it easier for the reader to get a quick overview of the proposal

    2) Complete this portion only after the rest of the document has been finished

    3) Highlight 14.9: Example of a Summary or Abstract

d. Narrative section

    1) Statement of the problem

        a) This should not only summarize the issue being addressed but also identify causative factors and past efforts to solve the identified difficulty

        b) Highlight 14.10: Example of a Problem Statement of a Grant Application

    2) Goals and objectives

        a) These are the end products of your grant project

        b) Highlight 14.11: Example of Goals and Objectives

        c) Outcome objectives—show what the result will be of our change efforts

        d) Process objectives—describe the steps you will take to accomplish the outcome objectives

    3) Methods

        a) These are the activities you will use to accomplish your objectives

        b) Highlight 14.12: Example of a Description of the Method

    4) Evaluation

        a) The evaluation section requires that you think carefully about your ultimate goals and exactly how you will prove that you have been successful

        b) Specify the purpose of the evaluation

        c) Specify the timetable for data collection

d)   Specify what happens when the grant period is over and the money is gone

e)   Highlight 14.13: Example of an Evaluation Section

5)   Bibliography

a)   List the references to which you referred in your proposal

b)   Highlight 14.14 Example of a Bibliography

e.   Budget section

1)   Line-item budget (the most common type for proposals)—identifies personnel costs, operating costs, travel, and capital costs

2)   Highlight 14.15: Example of a Line-Item Budget

3)   Functional (program) budgets—depict costs based upon specific proposed program elements or functions

4)   Highlight 14.16: Example of a Functional or Program Budget for a Peer Counselor and Drug Education Program

5)   Highlight 14.17: Example of Allocating Time and Space Costs

6)   Highlight 14.18: Example of a Budget Narrative

f.   Credentials of staff—describe the credentials of staff members carrying out the activities proposed in the grant

g.   Certification of compliance—if required, add a section discussing compliance with civil rights laws and protections for human subjects

h.   Cost sharing, matching funds, and indirect costs

1)   Cost sharing—an arrangement whereby both the agency receiving the grant and the organization dispensing the grant contribute to the proposed budget

a)   Indirect costs—often referred to as overhead, they compensate your agency for its expenses in operating the grant activity

          b)   Matching funds (cost-sharing grants)—assume that the receiving organization will contribute part of the total project costs

               (1)   Hard match—actual cash

               (2)   Soft match—allows an agency to provide its share of the costs through contributed services or activities (sometimes referred to as in-kind contributions)

               (3)   Figure 14.6: Calculating Soft Match

      i.   Agency or institutional endorsements—include a signature page for executives of the receiving agency

D.   Post-application phase

    1.   Positive factors in determining whether an agency receives grant funds or not

      a.   Shows a cost-effective operation

      b.   Supports other organizations in the community

      c.   Reflects cultural sensitivity and diversity

      d.   Focuses on primary prevention of the problem

      e.   Has a proven track record

      f.   Establishes new, innovative programs

      g.   Receives funding from other sources

      h.   Has a previous relationship with the foundation

      i.   Has a reputation that is not too radical

      j.   Has a competent and professionally trained staff

    2.   When funding is less than requested—generally requires major rethinking about whether the project is workable with the smaller amount

    3.   When the grant/contract runs out—you must plan either to continue the program by finding other sources of funds or to terminate it

Exercise 14.1: Working With the Media

A.	Brief Description
Students consider the ways in which the media may be useful or harmful to an agency.

B.	Objectives
Students will:
1.	Recognize the value of the media to an agency.
2.	Examine potential problems from using the media.

C.	Procedure
1.	Divide class into small groups of four to six students.
2.	Ask groups to address the questions shown in the box.
3.	Have each group report their responses to the questions to the entire class.

D.	Instructions for Students
Within small groups respond to the two questions shown in the box below. When requested by the instructor, share your responses with the rest of the class.

1.	Identify at least two ways in which the media can assist your agency in accomplishing its mission.
2.	In a proposed letter to the editor of the newspaper, a colleague says he believes that the Mayor is taking money earmarked for your agency and using it to conduct his re-election campaign. What would you advise your colleague about his letter and why?

E.	Commentary
The exercise can be completed with the entire class. It is also possible to construct other scenarios for students to consider.

Exercise 14.2: Press Releases

A.	Brief Description
Students will review a sample press release and identify its strengths and shortcomings.

B.	Objectives
Students will:
1.	Identify important elements in a press release.
2.	Critique an existing press release, identifying both its strengths and weaknesses.

C.	Procedures
1.	Review content on preparing a press release.
2.	Break students into small groups.
3.	Ask students to read the press release below and identify both its strengths and weaknesses.

D.	Instructions for Students
Read the press release shown below, compare it to the recommendations identified in the text, and list both its strengths and weaknesses.

274

Fremont Street Neighborhood Association

For Immediate Release:
    Neighborhood Association Pushes City for Action
    South Swampland, MO—August 1, 2005
The Fremont Street Neighborhood Association has filed suit against the City of South Swampland for failing to protect adequately children walking to school along East Doyle Avenue. The Association president said that two children were hurt in drive-by shootings during the past four weeks while the city does nothing about the problem. The Neighborhood Association Board of Directors voted yesterday to sue in Circuit Court, charging the Mayor and Police Chief with discrimination against the predominantly African-American neighborhood along Fremont Street. The Association is calling for increased police patrols and arrests of the gang members who frequent the area brandishing weapons and selling drugs to children. They also demand the city close the south end of Fremont Street to prevent drivers from racing down the street. "The city's failure to take action to alleviate the problem left us with no choice," said Chambers. "We are also considering filing a discrimination complaint with the state office of civil rights," she said. Chambers said a rally is scheduled for 10:00 a.m. Monday to draw attention to the problem. Following the rally, former Fremont Street resident and professional ballplayer Sam Malone will hold a news conference along with Association officers.

###

E.   Commentary
Not applicable.

Exercise 14.3: Preparing Sound Bites

A.   Brief Description
Students will practice preparing sound bites that increase the likelihood that their comments will be replayed by the media.

B.   Objectives
Students will:
1. Create sound bites that are more likely to be replayed by the media.

C.   Procedure
    1.   Briefly discuss with students the characteristics of sound bites and the media's use of them.
    2.   Divide the class into several small groups.
    3.   Ask each group to use the press release described in Exercise 14.2 to create a series of possible sound bites.
    4.   Ask each group to report on their sound bites.

D.   Instructions for Students
Read the information below and create a set of sound bites that are likely to meet the needs of radio and TV media.

A local television reporter has decided to interview you further about the news release you prepared above. Remember that the broadcast media tend to prefer comments that are short and to the point. Write four sound bites that take no more than 15 seconds to say and that convey key ideas about the program described in your news release.

1.

2.

3.

4.

E.   Commentary
       Not applicable.

Exercise 14.4: Draft a Letter to the Editor

A.   Brief Description
       Students will practice writing a letter to the editor on a topic of their choosing.

B.   Objectives
       Students will:
       1.   Develop skill in writing letters to the editor.

C.   Procedure
       1.   Ask students to pick a topic that was in the news within the past few days.
       2.   Review the information about writing letters to the media.
       3.   Ask students to prepare a draft letter to the editor regarding the topic.
       4.   Critique the strengths and weaknesses of the letters.

D.   Instructions for Students
       Prepare a letter to be sent to the editorial page of your local newspaper. Express your opinion on a topic that was covered in the paper during the last week. Turn in your letter and the original article or news item to which your letter relates.

E.   Commentary
       This can also be a graded written assignment.

Chapter 15
Stress and Time Management

I.   Introduction

II.   Stress and Stress Management

    A.   Stress—the comprehensive process by which external pressures affect individuals emotionally and physically, producing some internal tension

    B.   General Adaptation Syndrome

        1.   Alarm phase—the body recognizes the stressor and responds by preparing for fight or flight

        2.   Resistance or repair phase—bodily processes seek to return to homeostasis

        3.   Exhaustion phase—occurs only when the body remains in a state of high stress for an extended period of time

    C.   The macro context for stress

        1.   Burnout—a state of physical, emotional, and mental exhaustion that results from constant or repeated emotional pressure associated with an intense, long-term involvement with people

        2.   To avoid burnout and enhance your usefulness, good stress- and time-management skills are essential

    D.   Perceptions of stress

        1.   Physiological stress-related problems

        2.   Psychological stress-related problems

        3.   Behavioral stress-related problems

        4.   Figure 15.1: The Stress Process

    E.   Confronting stress: Flight or fight

    F.   Managing your stress

        1.   Changing your thinking about the stressful event

            a.   ABCDE theory of irrational thinking (Albert Ellis)

               1)   A—activating event (identify the stressor)

               2)   B—belief system (identify rational and irrational beliefs)

3)   C—consequences (mental, physical, behavioral)

4)   D—dispute irrational beliefs

5)   E—effect (change consequences)

6)   Figure 15.2: The ABCDE Theory of Stress Management

b.   Suggestions for changing your thinking about a stressful event

     1)   Accept that some stress cannot be avoided

     2)   Realize that the primary changeable element in your life is you

     3)   Separate insoluble problems from others

     4)   Examine your expectations

     5)   Avoid should/should not thinking

     6)   Analyze your needs

     7)   Emphasize your strengths—physical, emotional, and spiritual

2.   Changing the stressful event

a.   Inadequate or distressing work setting

b.   Frequent urgent deadlines

c.   Too much work and too little time

d.   Deterrents to accomplishing work

e.   Problematic interpersonal relationships

f.   Role ambiguity

g.   Poor match between staff and job

3.   Adopt stress management strategies

a.   Relaxation approaches

     1)   Deep breathing relaxation

     2)   Imagery relaxation

     3)   Progressive muscle relaxation

              4)   Meditative approaches

              5)   Biofeedback equipment

      b.   Exercise

      c.   Reinforcing activities

      d.   Social support

III. Managing Your Time

  A.   Highlight 15.1: Time "Troublers" and Controllers

  B.   How poor time management causes stress

      1.   Preoccupation

      2.   Poor task pacing

      3.   Stimulus overload

      4.   Stimulus underload

      5.   Anxiety

  C.   Styles of dealing with time

      1.   People who are bored

      2.   People who are happy-go-lucky

      3.   People who are nose to the grindstone type

      4.   People who perceive time as invaluable

      5.   People who look at time as something they can choose to manage

  D.   Time management approaches

      1.   Planning your time

            a.   Step 1: Figure out where the time goes

                1)   Figure 15.3: Where Does All the Time Go?

                2)   Time-mapping—keeping an hourly, half-hour, or 15-minute record of how you spend your time

                3)   Highlight 15.2: Time-Tracking

b.   Step 2: Establish goals for yourself

       1)   One reason that people fail to use time wisely is that they simply do not set goals for themselves

       2)   Highlight 15.3: Planning Time Management Goals

c.   Step 3: Prioritize your goals

       1)   ABC method of goal prioritization

       2)   Highlight 15.4: Prioritized Plan for "A Day in My Life"

       3)   Highlight 15.5: Prioritized Plan for a Professional Workday

d.   Step 4: Specify tasks for each goal

2.   Get control of your own behavior

a.   Look at yourself

b.   Understand your job

c.   Bunch similar activities together

d.   Use a calendar

e.   Handle each sheet of paper only once

f.   Delegate

g.   Don't do other people's work

h.   Bring order to your desk

i.   Develop a system

j.   Leave time for contemplation

k.   Designate leisure time for yourself

l.   Manage meetings effectively

m.   Manage your correspondence

n.   Use the phone efficiently

o.   Review your weekly progress

p.   Postscript

3. Procrastination—the tendency to put off doing something until a future time because it is perceived as being too onerous, unpleasant, or unappealing

    a. Reasons for procrastination

        1) Quest for flawlessness

        2) Worry that you will only fail at doing the task well anyway, so best avoid it altogether

        3) Feeling overwhelmed

        4) Nonassertive overacceptance of responsibilities

        5) Idling away your time with useless busyness

    b. Highlight 15.6: Self-Analysis of Procrastination

    c. The cons of procrastination

    d. Battling procrastination

        1) Break up a large, threatening task into a number of smaller, more manageable tasks

        2) Do the worst job first

        3) Complete whatever it is that you start

        4) Do it right now

Experiential Exercises and Classroom Simulations

Exercise 15.1: Summarizing the Stress in Your Life

A. Brief Description
Using a small group format, students identify the primary arenas of stress in their lives and formulate recommendations for stress reduction.

B. Objectives
Students will:
1. Recognize basic concepts inherent in conceptualizing stress.
2. Assess the process of stress as it affects specific individuals.
3. Propose methods for controlling stress.

C. Procedure
1. Review the material on the dynamics of stress and stress management discussed in the text.
2. Ask students to respond to directions *a, b,* and *c,* posed below under "Instructions for Students" (relating to the assessment of a personal stressful issue). Allow them 5 to 10 minutes to complete the task.

281

3.   Divide the class into small groups of three to four. Ask the groups to allow each member to share his or her responses briefly with the rest of the group. When all group members have finished, the group should address instruction *d*, posed below where they are asked to propose and discuss potential solutions for all group members' stress management issues.

4.   After 10 to 15 minutes, ask the small groups to terminate their discussions and participate in a full class discussion. Ask volunteers from each group to summarize the findings of their discussion.

D.   Instructions for Students

    1.   Take a sheet of scratch paper and jot down answers to the following:

> a.   Identify one of the three primary arenas of stress currently affecting your life. This may involve family, friends, significant other, illness, finances, school, work, or any other dimension of your life.
>
> b.   Explain the reasons for this stress.
>
> c.   Identify the reasons why you're having difficulty controlling this stress.

    2.   For each individual within your small group, propose and discuss ways for dealing with stress. Some suggestions are summarized in the box below.

> **Suggestions for Managing Stress**
>
> a.   Change the stressful event.
>   In a work setting, these may include:
>   1.   An inadequate work setting.
>   2.   Urgent deadlines.
>   3.   Too much work and too little time.
>   4.   Controlling distractions and interruptions.
>   5.   Problematic interpersonal relationships.
>   6.   Role ambiguity.
>   7.   Poor match between staff and jobs.
>
> b.   Change how you think about the stressful event.
>   1.   Accept that some stress cannot be avoided.
>   2.   Realize that the primary changeable element in your life is you.
>   3.   Separate insoluble problems from others.
>   4.   Examine your expectations.
>   5.   Avoid should/should not thinking.
>   6.   Analyze your needs.
>   7.   Emphasize your strengths—physical, emotional, and spiritual.
>
> c.   Adopt stress management strategies.
>   1.   Relaxation approaches (including deep breathing relaxation, imagery relaxation, progressive muscle relaxation, meditation, and biofeedback).
>   2.   Exercise.
>   3.   Reinforcing activities.

E.   Commentary
        Although students address their personal stress management issues individually, a subsequent small group format allows all students, including the quieter ones, to participate in discussion. It is suggested that small groups consist of only three to four members instead of four to six because of the time requirements involved when each group member discusses a personal stress management issue.
                You might direct students to choose a stressful issue that is not overly personal or painful to them for the purposes of this exercise.

Exercise 15.2: Assessing Your Stress Level

A.   Brief Description:
        Students fill out a questionnaire concerning current stress factors in their lives.

B.   Objectives:
        Students will:
        1.   Identify personal stress factors in their lives.
        2.   Evaluate the intensity of these factors.

C.   Procedure
        1.   Review the content on stress and stress management.
        2.   Instruct students to fill out the questionnaire below.
        3.   Initiate a full class discussion concerning areas causing minor and major stress.
        4.   Address the subsequent questions concerning what causes stress and how various people react to stress physically, psychologically, or behaviorally.

D.   Instructions for Students
        1.   Stress can be caused both by personal and work factors. Check the factors listed below, placing an X beside those that cause you stress. Indicate whether you consider the stress minor or major. On the blank lines at the end of each list, add any stressors that are not listed. Ignore factors that do not apply to you. Identifying your stress factors will help you begin to understand how to begin managing stress.

I. Personal Life Factors[1]	Minor	Major
Illness or injury (either yours or someone's close to you)............	___	___
Divorce or marital separation...	___	___
Getting married...	___	___
Marital reconciliation..	___	___
Pregnancy...	___	___
New member joins family...	___	___
Shift in financial status..	___	___
Change in the type or number of arguments with significant other..	___	___
Family member leaves family group....................................	___	___
Difficulty with in-laws...	___	___
Great personal accomplishment...	___	___
Beginning, quitting, or changing schools..............................	___	___
Alteration of living environment.......................................	___	___

---

[1]These items are derived from The Holmes & Rahe Life Changes Scale cited in the *Journal of Psychosomatic Research, Vol. 11*, 1967, pp. 213-18, figure 1-1.

Major changes in personal behavior or routine........................... ____ ____
Change in religious practices or activities................................ ____ ____
Change in social life or recreational activities......................... ____ ____
Debt.. ____ ____
Shift in sleeping pattern or practice.. ____ ____
Shift in eating patterns... ____ ____
Shift in interactions with other family members...................... ____ ____
Vacation.. ____ ____
Observing a major holiday.. ____ ____
Minor legal infractions (such as getting a speeding ticket)........ ____ ____
_____...................... ____ ____
_____...................... ____ ____
_____...................... ____ ____

II. Work Factors[2]   <u>Minor</u>   <u>Major</u>

Recent job loss .... ____ ____
Changing jobs.. ____ ____
Interpersonal difficulties with coworkers................................. ____ ____
Interpersonal difficulties with supervisor or administration........ ____ ____
Alteration of work schedule or conditions................................ ____ ____
Major change in workload... ____ ____
Lack of understanding of work role and responsibilities............ ____ ____
Unclear career path.. ____ ____
Generally hostile work environment.. ____ ____
_____...................... ____ ____
_____...................... ____ ____
_____...................... ____ ____

2.   Discuss with the class the following questions:
- What areas cause minor and major stress?
- What are the reasons that stress occurs?
- How do you tend to react to stress physically, psychologically, or behaviorally?

Exercise 15.3: Managing Stress

A.   Brief Description
Students are asked to explore ways to manage their stress levels.

B.   Objectives
Students will:
1. Identify areas causing stress.
2. Formulate plans to manage stress.

---

[2]These items are derived from The Holmes & Rahe Life Changes Scale cited in the *Journal of Psychosomatic Research, Vol. 11*, 1967, pp. 213-18, figure 1-1, and from those discussed in *The Stress Check* by G. L. Cooper (Englewood Cliffs, NJ: Prentice-Hall, 1981), pp. 175-91.

C.	Procedure
	1.	Review the material on stress management in the text.
	2.	Ask students to answer the questions posed below that identify causes of stress and urge students to propose stress management strategies for themselves.
	3.	Either using a small group format or a full class discussion, ask students to report their results.

D.	Instructions for Students
	1.	Managing stress often means reducing it or finding ways to keep it under control. Three primary approaches to stress management—whether in your macro setting at work or in your personal life—include (1) changing the stressful event, (2) changing the way you think about the stressful event, and (3) adopting specific strategies and techniques to help control your stress level. Read the following material and answer the subsequent questions.

Changing the Stressful Event

1.	At least five areas of problems in a work context can cause you undue stress which you need to control (Brody, 2005; Corey & Corey, 2007; Dolgoff, 2005; Gibelman & Furman, 2008; Sheafor & Horejsi, 2006). These include:

	A.	*Inadequate Setting:* Is your immediate work environment conducive to getting your work done? Do you have sufficient privacy? Is it quiet enough to concentrate? Do you have enough time to take care of necessary paperwork without interruption? Does your office look pleasant and feel comfortable?

	B.	*Urgent Deadlines:* Do you feel unable to catch up on your paperwork no matter what you do? How can you assume greater control of deadlines and paperwork? Is there any way to decrease the urgency of deadlines? To decrease the amount of paperwork you must do? Can you record less? Are you incorporating too much detail? Are there ways for you to become more efficient in your completion of paperwork? Can you find more lead time for accomplishing tasks and goals? Can you manage your time better? Can your supervisor help you better organize your priorities?

	C.	*Too Much Work and Too Little Time:* Do you clearly understand your job role? Are your expectations for your own performance appropriate? Are you spending your time on the most significant tasks? Or are you wasting time on overly repetitive or low-priority tasks?

	D.	*Distractions and Interruptions:* Are people constantly popping into your office? Does the phone ring incessantly? Do you feel you never have an opportunity to *think?* How can you get better control of your time? Can you shut your door during certain times of the day? Can you put up a "Please do not disturb" sign? Can you set aside some predetermined amount of time to finish your paperwork? Can an administrative assistant or secretary hold your calls and take messages so that you're not constantly distracted?

	E.	*Problematic Interpersonal Relationships:* Are there other personnel in the office whose poorly developed interpersonal skills continuously annoy you? Can you approach these people and try to work out your differences? Can you ask your supervisor to act as a mediator? If you don't think resolution is realistically possible, can you minimize your involvement or interaction with the individual without interfering with your own ability to do your job? Can you change your perspective on those you find annoying?

2. In the list below, check the events you feel are stressful in your life.

Inadequate Setting	_____	yes	_____	no
Urgent Deadlines	_____	yes	_____	no
Too much Work and Too Little Time	_____	yes	_____	no
Controlling Distractions	_____	yes	_____	no
Problematic Interpersonal Relationships	_____	yes	_____	no

3. Describe in detail the reasons each event you checked above causes you stress.

4. Think carefully about events and aspects of these events over which you might work to gain control. Explain in detail what you could do to change these stressful events.

Changing How You Think About the Stressful Event

1. If you can't change the stressful event or situation itself as discussed above, a second approach to stress management is changing how you think about the stressful event. Consider the following suggestions:
   - Accept that some stress cannot be avoided. Do you have to worry about every stressor? Or can you accept the fact that some stressors are going to exist regardless and put them out of your mind as much as possible?
   - Realize that the primary changeable element in your life is you. Appreciate the fact that you can control your thinking and your behavior.
   - Separate insoluble problems from others. If you can't solve the problem, can you put it out of your mind and stop worrying about it?
   - Examine your expectations. Put plainly, dump the unrealistic ones. Both positive thinking (reframing a negative event to look more positive) and talking to others about your expectations can be helpful. Try to become realistic.
   - Avoid *should/should not* thinking. This limits your options. Are you wasting time worrying about what you should be doing while you're not doing it? Either do it or don't, but don't waste time worrying about it.
   - Analyze your needs. What do you *really* need? How much does the stressful event really affect you? To what extent should you let it bother you? Are you wasting time and energy thinking about it?
   - Emphasize your strengths--physical, emotional, and spiritual. Could your time be better spent placing greater emphasis on positive aspects or your life instead of dwelling on the stress-producing negatives?

2. Select a stressful event or condition that you feel you cannot change. Describe the event or condition below.

3. Describe how you might change your thinking about this event or condition. (For example, is your instructor's grading scale exceptionally hard in your estimation? Can you change your thinking about this issue by, say, lowering your expectations from getting an A to getting a B?)

Adopting Stress Management Strategies

1.   Check any of the following relaxation responses you are willing to try.
   - _____ Deep breathing relaxation
   - _____ Imagery relaxation
   - _____ Progressive muscle relaxation
   - _____ Meditation

2.   Describe when and where you will begin (or explain why they won't work for you).

3.   Describe what kinds of exercise, if any, in which you are willing to participate (or explain why this approach won't work for you).

4.   When will you begin?

5.   Where will you exercise and under what circumstances?

6.   What reinforcing or enjoyable activities might you participate in that could help you relieve stress?

7.   Who might you turn to for social support in reducing stress?

Exercise 15.4: What Are Your Time "Troublers" and Controllers[3]

A.   Brief Description
Students assess the areas in which they have trouble managing their time.

B.   Objectives
Students will:
1. Assess problematic areas of time management.
2. Explore the reasons for these problems.

C.   Procedure
1. Review the material on time management in the text.
2. Ask students to answer the questions posed below.
3. Either using a small group format or full class discussion, ask students to report their findings.

D.   Instructions for Students
1. There are a number of elements that cause you and just about everyone else to waste time. Review the "time troublers," likely reasons, and possible options listed below. Then answer the subsequent questions.

---

[3]Most of this material is adapted from R. A. Mackenzie, *The Time Trap: Managing Your Way Out,* 1972. New York: AMACON.

Time Troublers	Likely Reasons	Possible Options
What a mess!	Confusion, disorder	Throw out, re-organize, file
Hurry, hurry!	Doing too much too fast, too little attention to detail	Undertake less, allow more time, just say no
I just can't decide.	Terror at making mistakes, cowering at responsibility, can't prioritize and set goals	Use decision-making, problem-solving, and goal-setting skills
Oops! Forgot to plan.	Just didn't think, things happened too fast	Take time to think things through ahead of time, allow time for thought
There's just too much to do!	Unable to say no, too much pressure to perform, can't prioritize	Prioritize goals, just say no, evaluate what is possible to accomplish
I'll do it later.	Being overwhelmed, don't feel like it, it's too hard	Prioritize tasks, plan how to accomplish the most significant
There's that phone again!	Can't resist answering, too nonassertive to not answer or speak briefly, can't control yourself	Talk briefly, stick to the main points, offer to return call later
Unwanted guests	Just can't say no, talking is fun, allows you to avoid work	Limit easy access and availability, be assertive

2. Now answer the following questions:

A. What is your #1 time troubler? _____

What are the likely reasons for this troubler?

What are your potential options for controlling this troubler?

B. What is your #2 time troubler? _____

What are the likely reasons for this troubler?

What are your potential options for controlling this troubler?

288

C.   What is your #3 time troubler? _____

What are the likely reasons for this troubler?

What are your potential options for controlling this troubler?

3.   Participate in a discussion concerning your findings.

Exercise 15.5: Identify Your Problems in Time Management

A.   Brief Description
Students assess the areas in which they have trouble managing their time.

B.   Objectives
Students will:
1.   Assess problematic areas of time management.
2.   Explore the reasons for these problems.

C.   Procedure
1.   Review the material on time management in the text.
2.   Ask students to answer the questions posed below.
3.   Either using a small group format or full class discussion, ask students to report their findings.

D.   Instructions for Students
1.   There are a number of elements that cause you and just about everyone else to waste time. They include (Curtis & Detert, 1981, pp. 190-91; Schafer, 1998):

- *"Preoccupation"* is being lost in thought over something other than what you are supposed to be doing.
- *Poor Task "Pacing"* means not allowing yourself adequate time to complete a set of necessary activities, goals, or tasks.
- *"Stimulus Overload"* occurs when you have so much to do that you could not possibly complete all of the tasks in the amount of time allowed.
- *"Stimulus Underload"* occurs when you don't have enough interesting things to do--things that hold your attention or concentration--so you don't get anything done.
- *"Anxiety"* is "a mood state wherein the person anticipates future danger or misfortune with apprehension" often involving "worry, unease, or dread" (Gray & Zide, 2008, p. 118).

2.   Which if any of the following problems characterize how you manage your work time. Check all that apply.

_____ Preoccupation   _____ Poor task pacing
_____ Stimulus overload   _____ Stimulus underload
_____ Anxiety

3.   Give specific examples of how the time management problems you checked above interfere with your ability to complete necessary tasks.

- What were you trying to accomplish?
- How did you react?
- What were the results?

Exercise 15.6: Where Does Your Time Go?

A.   Brief Description
Students track their time over a typical day and summarize the percentage of time they spend doing various activities.

B.   Objectives
Students will:
1.   Describe how they typically spend their time.
2.   Appraise the effectiveness of how they spend their time.

C.   Procedure
1.   Review the material on time management.
2.   Ask students to track their daily activities over a 24-hour period using the time-tracking format provided below.
3.   After they have tracked their time, ask them to summarize the approximate percentages of time they spend doing various things using the circles provided below. Also, ask them to fill in the circle provided below concerning how they would spend their ideal day.
4.   Instruct students to bring their findings with them to the next class period where they can participate in small group or full class discussions concerning their findings. (This may also be used as a take-home assignment.)

D.   Instructions for Students
1.   The time-tracking format illustrated below shows you how to begin tracking 30-minute time blocks. Select what you consider a "typical" workday. You may simply block or "x" out whatever period or periods of time you spend sleeping. Completing this exercise should help you pinpoint those periods when you waste time. Subsequently, this information can focus on those time periods over which you want to gain greater control.

Time-Tracking Format

Day: _____

Time Segment   **How Time Was Spent**

12:00 a.m.:

12:30 a.m.:

1:00 a.m.:

1:30 a.m.:

2:00 a.m.:

2:30 a.m.:

3:00 a.m.:

3:30 a.m.:

4:00 a.m.:

4:30 a.m.:

5:00 a.m.:

5:30 a.m.:

6:00 a.m.:

6:30 a.m.:

7:00 a.m.:

7:30 a.m.: _____

8:00 a.m.: _____

8:30 a.m.: _____

9:00 a.m.: _____

9:30 a.m.: _____

10:00 a.m.: _____

10:30 a.m.: _____

11:00 a.m.: _____

11:30 a.m.: _____

12:00 p.m.: _____

12:30 p.m.: _____

1:00 p.m.: _____

1:30 p.m.:

2:00 p.m.:

2:30 p.m.:

3:00 p.m.:

3:30 p.m.:

4:00 p.m.:

4:30 p.m.:

5:00 p.m.:

5:30 p.m.:

6:00 p.m.

6:30 p.m.:

7:00 p.m.:

7:30 p.m.:

8:00 p.m.:

8:30 p.m.:

9:00 p.m.:

9:30 p.m.:

10:00 p.m.

10:30 p.m.

11:00 p.m.:

11:30 p.m.:

2.   Using the information gained by the time-tracking exercise, fill in the empty circle B provided below concerning how you actually use your time. Circle A below illustrates how one individual spent a day.[4] Proportionate pieces of the 24-hour pie display how much time was spent doing what.

---

[4]This figure is adapted from an exercise in the *Student Manual of Classroom Exercises* and *Study Guide for Understanding Human Behavior and the Social Environment,* 2nd ed., by K. Kirst-Ashman & C. Zastrow, 1990, Chicago: Nelson-Hall, pp. 133-35.

CIRCLE A: AN EXAMPLE OF UNMANAGED TIME SPENT
IN A TYPICAL WEEKDAY

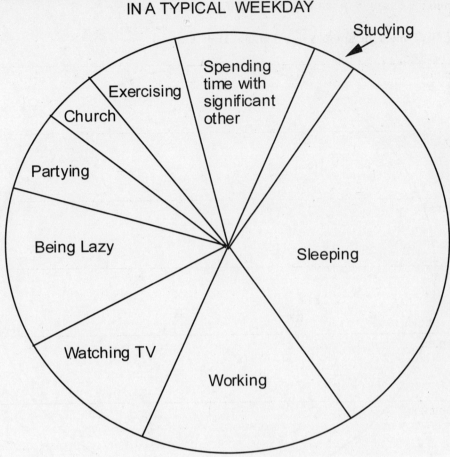

Proportionately, divide Circle B below to depict how you spent your time. The result might resemble the example of unmanaged time depicted in Circle A.

Circle B: How You Spent Your Typical Day

3. Scrutinize Circle B and determine (1) where you are wasting your time, and (2) how you ideally want to spend it.

4. Now divide Circle C below to reflect how you would *like* to use your time. It should provide you with a beginning plan for daily time management.

Circle C: How You Would Spend An Ideal Day

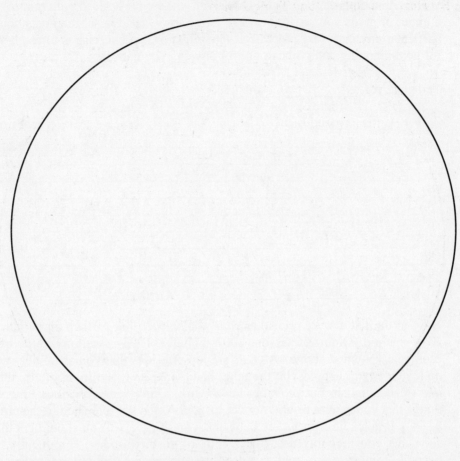

5.   Bring your results to class for discussion.

Exercise 15.7: Establish Your Time Goals

A.   Brief Description

Students establish goals for time management and specific strategies to achieve these goals.

B.   Objectives

Students will:

1.   Appraise how they would like to spend their time.
2.   Formulate a plan for time management.

C.   Procedure

1.   Review the material on time management.
2.   Instruct students to fill out the information requested below.
3.   Break the class down into small groups of 4 to 6 students and ask them to discuss their results. (This may also be used as a take-home assignment.)

D.   Instructions for Students

1.   Below list ten goals that you would like to accomplish in a given day. Remember that goals don't have to be set up on a daily basis. They can extend over weeks, months, or years, depending on the unit of time over which you wish to gain control. In reality, the number of goals you set for yourself is arbitrary. Likewise, the goals you set during any particular day may vary radically. The intent of this exercise is to teach you a procedure for goal-planning that you can use for any day you choose.

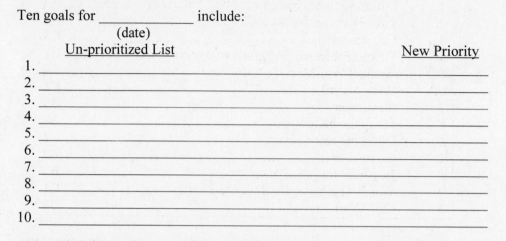

    Ten goals for _____ include:
                 (date)

Un-prioritized List   New Priority

1. _____
2. _____
3. _____
4. _____
5. _____
6. _____
7. _____
8. _____
9. _____
10. _____

2.   Now in the list above, prioritize your goals according to their importance by using the ABC method (Olpin & Hesson, 2007; Schafer, 1998). Assign a value of A, B, or C to each goal you cited above. A goals are top priorities that you absolutely want to get done no matter what. C goals, on the other hand, are relatively unimportant, things you would *like* to accomplish, but probably never will. Don't waste precious time worrying about things that you cannot or will not do. C goals often get relegated to the circular file.

    B goals lie somewhere between A and C goals. You should get them done pretty soon, but you probably don't have time to do them today. Frequently, today's B goal becomes tomorrow's A goal as a deadline approaches (or as your anxiety increases when you don't accomplish something you were supposed to). If you can't decide whether a goal should be A or B, automatically assign it a B. If you're not certain that it's critical enough to be an A goal, then it probably isn't.

    Category A, B, and C goals are then further prioritized by assigning them numbers: Goal A1 is the one you *absolutely* must get done today. Goal A2 is second in importance, A3 third, etc. When you finish prioritizing your A goals, go on to do the same thing with your B and C goals. This process will produce a clearly prioritized plan for your day. First, pursue goal A1, then A2, and so on down the line.

    Note that you can prioritize goals in at least three major life areas including diverse areas of your life including your personal life involving family, friends, and recreation, in addition to work. You can do this either separately or in one prioritized list. Box A below provides an example of prioritized goals using the ABC method.

3.   Looking at your new prioritized system, answer the following questions:

-       Which goals do you think you will actually achieve and which you will not?

-       Will you be able to complete all of your A goals in one day? If so, explain how you intend to do so. If not, explain why not. Discuss when you *will* accomplish them.

-       If you have listed any B goals, what do you think you will do about them? Explain when, if ever, you think you will complete them.   Discuss the consequences of completing them or not completing them.

-       If you have listed any C goals, what do you think you will do about them? Explain when, if ever, you will complete them. Discuss the consequences of completing them or not completing them.

4.   Now specify the respective steps you must follow in order to achieve the first 4 A goals listed above. Six task steps are arbitrarily listed for each A goal below. In reality, you may have more or fewer goals or tasks.

Goal A1

Task 1:

Task 2:

Task 3:

Task 4:

Task 5:

Task 6:

Goal A2

Task 1:

Task 2:

Task 3:

Task 4:

Task 5:

Task 6:

Goal A3

Task 1:

Task 2:

Task 3:

Task 4:

Task 5:

Task 6:

Goal A4

Task 1:

Task 2:

Task 3:

Task 4:

Task 5:

Task 6:

4.   Be prepared to discuss your findings in class.

D.   Commentary
Depending on the time available, only the beginning parts of this exercise need be completed.

Exercise 15.8: Changing Your Behavior to Improve Time Management

A. Brief Description
Students assess their own behavior and identify specific methods to improve their own time management skills.

B. Objectives
Students will:
1. Evaluate their own problems with time management.
2. Recommend specific means to improve their time management skills.

C. Procedure
1. Review the material on time management.
2. Ask students to select three or more of the time management techniques identified below.
3. Break the class down into small groups and ask them to explain how the use of the techniques selected could be used to their benefit and how they might implement the changes.

D. Instructions for Students
1. Review the following suggestions for improving time management skills:

SUGGESTIONS FOR IMPROVED TIME MANAGEMENT

1. *Understand Your Job and Work Responsibilities.* Effectively fulfilling your job responsibilities means fulfilling them at all levels--micro, mezzo, and macro. Discuss with your supervisor what your job description and specific responsibilities really involve (Sheafor et al., 1991).

2. *Bunch Similar Activities Together.* Try to block portions of time for completing similar types of tasks (Schafer, 1998).

3. *Use a Calendar.* Select a daily, weekly, or monthly format that works best for you, and plan your time on a longer term basis.

4. *Handle Each Sheet of Paper Only Once.* Don't waste time shuffling paper. Deal with the issue right away.

5. *Delegate.* Determine which tasks, if any, others can, will, or should do, and arrange for them to do so.

6. *Don't Do Other People's Work* (Sheafor & Horejsi, 2006). Especially if you tend to have high expectations for the quality of your work, be vigilant that you do not end up doing other people's work because you do it better than they do. View each individual as responsible for her or his own tasks, accomplishments, and failings.

7. *Bring Order to Your Desk.* Organize items on your desk so you can find them easily. (Sheafor & Horejsi, 2006). It is also useful to make certain that information you use frequently is readily available (Olpin & Hesson, 2007).

8. *Develop a System.* Devise some system for keeping track of your deadlines (Sheafor & Horejsi, 2006). For example, you could note deadlines on your regular monthly calendar or use a more sophisticated computer program. Try various methods. Whatever works for you is the best system.

9. *Leave Time for Contemplation.* Even with a busy schedule, allow yourself some "down" time each workday (Kottler & Chen, 2008; Schafer, 1998). You need time to organize your thoughts and evaluate the progress you have made toward your designated goals.

---

10. *Designate Leisure Time for Yourself.* To avoid burnout, regularly incorporate some leisure time into your schedule.

11. *Manage Meetings Effectively.* Plan ahead and consider following these suggestions:
    - *Start meetings on time*
    - *State the ending time at the start*
    - *Pre-schedule regular meetings*
    - *Distribute printed matter well before the meeting*
    - *Hold meetings in meeting rooms—not in your office*
    - *Don't hold meetings and eat simultaneously*

12. *Manage Your Correspondence.* Suggestions to facilitate the efficient handling of paperwork include:
    - *Write brief replies as quickly as possible*
    - *Use form letters for standard correspondence*
    - *Open second and third class mail once a week*
    - *Get rid of junk e-mail quickly*

13. *Use the Phone Efficiently.* Consider using conference calls instead of holding meetings. Outline what you want to accomplish during your phone calls before dialing.

14. *Review Your Weekly Progress.* At each week's end, review the extent to which you actually achieved your time management goals and make changes to increase effectiveness.

2. Which of the suggestions for changing your behavior mentioned above would be useful for you? Explain the reasons why each would be useful and how you plan to implement the change.

3. Break up into small groups and discuss your findings and suggestions.

Exercise 15.9: Self-Analysis of Procrastination

A. Brief Description
Students assess the reasons why they procrastinate and suggest methods for stopping procrastination.

B. Objectives
Students will:
1. Identify tasks over which they procrastinate.
2. Suggest ways to decrease procrastination.

C. Procedure
1. Review the content on procrastination.
2. Break the class into small groups of 4 to 6 and ask them to answer and discuss the questions posed below.

D. Instructions for Students
1. Answer the following questions:
   - Over what tasks do you procrastinate?
   - What are your reasons for procrastinating over them?
   - Why do you find them aversive?
   - What tactics can you employ to control your procrastinating behavior?
   - When will you begin implementing these tactics?

Exercise 15.10: Goal Planning

A.   Brief Description

Students are asked to identify their goals for the next day, week, month, year, and five-year period. They then participate in a full class discussion concerning their time priorities, time management approaches, and the relationship between time priorities and life goals.

B.   Objectives

Students will:

1.   Recognize the importance of time management in order to achieve goals.
2.   Assess their goal priorities.

C.   Procedure

1.   Review the material on time management discussed in the text.
2.   Ask students to respond to the questions posed below under "Instructions for Students." Allow them five minutes to work on this task.
3.   Initiate a full class discussion focusing on the following questions:

> a.   What goals did you establish during the five respective time frames?
> b.   What difficulties did you encounter identifying goals? What are the reasons for these difficulties?
> c.   What approaches might be useful in managing smaller chunks of time such as an hour, a day, or a week?
> d.   What approaches might be useful in managing longer chunks of time?
> e.   In what ways does this exercise help you to define your time priorities?
> f.   What goals can you establish based on these time priorities?

D.   Instructions for Students

To the best of your ability, answer the following questions.

> 1.   What goals would you like to achieve within the time frame of **tomorrow?**
> 2.   What goals would you like to achieve within the time frame of the **next week (Sunday through Saturday)?**
> 3.   What goals would you like to achieve within the time frame of the **next month (30 days)?**
> 4.   What goals would you like to achieve within the time frame of the **next year?**
> 5.   What goals would you like to achieve within the time frame of the **next five years?**

E.   Commentary

Students will likely find it difficult to address the goal questions posed. They may require some assistance regarding how to relate prioritizing their goals to managing blocks of time.

This exercise might also be conducted using the small group format described in earlier exercises.